The Anti-Bullying Handbook

2nd edition

Keith Sullivan

Los Angeles | London | New Delhi
Singapore | Washington DC

SAGE Publications Ltd
1 Oliver's Yard
55 City Road
London EC1Y 1SP

SAGE Publications Inc.
2455 Teller Road
Thousand Oaks, California 91320

SAGE Publications India Pvt Ltd
B 1/I 1 Mohan Cooperative Industrial Area
Mathura Road
New Delhi 110 044

SAGE Publications Asia-Pacific Pte Ltd
33 Pekin Street #02–01
Far East Square
Singapore 048763

Library of Congress Control Number: 2010923181

British Library Cataloguing in Publication data

A catalogue record for this book is available from the British
Library

ISBN 978-1-84920-479-8 (hbk)
ISBN 978-1-84920-480-4 (pbk)

Typeset by Dorwyn, Wells, Somerset
Printed in Great Britain by CPI Antony Rowe, Chippenham, Wiltshire
Printed on paper from sustainable resources

This publication was grant-aided by the Publications Fund of
National University of Ireland, Galway.

This book is dedicated to the memory of:

Dr Vahe Aslanian, late of Salinas, California, musical guide and mentor, wonderful friend and outstanding musician.

John Fisher, late of Oxford, England. John was a generous, thoughtful and warm-hearted friend and a deeply caring father and husband. I think of you often. Long live Tottenham!

My sorely missed brother, Terrence Francis Sullivan. Terry was an understated, caring and dedicated pastor who worked closely and well to support the spiritual and practical needs of convicted criminals in the prisons of California and Nevada.

CONTENTS

FIGURES

ABOUT THE AUTHOR

Keith Sullivan BA MPhil PhD DipBusStuds is the Established Professor and Head of the Discipline of Education at the National University of Ireland, Galway. He was educated at Hartnell College, Salinas, California, USA; Concordia University, Montreal, Canada; the University of Leeds, and St John's College, the University of Cambridge, England; and Massey University, New Zealand. Professor Sullivan's teaching and research focuses have been: educational psychology (with particular reference to bullying), the education of disadvantaged students, social and cultural processes, education policy and reform, and effective teaching, learning and managing.

At the secondary level, Keith has taught at schools in England and Canada and was a guidance counsellor in New Zealand. He also spent three years working in Government in New Zealand, first as a researcher in the Department of Justice, where he worked on criminal and civil justice issues (and had a particular interest in violence and its causes and effects); and second in the Department of Education, where he was working on education policy at the beginning of an era of extensive reforms.

In the tertiary sector, he has held appointments at the Open University in England and at Waikato and Massey Universities and Victoria University of Wellington in New Zealand, and at the University of the South Pacific in Kiribati. Professor Sullivan was given the opportunity to fully pursue his interests in school bullying when elected to the Charter Fellowship in Human Rights at Wolfson College, University of Oxford. Victoria University of Wellington provided him with a sabbatical so that he could take this up. He has since published extensively on the important topic of bullying. Oxford University Press published the first edition of *The Anti-Bullying Handbook* in 2000. It was reprinted four times and nominated for New Zealand's prestigious Montana Book Awards. Dr Sullivan also co-authored the Sage book *Bullying in Secondary Schools: What It Looks Like and How to Manage It* (2004) with high school principal Mark Cleary and anthropologist Dr Ginny Sullivan. This book was reprinted twice and translated into Spanish and Estonian.

Professor Sullivan's work has been well received by school practitioners and tertiary lecturers alike because it successfully bridges the gap between the scholarship and research processes of the university and the challenging, down-to-earth and immediate needs of busy schools. As well as writing books and articles, he has provided practical workshops and programmes for school principals, teachers, counsellors, psychologists, youth workers and administrators. He has also delivered keynote addresses for the Centre for Child Mental Health (London), the British Psychological Society, ISPA (the International School Psychologists Association), the New Zealand Police, and the NZ Special Education Services, the OECD, the Spanish Ministry of Education and Science, and UNESCO and the Israeli Ministry of Education. Furthermore, Professor Sullivan has lectured about school bullying at universities around the world including the Universities of Melbourne, South Australia and Flinders University (Australia); Die Pädagogische Hochschule Kärnten, Viktor Frankl Hochschule (Austria); the University of British Columbia, Toronto University's Ontario Institute for the Study of Education [OISE], McGill and Queen's Universities and York University's LaMarsh Centre for Research on Violence and Conflict Resolution (Canada); the Odense Socialpædagogiske Seminarium (Denmark); Brunel, Oxford, Queens University Belfast and Roehampton Universities (England and Ireland); the Åbo Akademi University, Vaasa (Finland); Auckland and Victoria Universities (New Zealand); and the University of Stavanger (Norway).

Dr Sullivan has a long-term interest in the philosophies and practices of the various martial arts, particularly in terms of the development and use of psychological self-defense skills. He has a black belt in and has been a teacher of Kyokushin Karate.

Keith's email address is: keith.sullivan@nuigalway.ie. His personal web pages can be found at: http:// www.nuigalway.ie/education/staff/keith_sullivan/index.html

ACKNOWLEDGEMENTS

I would like first of all to thank Marianne Lagrange, Publisher, Sage Publications Ltd, London for her advice and support in developing this project; Matthew Waters, Development Editor, for his encouragement in the early days; and Monira Begum, Editorial Assistant, who shepherded me along the way.

Many thanks to the Fellows of Wolfson College, Oxford, who elected me to the Charter Fellowship in Human Rights and supported my endeavours to research about and find solutions for addressing school bullying; and to Professors Richard Pring and David Phillips of the Department of Education, Oxford University who provided me with an academic home. Thanks also to the University for access to the Bodleian Library and the Radcliffe Camera, where I carried out much of the initial work, which resulted in the first edition of *The Anti-bullying Handbook*. I am indebted to Oxford University Press for releasing the rights to me so I could write a second edition.

Also in the UK, I extend my appreciation to the highly productive and creative duo of Barbara Maines and George Robinson of Bristol who have given permission for the use of 'A Circle of Friends' and 'The Support Group Method'. My thanks go also to Professor Peter Smith of Goldsmith College, University of London. Peter has created an immense body of work in his own right, has brought leaders in the field together via edited books, and over the years has mentored numerous emerging scholars, including the outstanding Dr Sonia Sharp. He also supported my initial work. Professor Helen Cowie of Roehampton University was similarly inspirational and has contributed vastly to our knowledge about bullying, especially in relation to counselling and mentoring in its various forms. The anti-bullying group of social workers, counsellors and psychologists involved in Dundee and the Greater Tayside area of Scotland in the 1990s were guiding lights for me, turning accessible theory into effective practice. The creative thinking of Val Besag, Professor David Hargreaves, formerly of Cambridge University and Scottish psychologist Alan MacLean, have provided important reference points for me.

In Scandinavia, I wish to acknowledge and thank the following people: in Finland, Professor Kaj Björkvist and Dr Karin Österman of the Abo Akademi University in Vaasa for their wonderful hospitality, for introducing me to the Finnish school system, and for their excellent anti-bullying work, particularly in terms of relational aggression; and Professor Christina Salmivalli and Dr Ari Kaukiainen of the Psychology Department at the University of Turku, who hosted me briefly and introduced me to their groundbreaking research, which now includes their cutting-edge KiVa project. In Norway, I wish to thank Dr Elaine Munthe and Professor Erling Roland who welcomed me to and supported my time at the Centre for Behavioural Research, University of Stavanger and introduced me to the Zero programme for combating school bullying. Tove Flack provided me with deep and insightful knowledge into how this excellent anti-bullying programme works in practice. It is important to acknowledge the seminal work of the University of Bergen's Professor Dan Olweus, which has served to inspire and provide direction to much of the excellent research that has emerged within the anti-bullying area, both in Norway and internationally. I also wish to thank the OECD and the Norwegian Government for inviting me to represent New Zealand at the 'Taking Fear out of Schools' Forum at the University of Stavanger in 2004 and for thereby providing me with the opportunity to meet world leaders in the anti-bullying area. In Sweden, I would like to thank Emeritus Professor Anatol Pikas of Uppsala University for allowing me to use his excellent Method of Shared Concern in this book.

In New Zealand, I wish to thank Owen Saunders, Gill Palmer and Inspector Morris Cheer of the New Zealand Police who twice invited me to carry out an evaluation of the New Zealand Police's *Kia Kaha* anti-bullying initiative and openly accepted my criticisms and recommendations for making radical changes in order to improve it significantly. I would also like to thank the counselling and administrative staff of Feilding High School for allowing me to use their school as a laboratory in which to do this. I also extend my appreciation to Yvonne Duncan and the New Zealand Peace Foundation for allowing the use of their Cool Schools programme in this book, to Barbara Craig and Dr Raymond Pelly for providing an inspiring location for writing in Otaki Forks, and Margaret and Richard Wheeler of Christchurch for inspiration and ongoing support.

My thanks go also to Mark Cleary and Ginny Sullivan, my co-authors for another Sage book, *Bullying in Secondary Schools: What It Looks Like and How to Deal With It,* for permission to incorporate and update materials from that book for this edition. I am also grateful to Paul Denford for his assistance with the application and use of the SWOTSS analysis in schools and to principal Hoana Pearson and pupils and parents of Newton Central School, Auckland, for permission to use their re-visualization and modification of ideas of space; and to Sharon Bowling and Jacob Sullivan for the diagrams and cartoons they respectively created and to my daughters, Amy and Hannah Sullivan for their illustrative contributions.

In Australia, Professor Ken Rigby arranged a Fellowship for me at the University of South Australia and generously shared his ideas and research findings, introducing me to the work being carried out in local schools and organisations and to the initiators behind them. Professor Phillip Slee co-hosted my visit and he and Professor Larry Owens (both of Flinders University) also shared their research and introduced me to their anti-bullying initiatives.

In Canada and the United States, I wish to thank Debra Pepler, Distinguished Professor of Psychology and member of the Lamarsh Centre for Research on Violence and Conflict Resolution at York University, Toronto; Professor Wendy Craig of the Department of Psychology of Queen's University, Kingston, Ontario; and Professor Shelley Hymel of the Department of Educational and Counselling Psychology, and Special Education of the University of British Columbia for hosting me and introducing to me an array of creative developments in Canada. They also allowed me to share my ideas with them and their students. I would particularly like to thank the Government of Canada for providing both Faculty Enrichment and

Canada–Asia–Pacific Research Awards to support my visits.

I am indebted to Pauline Tessler of Tessler, Sandmann & Fishman Law Offices, San Francisco, California, for the important work she has carried out in collaborative law: her ideas were very influential in my development of the CPR (Collaborative Problem-solving and Resolution) method. Thanks also to elementary school principal Cathy Baur and the students of Monta Loma Elementary School, Mountain View, California, for allowing the use of their playground rules.

In Ireland, I would like to thank Professor Mona O'Moore of Trinity College, Dublin, for the excellent work she has carried out in Irish schools and the workplace and for her ongoing support and encouragement. I owe a debt of gratitude to Una Kelly whose use of puppet theatre to address bullying in Irish primary schools inspired me to develop Interactive Puppet Theatre. Many thanks to the staff of the 12 Pins Hotel, Barna, Galway, who provided warmth, hospitality and a place to write during a cold, wet winter.

I am indebted to my colleagues in the School of Education at the National University of Ireland, Galway and to Professor Terry Smith, Vice-President for Research for their support; Anne Whelan, formerly of the Vice-President's Office, for providing advice and facilitating financial support for editing costs; and to Gwen Ryan, AHSS Research Support Librarian. I also extend my appreciation to the University for giving me sabbatical leave in 2009, which allowed me to research and write this second edition.

Many thanks to Charlotte Silke for her excellent assistance with research during summer 2009, to Geri Hughes Silke for bringing the area of collaborative law to my attention, for critiquing my chapter on CPR and for both ongoing and caring support and allowing me to use her lovely house in St Chinian, Langue d'Oc Roussillon, France as a writing base; to Anna Coffey for the wonderful diagrams she created, and to Dr Seamus O'Beirne and Gavin Davis for spiritual support and inspiration.

Lastly and most importantly, I would like to thank Dr Ginny Sullivan for editing this book. Ginny is a contract editor who not only pays attention to detail and expression but also exercises intellectual insight when editing. The quality of her wordsmithing, research abilities and structural realigning makes her, by far, the best editor I have ever worked with.

Keith Sullivan, Galway, Ireland, September 2010

FOREWORD

Bullying is a major problem in Irish schools and around the world. At the Anti-Bullying Centre at Trinity College, Dublin, we are constantly deluged with bullying problems that need to be solved. It is an uphill and difficult battle but one that must be fought. We have dedicated staff and research students here looking for answers and dealing with issues both at the chalkface and in the workplace. One enthusiastic and talented student arrived at my office one day and said she had found the best book that had ever been written about bullying. It was *The Anti-Bullying Handbook*. When I was speaking with Keith about his plans to write a second edition of this excellent and very successful book, he asked my opinion about what he should retain, update or drop. My honest response was that he should change nothing, that it was 'grand' as it was.

Having become familiar with the choices made, with the changes and updates and the creation of new strategies and programmes, however, I can honestly say that he has surpassed himself in the creation of an up-to-date book which answers the challenges bullying presents to us in a way that is creative, insightful, down to earth and completely appropriate for addressing this problem in its many forms.

I recommend this book to you most highly.

Congratulations and good luck. *Slainte go saol agat* (Irish for 'Health for life to you').

Professor Mona O'Moore
Trinity College, Dublin
Republic of Ireland

PART 1

DEFINING AND DESCRIBING BULLYING

CHAPTER 1

INTRODUCTION

School bullying has been identified as a major problem in many countries around the world. Everybody I know has a story they can tell about it.

It is imperative that bullying is stopped within our schools. It can create a hell on earth for someone who is victimized, and can seriously threaten that person's opportunities in life. Equally important, the social climate of a school is a model of the world outside. It is where people develop a large part of their morality, their understanding of how the world works and their sense of responsibility towards the society they live in.

Bullying is devastating in any shape or form, and cyberbullying is its newest expression. A number of young people have committed suicide as a result of cyberbullying. Suicide is tragic and final. Suicide as a result of bullying is a startling and hard-hitting indictment on the schools and societies in which it occurs. But there are many more cases of bullying that do not reach this utterly hopeless and irretrievable point but must still be dealt with if we are to live in just, egalitarian and humane societies in which children are able to reach their potential academically, socially and psychically.

Newspaper reports tend to focus on the tragedies, and on the type of bullying epitomized in *Tom Brown's School Days,* where large rough boys beat up smaller and cleverer boys who somehow do not fit the mould. Although these cases have the most visible impacts, bullying is much more than this. It can be psychological. It can include acts of exclusion and isolation, humiliation, name-calling, spreading false rumours and teasing. It can involve the extortion of money and the theft of possessions. It can be sexual. It can be done by and against girls. Although cuts and bruises are the external signs of physical bullying, research shows that the internal hurts from psychological bullying can be just as painful. Recent research also shows that reported cases of bullying are only the tip of the iceberg: the bulk is below the surface and hard to detect.

School bullying is a major problem in many countries. Maxwell and Carroll-Lind's (1997) study of first- and second-form pupils in the North Island of New Zealand asked its respondents to identify the three worst things they had ever experienced. The death of somebody close to them was the most often mentioned, but being bullied by other children came second.

Although the greatest worry parents may have for the safety of their children is in relation to their getting to and from school, and random attacks of the stranger-danger type, Maxwell and Carroll-Lind state that '90% of the incidents of emotional abuse and most of the physical violence between children occur at schools' (1997: 5).

The purpose of this book

This book has been written to provide an up-to-date and improved resource to combat school bullying. Its specific intentions are:

* To summarize what we know about bullying. Since the first edition of *The Anti-Bullying Handbook*, we have learned much more about the nature of bullying. The revised edition discusses this new information and combines it with what is known to work well in the provision of excellent, practical and effective resources to prevent, address and deal with bullying.
* To provide a guide for schools for the development, implementation and evaluation of effective anti-bullying philosophies, policies and programmes. In order to combat bullying, schools need to tackle it wholly and concertedly. Guidelines for the creation and clarification of school policy and practice are outlined. This book is intended to be a useful resource for all schools, from those just starting to consider setting up an anti-bullying initiative, to those with well-established programmes that wish to consider anti-bullying best practice.
* To recommend anti-bullying programmes that deal effectively with bullying. Choosing from the growing amount of materials on bullying is a difficult task. I have selected the most useful approaches and programmes, and in response to unmet needs have also created some new ones.
* To support a culture of problem-solving that uses the scholarship and research information available but also taps into the knowledge and experience of those involved (including teaching and administrative staff, students and the wider community) in developing and implementing anti-bullying programmes.

Although it is clear that anti-bullying programmes are useful tools, every school contains knowledge that must also be harnessed. This consists of the years of experience and knowledge of the school's teachers and administrative and ancillary staff, and the experience and potential for involvement of the students and parents in the creation of solutions.

What is the viewpoint of this book?

I have chosen to write this book from a constructivist and social-ecological perspective. Many studies of bullying, while providing important information, also tend to generalize about the components of the bullying dynamic, to make judgements about the individuals involved, and to deal more with the components than with the whole system. There is a tendency to make causal links between individuals and events, and to lock people into roles. This is commonly called the deficit perspective. Constructivism seeks instead to develop positive alternatives for those taking part in or subjected to bullying and social ecology provides a safe and healthy school environment in which to nurture and grow these more humane solutions.

This humanistic perspective aims to work hard to find solutions that improve everybody's chances, both bully and bullied. In the first instance, it seeks solutions for individuals in the short term, but also argues that such approaches will benefit our society as a whole in the long term.

Who has this book been written for?

In the literature on effective anti-bullying strategies, one issue stands out as being most important – the adoption of a whole-school approach, that is, developing an anti-bullying programme that is taken up and implemented wholeheartedly by the entire school community.

Those involved are, within the school, the students, the teaching staff and the administrative staff, and, outside the school, parents, and social and community agencies.

If all these people understand the dynamics of bullying, and know that something can be done about it, then there is a chance that it can be halted. Once a school decides to deal with bullying, as many people as possible must be included so that they can develop a sense of 'ownership' of the processes and programmes that are adopted. I will address specifically the concerns of these groups and of those who prepare teachers for their profession.

The teaching staff

The teacher's main job is effective classroom management and teaching of a group of children with whom they spend all day (in the case of primary/junior school teachers), or across a range of classes and at various levels (in the case of secondary/high school teachers). Many teachers are ill equipped to deal with relationship problems and specific antisocial behaviour like bullying, simply because they have not been trained to do so, and because teaching is so demanding.

Nonetheless, teachers want to handle bullying effectively, and these are some of the questions they may wish to ask about it:

- What counts as bullying? How do I detect it? What can I do about it?
- If I see what looks like bullying, when do I become involved? When should I let the children sort it out themselves? How do I know when things have gone too far?
- What resources are there to help me solve bullying problems effectively?
- Is it my job to handle bullying or should I go to somebody else?
- Who can I turn to for support when I do not seem to be handling things very well?
- How can I create a classroom that is safe for all of the children in my care?

Deputy or assistant principals are usually responsible for issues of crisis and discipline. They may ask:

- What do I need to do to make sure bullying is handled effectively?
- How will an anti-bullying strategy fit into our overall programme for dealing with disciplinary problems, such as disruptive behaviour, truancy and drugs at school?
- What programmes are available for dealing with bullying? How do I know what the best options are for our school?

The counsellor or pastoral staff may ask:

- What resources are available to inform me about the nature and dynamics of bullying?
- What anti-bullying strategies and programmes are available for dealing with bullying? How do I know which ones work best?
- If I am the person who will implement an anti-bullying policy, how can I best be prepared for this?
- With whom can I discuss how best to deal with the problem of bullying within the school community and/or the social services community?

The school administrators

Over and above their concerns to have a school that runs well and achieves in a variety of ways, the principal/head teacher, other administrators and governors of the school have a moral and legal responsibility to make their school a safe place. If a school has a reputation for being unsafe, parents may choose another school. Bullying is bad for any school. The concerns of administrators are therefore philosophical, legal and practical. Administrators may ask the following questions:

- What can I do to develop and support policies and programmes that will eliminate or reduce bullying in my school?
- What can I do to promote this school as a safe school?
- Providing an effective and proactive anti-bullying scheme is an excellent idea but can give the impression we have a major bullying problem. How can we adopt such schemes to show we are proactive and forward-looking rather than a 'bullying school'?

- What is our role as administrators in such developments – to provide support and structures, to implement or help implement the developments, to provide ongoing evaluations?
- What can best be done within the constraints of limited resources and competing demands?

The parents

Parents create the family environment of victims, bullies and onlookers to bullying. Their involvement in the adoption and implementation of any anti-bullying scheme is crucial. Parents may ask the following questions:

- Is my child involved in bullying in any way?
- What can I do to help?
- How do I know if my child is being bullied?
- How can I follow things up with the school? Who do I go to? What are the school's procedures?
- What should I do if I know bullying is taking place but I feel that the school is not doing enough about it?
- Who else can I go to for help?

Social and community agencies

Individuals in social and community agencies, such as counsellors, educational psychologists, police personnel, social workers and therapists, often work with the after-effects of bullying, school failure, and violent and disruptive behaviour. This may occur in the community; on other occasions, these people are brought into the school to share their expertise. The questions they may ask are:

- What can I find out about bullying in the school?
- How is it reflected in the family and society at large?
- How can I contribute my skills to help develop a school anti-bullying initiative that, if well implemented, will have beneficial effects in the community?

Teachers' college/university lecturers

Teachers' college and university lecturers who are helping to prepare future teachers also need to know about the bullying dynamic so that they can pass this knowledge on to their students. Teacher trainers may ask the following questions:

- What knowledge can I give my students so that they have a good understanding of peer group dynamics and how they work in relation to bullying?
- How can I help my students to develop skills to deal effectively with bullying?
- How can I best fit this understanding of bullying into the overall framework of classroom work?

The structure of the book

Part 1 defines and describes bullying in its many forms. Chapter 2 gives a definition of bullying and a general summary of what we know about it. Bullying can be complex in its development and its dynamic. Chapter 3 examines this. Chapter 4 looks at some specific and difficult types of bullying, namely, racist bullying, bullying of special educational needs children, homophobic bullying and sexual bullying. Chapter 5 examines the nature of cyberbullying and how to respond to it.

Part 2 provides the philosophical, developmental and concrete foundations needed to develop and implement an approach to bullying that works and is fair, humane and appropriately rigorous. Chapter 6, 'How to Create an Anti-Bullying Initiative', shows why schools need to be proactive in developing an anti-bullying initiative and provides a step-by-step plan for doing so. Chapter 7 argues that schools must be clear about their philosophical foundations before they can develop policies that have any chance of success. This includes looking inwards to determine the underlying values and beliefs of the school, and looking outwards to examine which anti-bullying strategies and programmes are consistent with the school's philosophy. Chapter 8, 'Planning and Information Gathering', describes two useful tools for gathering information about the school in general and about the extent of bullying in the school. First, a SWOTSS analysis process is outlined and illustrated with a case study. Second, a questionnaire has been designed to allow schools to gather and quantify information on bullying. Chapter 9, 'Creating a School Anti-Bullying Policy', discusses how to develop and establish an anti-bullying policy. It covers consultation, discussion, writing a policy document, implementation and monitoring, and maintenance.

Part 3 provides a variety of preventative strategies to help make schools safe places. Chapter 10, 'Strategies for Teachers: Practice, Pedagogy and Learning', discusses how teachers can help or stop a bullying culture by being reflective and authoritative in their practice. It also discusses cooperative learning as an effective strategy. Chapter 11 discusses what teachers can do to anticipate and better understand bullying through their use of puppet theatre, Circle Time and sociometry. Chapter 12 shows how interactive and experiential learning can be used to develop a deep understanding of bullying and to find solutions for it via 'On the Bus' (for younger students) and through social action drama (for adolescents). Chapter 13, 'Harnessing the Power of the Peer Group', outlines strategies to assist students to take some control and contribute towards making the school healthy and safe from bullying through the vehicles of a student leadership programme and peer partnering. In Chapter 14, there are suggestions for making the school a safer place aesthetically, environmentally and in terms of the use of space.

Part 4 offers information about interventionist anti-bullying programmes. Chapter 15, 'Peer Mentoring and Peer Mediation', describes two student-centred approaches to bullying that can be used to meet the needs of either bullies or victims. The Support Group Method has replaced what was known as the No Blame Approach, and is an excellent feelings-based programme designed to enlist onlookers and those who have bullied to find solutions to bullying. It is described in Chapter 16. Chapter 17, 'A Circle of Friends', outlines a programme that endeavours to create a supportive group around a child who is experiencing difficulties (and may be considered a bully or victim), so that prosocial behaviour is encouraged. Anatol Pikas is one of the seminal researchers in school bullying, and his Method of Shared Concern is described in Chapter 18. Collaborative problem-solving and resolution (CPR) Chapter 19, is a method aimed at solving bullying that is complicated or entrenched and needs a longer, intensive but constructive approach to restore harmony. Chapter 20 gives a selection of follow-up strategies that can be used: assertiveness training, anger management, and self-defence and martial arts training. This chapter also brings the threads of the book together.

The appendices contain a template for creating an anti-bullying policy (1), a selection of useful bullying scenarios (2), an account of the issues of ethics and confidentiality (3) and a selection of ice breakers (4).

Reference

Maxwell, G. and Carroll-Lind, J. (1997) *The Impact of Bullying on Children*. Wellington: Office of the Commissioner for Children Occasional Paper No. 6.

CHAPTER 2

WHAT WE KNOW ABOUT BULLYING

This chapter defines what bullying is and provides a summary of what we know about it. The most important questions about bullying are answered under the following headings: What is bullying? What are some common myths, misrepresentations and misunderstandings about bullying? Are schools safe? Are there gender and age differences in bullying patterns? How is it possible to tell if someone is being bullied? Can school bullying be stopped?

What is bullying?

In order to deal effectively with bullying, it is important, first, to know what it is.

How is bullying defined?

Definition: Bullying is a conscious, wilful and repetitive act of aggression and/or manipulation and/or exclusion by one or more people against another person or people.

Bullying contains the following elements:

- Bullying is abusive and cowardly.
- Harm is intended.
- It is repetitive and can occur over a short or a long period of time.
- The person(s) doing the bullying has more power than the one(s) being victimized.
- It is often hidden from people in authority.
- Bullies do not expect either to be caught or to suffer any consequences.
- Those who bully are often feared for their bullying behaviour.

- Bullying can gradually undermine and damage the physical and mental well-being of the person being bullied.
- Bullying can be premeditated, organized and systematic, or it can be opportunistic. Once it starts, however, it is likely to continue.
- Although bullying may be directed towards one victim, it also may communicate a sense of menace to those who are witnesses but not contributors to it.
- Hurt experienced by a victim of bullying can be external (physical) and/or internal (emotional/psychological).
- All bullying causes psychological damage.

There are many definitions of bullying and various ways of understanding it (see Smith et al., 2002). In parts of Europe, particularly in Scandinavia, the term 'mobbing' is often used instead of bullying. Rather than being a synonym for bullying, mobbing is a subcategory that refers specifically to a group's ganging up on an individual. A good example from the animal world is when chickens establish a 'pecking order' whereby all chickens peck the weakest one.

What forms does bullying take?

Bullying can take a number of forms, both physical and non-physical. Physical bullying often causes visible hurt such as cuts and bruises, and is tangible and easy to identify. Non-physical bullying is sometimes more difficult to detect and identify because the damage it does is harder to see. There are different complexions of bullying, from the mildest to the most extreme. Sometimes, what has started as physical bullying has escalated into brutality and ended in murder. Bullying, both physical and non-physical, has made some children so desperate that they have attempted or succeeded in committing suicide.

The different forms of bullying are as follows:

- **Physical bullying** (also called direct bullying/aggression) includes biting, choking, hair pulling, hitting, kicking, locking in a room, pinching, punching, pushing, scratching, spitting, stalking or any other form of physical attack and intimidation. It also includes damaging a person's property.
- **Psychological bullying** (also called indirect bullying/aggression) is an attack 'inside' the targeted person. The intention is to harm the individual under attack, but as there are no physical marks it is often assumed to be less harmful. Goldstein et al. (2007) and others argue that psychological bullying can be just as damaging as physical bullying.

Psychological bullying can be verbal and non-verbal:

- **Verbal bullying** includes abusive telephone calls, extorting money, using sexually suggestive or abusive language, making cruel remarks, name-calling, sending (often anonymous) poisonous notes or messages, spiteful teasing, and spreading false and malicious rumours.

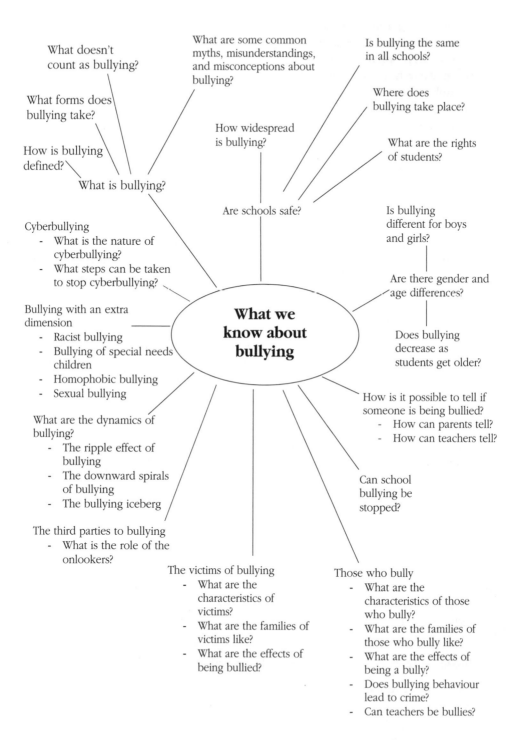

Figure 2.1   What we know about bullying

- **Non-verbal bullying** can be direct or indirect:
  - **Direct non-verbal bullying** often accompanies physical or verbal bullying and includes mean faces and rude gestures. Although this behaviour may not seem significant, it can be part of a process and reinforce bullying that is already going on.
  - **Indirect non-verbal bullying** is sneaky and subtle, and includes manipulating relationships and ruining friendships; and purposely and often systematically excluding, ignoring and isolating someone. When bullying is used to undermine relationships or diminish status, it is known as relational bullying.

Bullying can be any one of the above or a combination of them.

What does not count as bullying?

It is important to be clear about what is *not* bullying. Some incidents that at first appear to be bullying may be something else – criminal offending, sub-bullying or non-bullying behaviour.

Criminal behaviour

Bullying is antisocial and damaging but it is not criminal behaviour. Some acts of aggression have all the hallmarks of bullying (they may be repetitive, and involve violence and an abuse of power, for instance), but in intensity and severity they go beyond the boundaries of what constitutes school bullying and are thus outside the jurisdiction of the school; for example:

- seriously assaulting someone or attacking them with a weapon or an object such as a broken bottle, knife or razor;
- significant theft;
- seriously threatening to cause grievous bodily harm or to kill;
- sexually violating someone (including unwanted sexual touching).

These are criminal offences and should be handled by the police or juvenile authorities, depending on the age of the offenders.

Sub-bullying and non-bullying behaviour

Children often play exuberant physical and verbal games that may appear aggressive and unruly to adults. These activities include play-fights, rough-and-tumble play, and teasing and name-calling between children of equal status. If such activities and events are not repetitive or intended to cause harm, then they may be regarded at worst as sub-bullying behaviour and monitored for escalation and frequency.

Children, especially boys, sometimes end up in full-scale, one-off physical conflicts when a play-fight or verbal sparring has got out of hand. An aggressive attack that occurs once (be it an assault, harassment, intimidation or exclusion) can be hurtful and traumatic. Although these may be considered disciplinary matters, they are not necessarily instances of bullying.

It is important for teachers to be aware that children who are in fact bullying can pretend that fights and teasing are fun and make them appear to be conflicts between equals (when bullying is between people of unequal power). In doing so, they discredit the person being bullied, assert their power and maintain the veil of secrecy that usually surrounds bullying. The person being bullied often concurs with this interpretation of events in order to be accepted by the group doing the bullying.

Teachers need to learn to tell the difference between bullying, criminal acts, and sub-bullying and non-bullying behaviour.

What are some common myths, misrepresentations and misunderstandings about bullying?

There are a number of commonly held myths (long-standing societal 'truths'), misrepresentations (when someone argues in favour of something they know is not the truth) and misunderstandings (when people genuinely believe something to be the case when it actually is not) about bullying that need to be dispelled.

We do not have bullying in our school

This is a common myth. Bullying is seen as something that happens only in 'other' schools, usually those in 'rough' areas.

The Bully Online website makes the following point, however:

> It's in schools which say 'there's no bullying here' that you are most likely to find bullying. Bullying happens in every school; good schools are proactive in their approach and deal with incidents of bullying promptly, firmly and fairly. Bad schools deny it, ignore it, justify it, rationalize it, handle it inappropriately, sweep it under the carpet, blame the victim of bullying, blame the parents of the victim of bullying, say they've 'ticked all the boxes' and make lots of impressive noises but take no substantive action. (http://www.bullyonline.org/schoolbully/myths.htm)

Bullying occurs in all schools and to a greater degree than most people realize. Acknowledging that it occurs is the first step towards preventing it.

You have to learn to stand up for yourself in life: being bullied is character-forming/part of growing up

This is probably the most dangerous myth because it suggests that victims of bullying are to blame for the bullying because they do not stand up for themselves.

Swearer et al. (2009) challenge the myth that bullying is a normal part of growing up: bullying is not normal, natural or acceptable, and young victims are hurt physically and emotionally by it.

Can be mistaken for but is not bullying	←————— Bullying —————→	Criminal activity

- playful teasing
 	
- a one-off fight
 	
- rough and tumble or playfighting with no intention of causing damage
	PHYSICAL
	
	  - biting
	  - hair pulling
	  - hitting
	  - kicking
	  - locking in a room
	  - pinching
	  - punching
	  - pushing
	  - scratching
	  - spitting
	  - any other form of physical attack
	  - damaging a person's property
	
	NON-PHYSICAL
	
	Verbal
	  - abusive language
	  - abusive telephone calls
	  - extorting money or possessions
	  - intimidation/threats of violence
	  - name calling
	  - racist remarks/teasing
	  - sexually suggestive language
	  - spiteful teasing (cruel remarks)
	  - spreading false/malicious rumours
	
	Non-verbal
	
	Direct:
	  - mean faces/rude gestures
	Indirect:
	  - manipulating/ruining friendships
	  - systematically excluding, ignoring and isolating
	  - sending (often anonymous) poisonous notes
	
	Bullying can be any of the above or a combination of these.
	
	Bullying is mean-minded, intentional, cowardly and an abuse of power.
	
	Bullying is a repetitive process.
		- assault with a weapon
		
		- grievous bodily harm
		
		- seriously threatening to cause harm or kill
		
		- serious theft
		
		- sexual abuse

Schools should handle such incidents constructively but not treat them as bullying.	**Schools should address bullying in all its forms.**	**The police or juvenile authorities should handle these criminal offences.**

Figure 2.2   What is and is not bullying

Part of the process of bullying is the almost imperceptible isolating or discrediting of those who are bullied. Their self-esteem is gradually lowered until they feel worthless, and this sense is conveyed to others both through their own worsening perception of themselves and the relentless negativity that is expressed towards them.

Bullies have power over their victims. The process of exclusion and humiliation that is inherent in bullying almost guarantees that victims will not be able to stand up to bullies. Any efforts to do so become part of the fuel that inflames them. The situation is characterized by menace and an imbalance of power, which invites further humiliation for the victim and, in the case of physical bullying, an escalation of violence.

It was just a bit of fun. No harm was done. Can't you take a joke? Boys will be boys!

These are all representations of a similar theme: that it is OK to bully, that it is part of life and that it is natural for boys to act 'tough'. These are all misrepresentations of the truth. Bullying is not fun and it is not harmless. Schools need to develop policies and programmes that reinforce this message and create safer environments.

They were asking for it. They got what they deserved

This is a misrepresentation. A common response, when people are caught bullying, is to say that the victims were asking for it, that they did something provocative and got what they deserved. Bullying is not about justice, however: it is about victimization.

Sometimes a child is annoying and provokes other students. Olweus (1993: 33) calls such children 'provocative victims'. Provocative and annoying behaviour needs to be looked at carefully and treated gently, perhaps with the help of counselling and other interventions (see Chapter 17, 'A Circle of Friends'). It is important to note that victims, like bullies, come in all shapes and sizes, and some people can become victimized only by being in the wrong place at the wrong time.

Teachers know how to handle bullying. It's their job!

This is a misunderstanding. Bullying is only one of many things teachers have to deal with, and usually they have no training for doing so. The majority of bullying purposely occurs out of their sight, and the fact that most children do not report the problem makes it doubly difficult for teachers to handle.

Bradshaw et al. (2007) conducted a study among teachers in the USA and found that teachers seriously underestimated rates of bullying. For example, 57 per cent of school staff thought that less than 10 per cent of their pupils had been victimized, when bullying rates were nearer one-third to half.

Bullies are thick kids from dysfunctional families picking on academic, nerdy kids with glasses

This is a myth. Bullies come in all shapes and sizes – they can be star athletes, popular girls, teachers' pets or the kids who always get into trouble. Contrary to the myth, research suggests that many bullies are socially adept and possess an adequate range of social skills that allow them to manipulate the group to achieve their goals (Besag, 2006).

Schools and their communities must develop a better understanding of bullying so that they can deal effectively with all its protagonists and all its forms.

Are schools safe?

How widespread is bullying?

Recent international research indicates that school bullying is a widespread and specific phenomenon of school violence that affects schools around the world, regardless of national borders, geography, culture or politics (Carney and Merrell, 2001; Craig et al., 2009; Griffin and Gross, 2004). In their introduction to a study of international bullying (Smith et al., 1999), Smith and Morita (1999) say that wherever institutionalized schooling has been established, bullying occurs: all the countries described in this book show a high incidence of bullying.

Of the hundreds of studies of the prevalence of bullying in schools around the world, none of them has reported zero. Instead, they have found that a substantial proportion of all students (8–20 per cent) are 'chronic' victims who are bullied at least once per week (Avilés and Monjas, 2005; Benitez and Justicia, 2006; Bradshaw et al., 2007; Wong et al., 2008).

In Australia, one child in six or seven (20.7 per cent of boys and 15.7 per cent of girls) is bullied at least once a week (Rigby and Slee, 1999). Bullying has been reported as occurring in every school, kindergarten or day-care environment in which it has been investigated (Ken Rigby's website, 2006, kenrigby.net).

A survey published by the Association of Teachers and Lecturers in the UK involving more than 2,500 secondary school pupils in England and Wales suggested that a significant number of pupils were frightened of being bullied at school and believed teachers were unaware of the problem. Of the total, a third said they had been bullied in the past 12 months, a quarter said they had been threatened with violence at school and more than one in 10 said they had actually been attacked (*BBC News*, 16 April 2000).

In another survey of 4,700 children aged 11–16 conducted a couple of years later, approximately 75 per cent reported being the victim of some variety of physical bullying within the school year and 7 per cent reported being the perpetrator or victim of more severe forms of bullying (that is, repeated verbal or physical bullying, property damage or social exclusion) (Glover et al., 2000; Griffin and Gross, 2004).

Sanders and Phye (2004) note that bullying is considered the most predominant form of aggression found in American schools and impacts on the largest number of students when compared to other forms of violence. A 2001 study involving more than 15,000 US students in grades 6 to 10 found that 29.9 per cent of students were involved in moderate or frequent bullying, as a bully (13 per cent), one who has been bullied (10.6 per cent) or both (6.3 per cent) (Nansel et al., 2001). Other research has found that as many as 33.7 per cent of US elementary school students report being bullied frequently at school (Bradshaw et al., 2007; Swearer et al., 2009); and that a quarter of children and adolescents admit to bullying another student at least once in the academic year (Ollendick and Schroeder, 2003).

These examples are given not to suggest that the countries referred to have worse bullying problems than others: the literature on bullying rates throughout the world is enormous, and what all the research has in common is the fact that bullying occurs everywhere. The differences are in the details rather than in this fact.

Is bullying the same in all schools?

The *extent* of bullying can differ from school to school, even within the same community (Olweus, 1993).

Why does the rate of bullying differ from school to school? Three reasons have emerged from the literature:

1. Bullying occurs more frequently in poorer areas. It is sometimes suggested that, in economically depressed areas, there are higher levels of alcoholism, drug use, theft, unemployment and vandalism; a higher percentage of one-parent families; and a general breakdown of the cement that holds society together (Ollendick and Schroeder, 2003). In the Sheffield study, Whitney and Smith (1993) found there was some truth to this perception: it seemed to account for a 10 per cent difference in the level of bullying.
2. Bullying occurs less in more academically focused schools. In support of this suggestion, in Germany, Lösel and Bleisener (1999) found there was less bullying in the more academic grammar schools than in secondary general schools and special schools. Similarly, in Switzerland, bullying was found to occur least in the highest academic school, the gymnasium (Alsaker and Brunner, 1999). The underlying argument is that, in more academically orientated schools, students are more focused, more successful in their studies, and more prosocial in their attitudes and behaviours (and probably socio-economically better off). Consequently, the incidence of bullying (and other antisocial behaviour) is thought to be lower in these settings. Although there is some evidence to support this hypothesis, it is inconclusive (Almeida, 1999; Olweus, 1993; Ortega and Mora-Merchan, 1999).
3. A school's ethos determines the extent of bullying. If a school ethos is developed that promotes qualities such as trust, mutual respect, caring and consideration for others, then bullying is more likely to be marginalized (Elliott, 2002). In relation to the Sheffield study, Whitney and Smith (1993) argue that a good school ethos and effective anti-bullying policies are more important than a school's socio-

economic classification in determining the rate of bullying. Smith and Sharp (1994), too, found that those schools with a good ethos were the most successful in making their schools safe from bullying. In Holland, Mooj's research, cited in Junger-Tas (1999), provides evidence that effective management and teaching methods can produce a positive school ethos at the classroom level. He found schools that encourage cooperative teaching methods and small group learning, and employ teachers who offer a high level of both academic and social group supervision, are more likely to have relatively low levels of bullying. Student welfare policies that stress respect and social health are also more likely to help sustain a non-bullying culture (Soutter and McKenzie, 2000).

While it is difficult to attribute causes to rates and severity of bullying, it is possible to suggest some differences in frequency that may be tied to age and gender differences, and to class composition, and types and cultures of schools. Among many other studies that concluded that bullying is more common in younger groups of children, Nansel et al. (2001) found that bullying occurs most frequently in the sixth through to the eighth grade. A large international study discovered that boys are more likely to be bullied if they attend single-sex government schools, and girls are more likely to be bullied if they attend co-educational private schools (Delfabbro et al., 2006). Rigby (2007) concluded, particularly in relation to Australia, but also more generally, that boarding schools provide more opportunities for sustained bullying to occur without respite.

In conclusion, although there is some evidence that socio-economic difference and the academic nature of a school can influence bullying levels, the presence or absence of bullying in any setting is never a given. The most important finding to emerge from the research is that the development and maintenance of a positive school ethos *in any setting* are the most effective deterrents to entrenched bullying.

Where does bullying take place?

In order to deal effectively with bullying, it is important to know where it most often occurs.

Rigby (2007) suggests that bullying primarily occurs in the playground, classrooms, corridors, outside the school buildings at lunch, or on the way to and from school. With variations, similar findings are made in relation to: Belgium (Vettenburg, 1999), Canada (Craig et al., 2000; Zeigler and Rosenstein-Manner, 1991), England and Wales (Smith, 1999; Wolke et al., 2001), Germany (Lösel and Bleisener, 1999; Wolke et al., 2001), Portugal (Almeida, 1999), Spain (Ortega and Mora-Merchan, 1999) and Switzerland (Alsaker and Brunner, 1999).

In areas where there is less teacher surveillance there is likely to be more bullying (Rigby, 2007), such as when large groups of students are supervised by a small number of adults, including during lunchtime, recess, physical education and when students change classes (Espelage and Asidao, 2001). But whereas large numbers of students surveyed say that bullying is more prevalent in the open and less super-

vised areas of the school (and also on the way to and from school), significant numbers reported a high incidence of bullying in the classroom (http://njbullying.org/
documents/samplenewsletterarticle.pdf; Rigby, 2007). For example, in a comparative
study of primary schools in England and Germany, around 90 per cent of students
cited the playground as the most bully-prone area but about 30 per cent also named
the classroom (Wolke et al., 2001: 683). The same findings have been made by other
researchers on elementary school bullying, for example, Craig et al. (2000) for
Canada, and Espelage and Asidao (2001) for the USA.

Lösel and Bleisener (1999: 232) give an interesting proportional analysis of violent bullying in Germany: 60.1 per cent occurs in the playground, 17.3 per cent on
the way to and from school, 10.4 per cent in the school corridors and 9.2 per cent
in the classroom. The washrooms and toilets are another location for bullying. In a
South Australian survey by Venu Sarma, 21 per cent of primary school students
reported that they did not feel safe from bullying in the playground and 12 per cent
reported not feeling safe in the classroom (Rigby, 2007: 185).

Generally, it is clear that bullying can occur wherever children interact. What is
important is for schools to identify hotspots, to keep those areas under surveillance,
but most of all to educate staff and students about the dynamics of bullying and
what can be done to understand and disarm them (Rapp-Paglicci et al., 2005).

What are the rights of students?

The United Nations Charter of Rights for Children states that every child has the right
to an education and every child has the right to be safe. It is a basic human right in
a democratic society to be safe at school and in the classroom, and as part of the
increasing human rights agenda of the last century, the individual right not to be
bullied or harassed in school has gathered considerable academic, social and political attention. Bullying behaviour infringes upon the child's right to human dignity,
privacy, freedom and security, and has an influence on the victim's physical, emotional, social and educational well-being.

Most countries have legislation and government guidelines to safeguard the rights
of students in their care. (It is easy to find out what the rules and regulations are from
government documents and websites and from local libraries.) In New Zealand, for
example, through the legislation in Section 60 of the Education Act 1989, the government directs that schools are to provide a safe physical and emo-tional atmosphere for their pupils. Schools are also required to analyse and find ways to remove
any barriers to learning. In the State of Victoria, Australia, 'all students have the right
to be treated with respect, and to learn in a safe and supportive environment, that is
free   from   bullying   and   harassment'   (http://www.youthcentral.vic.gov.au/
Know+Your+Rights/Discrimination+&+harassment/Bullying/).

The fact that bullying has become a human rights issue has meant in some cases
that prosecutions, especially of serious instances of bullying, have occurred. While
some of these have clearly been instances of criminal behaviour, others have been
identified because of the psychological as well as physical harm inflicted on the vic-

tims. Smith (1999: 86) cites several cases in which people in Britain have been prosecuted for bullying. A girl was jailed for three months for leading a gang attack on another girl who later committed suicide. A 20-year-old woman received an out-of-court settlement of £30,000 from a London school where she had been victimized as a student for four years. In certain states in the USA, a civil action can be brought against a school or district for some failure in its duty to take reasonable measures to protect a student from harm or bullying (McGrath, 2006).

It seems likely that infusing a human rights framework into bullying prevention efforts may strengthen and facilitate their effective implementation (Greene, 2006). Undoubtedly, many of the myths about bullying will not be able to stand in the face of a strong human rights perspective, and its upholding by constitution and law.

Are there gender and age differences in bullying patterns?

Is bullying different for boys and girls?

Boys bully and are bullied more than girls

An extensive body of literature has revealed that boys are more likely to bully and be bullied than girls (Craig et al., 2009; Juvonen et al., 2003; Nansel et al., 2001; Sanders and Phye, 2004).

In addition, boys carry out a large percentage of the bullying to which girls are subjected. In a study conducted in Bergen, more than 60 per cent of bullied girls reported being bullied mainly by boys, and 80 per cent of boys were bullied by boys (Olweus, 1993, 1995).

Boys tend to use more physical bullying and girls more psychological bullying

Comparative studies of the bullying experiences of boys and girls indicate that there may be significant differences. For example, Smith (1999) and Smith and Sharp (1994) report that, for both primary and secondary schools in the Sheffield project, boys were more likely to be physically bullied and threatened than girls, and girls were more likely to experience indirect forms of bullying, such as being purposely left out and having false rumours spread about them.

There are cases, however, of serious physical bullying among girls in which the victims have been very badly hurt (O'Neil, 2008). Boys, too, use psychological bullying, especially as they get older (Boulton and Hawker, 1997).

While boys tend to use physical means, girls often engage in 'covert bullying' or 'relational aggression' (Crick et al., 1996), which relies on a range of psychological weapons such as isolation from the group (Seals and Young, 2003), persistent teasing and spreading malicious rumours (Besag, 2006).

Boys and girls bully differently and this reflects their friendship patterns

Owens (1996) argues that differences in aggression between boys and girls are linked to differences in friendship patterns. His study shows that boys use more physical and verbal aggression than girls, and that older girls in particular use more verbal aggression and indirect aggression in the form of exclusion and the destruction of friendships. He links this to early socialization, in which boys tend to play in large hierarchically dominated groups, and girls in smaller, more intimate groups.

Sociocultural and developmental theories have been used to explain the differences in aggressive behaviours and conflict strategies between boys and girls. Whereas gender differences in aggression are not very great in infancy and toddlerhood, they increase from preschool years onwards (O'Neil, 2008). In Western cultures, boys and men are socialized and encouraged to be domineering, and to exhibit overt physical and verbal aggression. Research shows that 'parents positively reward verbal and physical aggression in sons and positively reward interpersonal and social skills in daughters' (Wood, 2007: 164–5).

Recent studies of girls' aggressive behaviour have produced consistent findings: girls are aggressive towards each other but usually in more covert, indirect ways, which are motivated by the relational goals concerned with the making and breaking of friendships (Archer and Coyne, 2005; Björkqvist et al., 1992; James and Owens, 2005; Owens et al., 2000; Underwood, 2003).

Boys' relationships tend to be held together by common interests, and they are loose and relatively conflict-free. Besag (1989: 40) suggests that, in their relationships, 'boys seek power and dominance, whereas girls need a sense of affirmation and affiliation, a feeling of belonging and shared intimacy expressed in exchanging confidences and gossip'.

Indirect bullying can be as harmful for girls as physical bullying is for boys

Owens (1996) argues that, with the focus on boys' physical aggression, indirect aggression by girls gets overlooked, probably because it is subtle and there is no outward sign of damage (see also, Sullivan, 1998). It is, however, as harmful for girls as physical bullying is for boys, and more attention needs to be paid to it.

As one middle-school student expressed it, 'There is another kind of violence, and that is violence by talking. It can leave you hurting more than a cut with a knife. It can leave you bruised inside' (National Association of Attorneys General, 2000).

Boys and girls respond differently to being bullied

In an Australian study, Rigby (2007) found that girls tend to respond to bullying with sadness and to believe they are to blame for the bullying. They are more likely to tell someone than boys are. Rigby found that boys tend to respond with anger.

Girls are more willing defenders than boys

Finnish researchers Salmivalli et al. (1998) provide interesting information about the roles of boys and girls in bullying. They found that whereas lots of boys were prepared either to assist with or to reinforce acts of bullying, almost no girls were. Few boys were prepared to become defenders of the victim, but at least five times as many girls were. And five times as many girls were totally uninvolved in or unaware of the bullying.

Does bullying decrease as students get older?

The incidence of bullying seems to peak during middle school years (Benitez and Justicia, 2006; Eslea and Rees, 2001; Pellegrini, 2002), and is highest when children start secondary school (Pellegrini and Long, 2002), but the majority of studies indicate a decreasing prevalence of bullying and victimization (and bully/victims) with increasing age (Gofin et al., 2002; Nansel et al., 2001; Whitney and Smith, 1993).

The apparent discrepancy in these findings may be explained by several factors. Children tend to *report* being bullied less with increasing age – it is more acceptable to admit being bullied as a young child (Rigby, 2007). It is also possible that research findings are skewed by the confusion that surrounds reporting of bullying, interpretation of bullying behaviour, and memories of unpleasant and/or traumatic events.

The increase in bullying during the transition from primary to secondary school is more easily understood. This can be a difficult time due to the onset of puberty and changes in social hierarchy (Benitez and Justicia, 2006; Pellegrini and Long, 2002). Pellegrini and Bartini (2000: 700) refer to this transition as a 'brutalizing period', and Pellegrini and Long (2002) draw upon dominance theory to explain this increase in bullying: it is used as a strategy to gain status in an environment in which establishing new social groups is imperative (Espelage and Swearer, 2004; Salmivalli, 2010). It is also the case that by the time the upper levels of the school are reached, some of the disruptive and bullying students have either been expelled or dropped out, with those left focusing on their final examinations.

How is it possible to tell if someone is being bullied?

Because the great majority of bullying is not reported, in many cases it is driven underground and the victims are left powerless and trapped. This makes the school, and the world in general, a very unsafe place.

It is important, therefore, that we become familiar with the signals that tell us someone is being bullied. A single sign may be nothing more than a temporary aberration, a passing mood or, in the case of teenagers, a symptom of adolescent angst. But if several of these symptoms occur together, bullying may be occurring (Rigby, 2007).

The following is an overview of some of the symptoms of bullying that parents and teachers should look out for in children.

How parents can tell

- Anxiety about going to school; finding reasons to be late in leaving; or going to school via some obscure, roundabout route.
- Other signs of anxiety, such as bed-wetting and nightmares; and headaches and stomach aches, particularly in the morning when it is time to go to school.

- Coming home with books or clothes ripped, or with bruises and cuts.
- Losing possessions.
- Asking for (or even stealing) extra money, sometimes to replace goods or money stolen from them.
- Receiving mysterious and upsetting telephone calls.
- Never bringing children home, and seldom being invited to social functions with classmates.
- Being irrational and angry with parents and siblings.
- Seeming depressed, sad, and even threatening or attempting suicide.
- Being unable to concentrate on homework, and a decline in school work.
- Refusing to talk about what is wrong or being evasive.
- Taking or attempting to take 'protection' to school (a stick, knife, gun, and so on), and displaying 'victim' body language, for example, avoiding eye contact, hunching shoulders.
- Truanting.
- Doing things that are out of character and getting into trouble.

How teachers can tell

- When a child is getting a lot of negative attention and being teased.
- Sitting alone at lunchtime, having no friends to play with and being ignored by peers except to be taunted.
- Never being chosen when sports or classroom teams are selected.
- Not speaking up in class, lacking confidence when forced to participate and eliciting snide remarks when they do.
- When a physical problem develops or becomes worse, for example, a stutter.
- When someone seems to be drawn into conflict, but then flounders and appears stupid.
- When classwork deteriorates in an unaccountable way.
- Unhappiness, distress and withdrawal.
- Irregular attendance or frequent absence.
- When a child is small and not strong, yet seems to be at the centre of fights and gets blamed for starting them.

Can school bullying be stopped?

Bullying can be stopped. The schools that do this most successfully are those that act with purpose, thoroughness and integrity. Like the first edition, this book adopts a socio-ecological approach that is founded in a whole-school/whole-community perspective. This means that, while it is important to deal specifically with incidents of bullying, it is crucial to be aware of the wider context of community, culture and society in order to be effective and constructive (Espelage and Swearer, 2004).

Central to effective anti-bullying initiatives is the concept of a whole-school approach: all who are affected by bullying are included in developing an initiative and educated about it at the same time. There are many success stories of schools handling bullying effectively. Parts 2–5 of this book show how schools can produce such success for themselves.

References

Almeida, A.M. (1999) 'Portugal', in P.K. Smith, Y. Morita, J. Junger-Tas, D. Olweus, R. Catalano and P. Slee (eds), *The Nature of School Bullying: A Cross-national Perspective*. London: Routledge.

Alsaker, F. and Brunner, A. (1999) 'Switzerland', in P.K. Smith, Y. Morita, J. Junger-Tas, D. Olweus, R. Catalano and P. Slee (eds), *The Nature of School Bullying: A Cross-national Perspective*. London: Routledge.

Archer, J. and Coyne, S.M. (2005) 'An integrated review of indirect, relational and social aggression', *Personality and Social Psychology Review*, 9: 212–30.

Avilés, J.M. and Monjas, I. (2005) 'Study on the incidence of intimidation and bullying in compulsory secondary education, using the CIMEI questionnaire on intimidation and bullying' (in Spanish), *Anales de Psicología*, 21(1): 27–41.

Benitez, J.L. and Justicia, F. (2006) *Bullying: Description and Analysis of the Phenomenon*. Granada: University of Granada, Department of Developmental and Educational Psychology.

Besag, V. (1989) *Bullies and Victims in Schools: A Guide to Understanding and Management*. Milton Keynes: Open University Press.

Besag, V.E. (2006) 'Bullying among girls: friends or foes?', *School Psychology International*, 27: 535–51.

Björkqvist, K., Lagerspetz, K.M.J. and Kaukiainen, A. (1992) 'Do girls manipulate and boys fight? Developmental trends in regard to direct and indirect aggression', *Aggressive Behavior*, 18: 117–27.

Boulton, M.J. and Hawker, D.S. (1997) 'Non-physical forms of bullying among school pupils: a cause for concern', *Health Education*, 97(2): 61–4.

Bradshaw, C., Sawyer, A. and O'Brennan, L. (2007) 'Bullying and peer victimization at school: perceptual differences between students and school staff', *School Psychology Review*, 36: 361–83.

Carney, A.G. and Merrell, K.W. (2001) 'Bullying in schools: perspectives on understanding and preventing an international problem', *School Psychology International*, 22(3): 364–82.

Craig, W., Harel-Fisch, Y., Fogel-Grinvald, H., Dostaler, S., Hetland, J., Simons-Morton, B., Molcho, M., Gaspar de Mato, M., Overpeck, M., Due, P., Pickett, W. (2009) 'A cross-national profile of bullying and victimization among adolescents in 40 countries', *International Journal of Public Health*, 54(2): 216–24.

Craig, W., Pepler, D. and Atlas, R. (2000) 'Observations of bullying in the playground and in the classroom', *School Psychology International*, 21(1): 22–36.

Crick, N.R., Bigbee, M.A. and Howe, C. (1996) 'Gender differences in children's normative beliefs about aggression: How do I hurt thee? Let me count the ways', *Child Development*, 67(3): 1003–14.

Delfabbro, P., Winefield, T., Trainor, S., Dollard, M., Anderson, S., Metzer, J., et al. (2006) 'Peer and teacher bullying/victimization of South Australian secondary school students: prevalence and psychosocial profiles', *British Journal of Educational Psychology*, 76: 71–90.

Elliott, M. (2002) *Bullying: A Practical Guide to Coping for Schools*. 3rd edn. London: Pearson Education.

Eslea, M. and Rees, J. (2001) 'At what age are children most likely to be bullied at school?', *Aggressive Behavior*, 27: 419–29.

Espelage, D.L. and Asidao, C. (2001) 'Interviews with middle school students: bullying, victimization, and contextual variables', *Journal of Emotional Abuse*, 2: 49–62.

Espelage, D.L. and Swearer, S.M. (2004) *Bullying in American Schools: A Social-Ecological Perspective on Prevention and Intervention*. Mahwah, NJ: Erlbaum.

Glover, D., Gough, G. and Johnson, M., with Cartwright, N. (2000) 'Bullying in 25 secondary schools: incidence, impact and intervention', *Educational Research*, 42(2): 141–56.

Gofin, R., Palti, H. and Gordon, L. (2002) 'Bullying in Jerusalem schools: victims and perpetrators', *Public Health*, 116: 173–8.

Goldstein, S.E., Young, A. and Boyd, C. (2007) 'Relational aggression at school: associations with school safety and social climate', *Journal of Youth and Adolescence*, 37(6): 641–54.

Greene, M.B. (2006) 'Bullying in schools: a plea for measure of human rights', *Journal of Social Issues*, 62(1): 63–79.

Griffin, R. and Gross, A. (2004) 'Childhood bullying: current empirical findings and future directions for research', *Aggressive and Violent Behaviour*, 9: 379–400.

James, V.H. and Owens, L.D. (2005) 'They turned around like I just wasn't there: an analysis of teenage girls' letters about their peer conflicts', *School Psychology International*, 26: 71–88.

Junger-Tas, J. (1999) 'The Netherlands', in P.K. Smith, Y. Morita, J. Junger-Tas, D. Olweus, R. Catalano and P. Slee (eds), *The Nature of School Bullying: A Cross-national Perspective*. London: Routledge.

Juvonen, J., Graham, S. and Schuster, M.A. (2003) 'Bullying among young adolescents: the strong, the weak, and the troubled', *Pediatrics*, 112(6): 1231–7.

Lösel, F. and Bleisener, T. (1999) 'Germany', in P.K. Smith, Y. Morita, J. Junger-Tas, D. Olweus, R. Catalano and P. Slee (eds), *The Nature of School Bullying: A Cross-national Perspective*. London: Routledge.

McGrath, M.J. (2006) *School Bullying: Tools to Avoid Harm and Liability*. Thousand Oaks, CA: Corwin.

Nansel, T.R., Overpeck, M., Pilla, R.S., Ruan, W.J., Simons-Morton, B. and Scheidt, P. (2001) 'Bullying behaviors among US youth: prevalence and association with psychosocial adjustment', *Journal of the American Medical Association*, 285: 2094–100.

National Association of Attorneys General (2000) *Bruised Inside: What our Children Say about Youth Violence, What Causes It, and What We Should Do About It*. Washington, DC: National Association of Attorneys General.

O'Neil, S. (2008) *Bullying By Tween and Teen Girls: A Literature, Policy and Resource Review*. Toronto: Kookaburra Consulting.

Ollendick, T.H. and Schroeder, C.S. (eds) (2003) *Encyclopedia of Clinical Child and Pediatric Psychology*. New York: Kluwer Academic.

Olweus, D. (1993) *Bullying at School: What We Know and What We Can Do about It*. Oxford: Blackwell.

Olweus, D. (1995) 'Bullying or peer abuse at school: facts and intervention', *Current Directions in Psychological Science*, 4(6): 196–200.

Ortega, R. and Mora-Merchan, J. (1999) 'Spain', in P.K. Smith, Y. Morita, J. Junger-Tas, D. Olweus, R. Catalano and P. Slee (eds), *The Nature of School Bullying: A Cross-national*

Perspective. London: Routledge.

Owens, L. (1996) 'Sticks and stones and sugar and spice: girls' and boys' aggression in schools', *Australian Journal of Guidance and Counselling*, 6: 45–57.

Owens, L., Shute, R. and Slee, P. (2000) '"Guess what I just heard!": indirect aggression among teenage girls in Australia', *Aggressive Behaviour*, 26: 67–83.

Pellegrini, A. (2002) 'Bullying, victimization, and sexual harassment during the transition to middle school', *Educational Psychologist*, 37(3): 151–64.

Pellegrini, A. and Bartini, M. (2000) 'A longitudinal study of bullying, victimization, and peer affiliation during the transition from primary school to middle school', *American Educational Research Journal*, 37(3): 699–725.

Pellegrini, A. and Long, J. (2002) 'A longitudinal study of bullying, dominance, and victimization during the transition from primary school through secondary school', *British Journal of Developmental Psychology*, 20: 259–80.

Rapp-Paglicci, L., Dulmus, C.N., Sowers, K.M. and Theriot, M.T. (2005) '"Hotspots" for bullying: exploring the role of environment in school violence', *Journal of Evidence-based Social Work*, 1(2 and 3): 131–41.

Rigby, K. (2007) *Children and Bullying: How Parents and Teachers Can Reduce Bullying*. Oxford: Blackwell.

Rigby, K. and Slee, P. (1999) 'Australia', in P.K. Smith, Y. Morita, J. Junger-Tas, D. Olweus, R. Catalano and P. Slee (eds), *The Nature of School Bullying: A Cross-national Perspective*. London: Routledge.

Salmivalli, C. (2010) 'Bullying and the peer group: a review', *Aggression and Violent Behavior*, 15(2): 112–20.

Salmivalli, C., Kaukiainen, A. and Lagerspetz, K. (1998) 'Aggression in the social relations of school-aged girls and boys', in P.T. Slee and K. Rigby (eds), *Children's Peer Relations*. London and New York: Routledge.

Sanders, C.E. and Phye, G.D. (eds) (2004) *Bullying: Implications for the Classroom*. San Diego, CA: Academic Press/Elsevier.

Seals, D. and Young, J. (2003) 'Bullying and victimization: prevalence and relationship to gender, grade level, ethnicity, self-esteem, and depression', *Adolescence*, 38(152): 735–40.

Smith, P.K. (1999) 'England and Wales', in P.K. Smith, Y. Morita, J. Junger-Tas, D. Olweus, R. Catalano and P. Slee (eds), *The Nature of School Bullying: A Cross-national Perspective*. London: Routledge.

Smith, P.K. and Morita, Y. (1999) 'Introduction', in P.K. Smith, Y. Morita, J. Junger-Tas, D. Olweus, R. Catalano and P. Slee (eds), *The Nature of School Bullying: A Cross-national Perspective*. London: Routledge.

Smith, P.K. and Sharp, S. (eds) (1994) *School Bullying – Insights and Perspectives*. London: Routledge.

Smith, P.K., Cowie, H., Olafsson, R. and Liefooghe, A. (2002) 'Definitions of bullying: a comparison of terms used, and age and gender differences, in a fourteen-country international comparison', *Child Development*, 73: 1119–33.

Smith, P.K., Morita, Y., Junger-Tas, J., Olweus, D., Catalano, R. and Slee, P. (eds) (1999) *The Nature of School Bullying: A Cross-national Perspective*. London: Routledge.

Soutter, A. and McKenzie, A. (2000) 'The use and effects of anti-bullying and anti-harassment policies in Australian schools', *School Psychology International*, 21(1): 96–105.

Sullivan, K. (1998) 'Isolated children, bullying and peer group relations', in P.T. Slee and K. Rigby (eds), *Children's Peer Relations*. London and New York: Routledge.

Swearer, S.M., Espelage, D.L. and Napolitano, S.A. (2009) *Bullying Prevention and*

Intervention: Realistic Strategies for Schools. New York: Guilford.

Underwood, M.K. (2003) *Social Aggression Among Girls.* New York: Guilford.

Vettenburg, N. (1999) 'Belgium', in P.K. Smith, Y. Morita, J. Junger-Tas, D. Olweus, R. Catalano and P. Slee (eds), *The Nature of School Bullying: A Cross-national Perspective.* London: Routledge.

Whitney, I. and Smith, P.K. (1993) 'A survey of the nature and extent of bully/victim problems in junior/middle and secondary schools', *Educational Research*, 35: 3–25.

Wolke, D., Woods, S., Stanford, K. and Schulz, H. (2001) 'Bullying and victimization of primary school children in England and Germany: prevalence and school factors', *British Journal of Psychology*, 92: 673–96.

Wong, D.S.W., Lok, D.P.P., Wing Lo, T. and Ma, S.K. (2008) 'School bullying among Hong Kong Chinese primary schoolchildren', *Youth and Society*, 40(1): 35–54.

Wood, J. (2007) *Gendered Lives: Communication, Gender, and Culture.* Florence, KY: Thomson Wadsworth.

Zeigler, S. and Rosenstein-Manner, M. (1991) *Bullying at School: Toronto in an International Context.* Toronto: Toronto Boards of Education, No. 196R.

CHAPTER 3

THE BULLYING TRIANGLE AND THE BULLYING DYNAMIC

Introduction: identifying the protagonists and placing them in context

Very often people think of bullying as a one-to-one relationship, but in fact there are three main roles: bullies, victims and bystanders. Understanding this triangle goes some way towards understanding that bullying does not exist in isolation but occurs in a social context and a wider environment in which not only schools but also families and whole communities are involved. It is in this context that the dynamics of bullying can best be understood.

Three concepts that give us a better grasp of the complexities of bullying are provided in this chapter: the ripple effect, the downward spirals and the bullying iceberg.

Those who bully

What are the characteristics of those who bully?

Bullies tend to be characterized as aggressive, domineering, having a positive view of violence, impulsive and lacking empathy with their victims (for example, Benitez and Justicia, 2006; Carney and Merrell, 2001; Lösel and Bleisener, 1999). While such profiles are accurate for confident bullies, they do not account for anxious bullies, who hit out because they are insecure; for passive bullies, or bully/victims, who are bullies in some situations and are bullied in others (Stephenson and Smith, 1989); for the differences between boy and girl bullying; and for most types of psychological bullying.

Anxious bullies are usually boys who are weak academically and are generally unpopular. Their bullying takes the form of skirmishes that evoke a reaction and give a momentary sense of power. Bully/victims or passive bullies are likely to exist in an emotionally and socially chaotic environment in which they are disruptive, hostile and at the same time disturbed. They are inclined to victimize some children and to be victimized by others (Veenstra et al., 2005).

In the case of boys, dominance is often claimed by physical prowess (Espelage et al., 2001); and in the case of girls, through the use of indirect aggression (Owens, 1996) and control over and the creation and dissolution of cliques and friendships (Owens and MacMullin, 1995).

It is difficult to typify the sorts of children who are bullies, but because all forms of bullying are dependent on unequal power relationships, it is accurate to say that most bullies are individuals who seek dominance and status in the peer group (Salmivalli, 2010). A constructivist argument is that if the dominant behaviour of bullies is channelled into leadership and prosocial acts, the apparent deficits may be reformed into better peer relations and an improvement in attitudes to, and performance at, school.

What are the families of bullies like?

Family influences (for example, rearing practices, parental modelling) on aggressive behaviour in children have been recognized for a long time, and recent research suggests there may be links between bullying and family practices.

Bullying can be passed on from generation to generation, and intergenerationally within families between peers. Farrington (1993) states that males who are bullies and are aggressive at school are likely to have sons who will repeat this behaviour. But transmission of influences between siblings, through acting as 'key pathogens' and/or 'partners in crime', is also responsible for the aggregation of delinquent behaviour.

For most children, the family is the agent of socialization, and a child who is not cared for is unlikely to care for others, to develop empathy or to learn to cooperate (Rigby, 2007). An adolescent in a dysfunctional family where communication is minimal or non-existent and where the relationships are poor is prone to developing feelings of inferiority and resentment that can lead to the need to dominate others. In an earlier study, Rigby (1994) found that a majority of self-reported male bullies came from dysfunctional families, which were characterized by little sense of belonging, and a lack of love or support.

Bowers et al. (1992) suggest that families with strong hierarchical power structures (where a father controls a child through harsh physical punishment) predispose a child towards aggressive behaviour. Similarly, families that do not provide monitoring and boundaries are likely to produce children with poor relationship skills who know little except haphazard reactions and random antisocial behaviour. This is reflected in how they deal with peer relationships. Others bully because they are isolated and have a deep need for belonging, but do not have the social skills to keep and maintain friendships (Williams et al., 2005).

Researchers at the Institute of Psychiatry, King's College London, have published new findings that highlight the influence of family factors, such as maltreatment, domestic violence or abusive parenting, as important risk indicators for children going on to become involved in bullying once they reach school age. A nationally representative cohort of 2,232 children took part in the research, and their mothers and teachers were questioned to identify factors that make children more likely to be bullied or to bully others. The researchers found that children who experienced abuse, were maltreated or witnessed family violence were twice as likely to be bullied, engage in bullying, or be both a bully and a victim of bullying. Children who showed symptoms of anxiety or depression (for example, being shy or fearful or crying a lot) were more likely to be involved in bullying as victims or bullies, and children were more prone to being bully/victims if their mother was depressed. The study demonstrated that there are environmental factors that influence childhood bullying and concluded that the inclusion of families in bullying interventions may help reduce the prevalence of bullying during the early school years (Bowes et al., 2009).

While there are apparent links between bullying and the family, a person may bully for a variety of other reasons: because of life events, because of the power of an antisocial peer group, because of the social climate of the school or surrounding community, because of personality characteristics, or a combination of these and other factors. It is important not to assume that a certain type of family will produce bullies, but to bear the research findings in mind and to use them wisely and with discretion.

What are the effects of being a bully? Does bullying behaviour lead to crime?

Bullying among primary school-age children is now recognized as an antecedent to progressively more violent behaviour in later grades (Saufler and Gagne, 2000). Bowes et al. (2009) found that children who showed antisocial behaviours such as aggression or delinquency (for example, stealing, vandalism and lying) were more likely to be bullies or bully/victims. A study by Rigby and Cox (1996) concluded that adolescents identified as bullies were prone to involvement in other forms of antisocial behaviour such as shoplifting, truancy, writing graffiti and getting into trouble with the police. In addition, several studies have linked bullying with depression and post-traumatic stress disorder, especially later in life (Kaltiala-Heino et al., 1999; Klomek et al., 2007, 2009; Tehrani, 2004). Does this mean that there is a progression from the antisocial behaviour of bullying to psychopathology and/or criminal offending?

Several researchers have found a strong relationship between bullying, criminal offending and recidivism. Bullying in early childhood has been posited as a critical risk factor for the development of future problems with violence and delinquency

(Ross, 2003). A study of more than 500 American children found that those identified as bullies at the age of eight had a 25 per cent chance of having a criminal record by the age of 30 (Eron et al., 1987). In a follow-up to his 1980s study in Norway, Olweus (1993) found that around 60 per cent of boys considered bullies in his grade 6 to 9 cohorts had at least one criminal conviction by the time they were 24. As many as 35 to 40 per cent of former bullies had three or more convictions by this age, as compared with those who were not bullies.

Researchers have also found that, while their criminal informants may have been bullies, they were just as likely to have been victims of bullying (Cullingford and Morrison, 1995). The Finnish 'From a boy to a man' study that analysed the life patterns of over 2000 males born in 1981 (Sourander et al., 2007, 2009) makes a clear link between bullying and other pathologies, including criminal behaviour, and personality and psychiatric disorders. All of the research suggests that the issue is a complex one: it underlines the destructive character of bullying.

Can teachers be bullies?

Although the vast majority of adults in authority interact respectfully with students, some physically and psychologically bully students (Whitted and Dupper, 2008). In Maxwell and Carroll-Lind's New Zealand study (1997) of lower secondary school students, 14 per cent reported being treated unfairly or bullied by adults at school. This finding is not uncommon.

The most frequently reported types of maltreatment perpetrated by adult educators include students being prohibited from using the bathroom, and being grabbed, pushed, yelled at, unfairly disciplined, called names and isolated from peers (Whitted, 2005). In a study of 50 alternative education students, 86 per cent reported at least one incident of adult physical maltreatment in school and 88 per cent reported at least one incident of adult psychological maltreatment in school (Whitted and Dupper, 2008). Almost twice as many students reported that an adult, rather than a peer, was involved in their worst school experience (64.4 per cent), with several indicating that this involved being physically mistreated by an adult; half reported being upset by the experience 'a lot'. These findings indicate that students are being bullied by teachers in a wide range of destructive and harmful ways (Delfabbro et al., 2006).

Until recently, teachers had authority by virtue of their role. Although corporal punishment at school has been made illegal in many countries, teachers are not barred from being abusive, derisory or insensitive (Garbarino and deLara, 2003).

Olweus (1999) makes the point that the issue of teachers who bully is serious and deserves more attention than it currently receives. Anyone who bullies students is not going to be good at solving student-on-student bullying, and is likely to be a negative role-model. Olweus further suggests that when students are bullied by teachers, they may develop anti-teacher and anti-school attitudes.

The victims of bullying

What are the characteristics of victims?

Victims of bullying are usually characterized as depressed, anxious, shy and lonely (Drake et al., 2003). They are typically insecure, unassertive and cautious, and rarely defend themselves or retaliate when confronted by students who bully them. They have a tendency to self-depreciation, indecisiveness and approval-seeking, and may lack social skills and friends, thus often being socially isolated (Field, cited by Rigby, 2002; http://www.parentspress.com/edubullying.html). Because they play less with other children, their social skills tend to be less developed than those of their peers. Their isolation also means that they are targets (Smith, 1999).

Byrne (1999) found that victims of bullying feel guilt, shame and a sense of failure because they cannot cope with the bullying. They are often worried, unhappy and fearful, and significantly more neurotic than the norm. While research has shown that victims as a rule score lower on measures of self-esteem (Rigby, 2002), it is not clear whether they are bullied because of low self-esteem or have low self-esteem because they are bullied.

A frequently cited defining characteristic of victims of bullying is that they tend to be physically weaker than their peers (Batsche and Knoff, 1994). However, this would suggest that retaliation is a matter of muscles rather than confidence and social intelligence. While some of the literature has suggested that bullies frequently target victims who are disabled, overweight, underweight or physically unattractive (see Chapter 4), other research argues that such physical characteristics do not appear to be significant factors that can be correlated with victimization (Ross, 2003).

At least three types of victims have been identified: passive victims, who lack confidence and are generally unpopular (Carney and Merrell, 2001); provocative victims, who are confrontational and cause tension and irritation around them (Olweus, 1978, 1984, 1991, 1994; Veenstra et al., 2005); and bully/victims, who provoke aggression in others and instigate aggressive acts (Griffin and Gross, 2004; Stephenson and Smith, 1989). While these typologies are useful, they can be used unhelpfully to label and blame victims rather than to unravel the bullying dynamic.

Bullying dehumanizes victims and makes it easy for bullies to act without conscience towards them (Perry et al., 1990, and Troy and Sroufe, 1987, both cited in Harachi et al., 1999). A constructivist approach to bullying would challenge the thinking underlying the classification of victims because such classifications focus on symptoms rather than dealing with the whole bullying system. This is examined more fully later in this chapter under the heading 'What are the dynamics of bullying?'.

What are families of victims like?

Because children acquire their primary socialization from the family, some researchers have looked to the family for some of the causes of bullying and victimization (Dautenhahn et al., 2007). Families are important in helping children develop the skills necessary for positive peer interactions: it is through the family that the child will learn interpersonal skills, what to expect in relationships and how to behave (Espelage and Swearer, 2004).

Sometimes children who are victims come from families under stress (for example, illness, Maines and Robinson, 1998; immigration and/or large families, Fabre-Cornali, 1999; and marriage breakup, Mellor, 1999). It is relatively easy to see how such life events may make a child sad and withdrawn, or aggressive and angry, and thus open to being victimized. Other researchers have made causal links between school bullying and over-protectiveness in mothers (Espelage and Swearer, 2004), and physical or emotional absence in fathers (Fosse and Holen, 2007).

While these findings may be interesting, some of them are psychological and measurement based, operating out of a deficit mode that tries to align problems with parents and families causes and so to advocate the need for a change in the behaviour of individuals rather than addressing the system. If teachers assume that such studies are correct, then they may add to the child's predisposition to being bullied by characterizing them as overprotected, blaming not only them but also their parents. This also means that teachers do not have to take the bullying seriously.

Other researchers (for example, Rigby, 2002) have focused on the fact that, when there is support from parents, the negative effects of bullying can be greatly reduced. Clearly, it is more sensible to harness the support that resides in the protectiveness of these families than to blame them for the fact that their children are being victimized.

What are the effects of being bullied?

Research indicates that those who have been bullied severely tend to suffer long-term consequences, including increased levels of depression, anxiety and psychosomatic symptoms (Arseneault et al., 2006; Campbell and Morrison, 2007; Kaltiala-Heino et al., 2000; Tehrani, 2004), as well as suicidal ideation (Kaltiala-Heino et al., 1999). Even more tragically, many studies link bullying and suicide: for example, the Victoria Coroner in 2007 indicated that 40 per cent of suicide victims have been bullied in school (cited on http://www.schoolangels.com.au/bm/resources/bullying/what-is-school-bullying-100508.shtml).

The isolation and exclusion that often accompany bullying not only deny children company, friendship and social interaction, but also cause them to feel incompetent and unattractive. Those who have been bullied often have difficulty forming good relationships and tend to lead less successful lives. Even though they may be very capable, bullied children sometimes appear unintelligent and as a result suffer academically (Kupersmidt et al., 1990; Olweus, 1978; Sanders and Phye, 2004).

In an Australian study, Rigby (1994) found that frequently bullied students were more likely than others to suffer poor health. In a study of over 700 English secondary school students, Sharp (Sharp, 1996; Sharp and Thompson, 1992) found that 43 per cent of the respondents had been bullied in the past year; of this group, 20 per cent said that they would truant to avoid bullying, 29 per cent that they found it hard to concentrate on their schoolwork, 22 per cent that after they had been bullied they felt physically sick and 20 per cent that they had sleeping difficulties.

Emotionally, victims of bullying may feel any of the following: afraid, alienated, angry, ashamed, depressed, disempowered, dumb, hurt, sad, stupid, subhuman, trampled on, ugly and useless.

Physically, the effects of bullying are often severe: broken bones, broken teeth, concussion, damaged eyes and even permanent brain damage. Other physical effects include bites, bruises, cuts, gouges and scratches. The most serious effect of bullying is suicide, instances of which are cited by most anti-bullying researchers (for example, Kim and Leventhal, 2008; Klomek et al., 2009).

Bullying clearly affects learning, mental and physical health, and safety and well-being. It has been linked to serious school violence, including shooting and hazing incidents in American schools (Nansel et al., 2001). An estimated 160,000 children miss school every day in the USA because of intimidation by their peers (Lumsden, 2002); and as many as 7 per cent of America's eighth graders stay home at least once a month because of bullies (Banks, 1997). Twenty per cent of students carry weapons to school to feel safer, and 50 per cent knew of a student who had switched schools to feel safer (Newman, 2004).

Abraham Maslow (1970) developed a theory that human beings have certain basic needs that must be met before higher-order (or growth) needs can be addressed. Our physiological needs are for food, water and shelter. Our safety needs require us to protect ourselves from the world at large. Our relationship needs are for social contact, friendship and love.

Our higher-order or growth needs involve gaining the approval and love of others so that self-esteem and self-respect are formed and nurtured. The need to be creative and to be able to reach our potential is achieved only after the four other needs have been met.

Maslow's model is useful for explaining some of the possible effects of bullying. If children are bullied, their safety needs have not been met. If they are being emotionally bullied, excluded or isolated, then they are being denied the opportunity of making friends and experiencing the normal interactions of the school years. They are being barred from the relationship growth that leads to the development of social intelligence. It may also mean that they are being denied access to full cognitive development.

The third parties to bullying

What roles do the onlookers to bullying play?

Bullies derive power from a public display. In fact, if they are motivated by a wish for dominance and status, then bullying will have to occur in front of an audience, and the onlookers, whether directly involved or only present passively, form the main part of this audience (Salmivalli, 2010). Research in Canada claims that peers are present in 85 per cent of bullying episodes in the playground and in the classroom (Canada Safety Council websites), and may be critical in instigating, maintaining and exacerbating bullying episodes (Craig and Pepler, 1995).

When bullying occurs, onlookers can choose to observe passively, to become participants in the bullying, to walk away or to intervene (Salmivalli, 2010). Children may indicate support for bullying either passively, via not intervening, remaining friends with the bully or gossiping about the incident; or actively, via providing verbal encouragement, holding the victim or adopting the role of lookout (Cowie and Sharp, 1994; Reid et al., 2004).

Adair's New Zealand research found that 42 per cent of onlookers to bullying chose not to intervene. She identified three reasons for this: 'the victim was not liked or not a friend; fear of being a target; belief that it was probably deserved' (Adair, 1999: 35). This suggests that some children will intervene if a friend is being bullied (even if it means risking becoming a target), but those who are not friends or who are deemed to have deserved it will not be helped. This is a highly selective and entrenched response. Adair et al. (2000) identified a general malaise and sense of powerlessness among many onlookers. This was because they had neither strategies for combating bullying nor faith that it could be stopped.

On the other hand, the same research showed that 32 per cent of students did stand up for victims of bullying and 22 per cent told a teacher or got help. Studies generally show that those willing to intervene are more likely to be primary rather than secondary students (Vettenburg, 1999), and much more likely to be girls than boys (Adair, 1999; Salmivalli et al., 1998).

Several studies suggest that many people are uncomfortable with bullying and are eager to find ways to deal with it. Results from the Sheffield study (Smith and Sharp, 1994) showed that after bullying programmes had been introduced to participating schools, onlookers became more active in trying to combat bullying, with an average of 9 per cent more secondary pupils reporting that they would not join in bullying. This is an indication that if schools encourage interventions and have clear anti-bullying policies, more children will feel able to dissociate themselves from the bullying and to offer support to those being bullied. The role of the peer group in objecting to or stopping bullying is potentially of huge importance.

Who else is affected by bullying?

Bullying occurs in a social context. It affects the person being bullied most of all, but it affects others as well. It is like a stone thrown into the middle of a pool: the ripples that come from the point of impact spread outwards toward the edges of the pool (see Figure 3.1). More specifically, this occurs as follows.

The first level: point of impact

The bullied person is the primary victim and feels the brunt of the bullying, not only when it occurs but beyond.

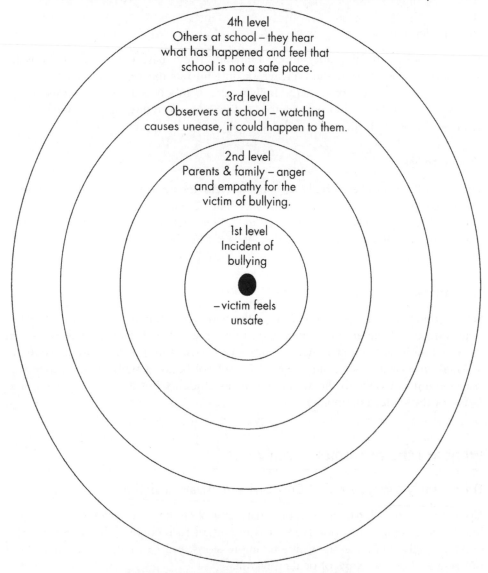

5th level
The wider community – if students are not safe in school, why should they be
safe in the wider community? The school is a microcosm of the community.

4th level
Others at school – they hear
what has happened and feel that
school is not a safe place.

3rd level
Observers at school – watching
causes unease, it could happen to them.

2nd level
Parents & family – anger
and empathy for the
victim of bullying.

1st level
Incident of
bullying

– victim feels
unsafe

Although bullying most affects those being victimized,
there are second-, third-, fourth- and fifth-level effects.
Bullying can be said to have a ripple effect.

Figure 3.1   The ripple effect of bullying

The second level

Parents and families are the secondary victims of bullying. They will have mixed feelings, ranging from helplessness to anger to wanting revenge. When parents approach the school, it is important they are listened to and kept informed.

The third level

The bystanders are also affected by bullying. They may feel afraid and unsafe, ashamed for not stopping the bullying, or drawn to its meanness and cruelty. What the school does in response to the bullying is a symbolic statement for this group. If they feel the school cares enough to act effectively, then they may be able to show disapproval of the bullying (or at least to tell an adult – parent or teacher).

The fourth level

The school's response to bullying sends a clear message to others in the school. If it reacts proactively, it conveys the fact that bullying will not be tolerated. If it handles it poorly, it sends a message to bullies that they may continue to bully with impunity. If it does not act, then it is a direct contributor to the culture of bullying.

The fifth level

Several things can happen in relation to the wider community. If bullying is neither detected nor effectively dealt with, then there is a sense that those who bully can carry out their bullying anywhere – on the way to and from school, in the street, at a youth club or at a shopping centre. If a school handles bullying well, then it is contributing not only to the well-being of its students but also to the health and safety of the wider community.

What are the dynamics of bullying?

Once a bully always a bully? Once a victim always a victim?

Up to this point, I have focused on what researchers have discovered about bullying, bullies, victims and observers. It is important to recognize that these descriptions are only guidelines that give us impressions and can help us to understand bullying and devise ways of dealing with it.

Much of our reaction to bullying is founded in the deficit mode that emphasizes faults and weaknesses in the individual, and offers remediation as a solution. This approach tends to deal only with symptoms. A more dynamic alternative is the systems perspective where meaning is seen as socially constructed, with a strong emphasis on competency, success and individual strength.

This approach deals with the whole problem in all its complexity rather than focusing on symptoms.

'The mind set of "Once a bully always a bully" or "Once a victim always a victim" only serves to keep us stuck in thinking that these are fixed traits in individuals' (Swearer et al., 2009).

I would suggest that, in dealing with bullying, it is important to focus on changing behaviour and to avoid labelling the participants. This allows people to move out of negative roles. I know of situations where, as a result of such a dynamic approach, former bullies have become defenders of a school's anti-bullying stance. The important points to remember are that:

- Each situation is unique and needs a specific solution.
- In our lives we can be victims of bullying, perpetrators of bullying and bystanders/onlookers. A person may be a victim of bullying but not a victim in a general sense. Similarly, a person may bully in a particular situation but not be a bully in general.
- Labels can stick. It is important, when dealing with a bullying incident, to try to find a solution rather than to label the participants. The incident should be dealt with, but not by blame and condemnation.
- It is crucial to provide opportunities for people to change their behaviour. If the first strategy does not work, there should be back-up responses.

The downward spirals of bullying

To suggest that people who are bullied should stand up for themselves is not only unfair, it is also unrealistic. If they could have stood up for themselves, they would not have been bullied. Bullying undermines anyone's ability to stand up to torment. The most compelling reason why it is so hard for someone to defend themselves is the fact that what they are now experiencing is part of a process that has been gradually and purposely created, in which the bully has power and the victim has not. This tends to be self-perpetuating, a downward spiral (see Figure 3.2).

Stage 1: watching and waiting

At the beginning of the year, students settle into the school culture. During this early stage, they are quietly gaining a sense of the characteristics of their classmates and the dynamics of the classroom. Those who will bully are observing and gathering information, picking who will be easy to bully and who will be bully-proof. Those who are prone to be bullied may have no idea they are being singled out. Those who will become bystanders may have given signs that they are not easy targets. Research indicates that early in the school year, single acts with bullying potential are visited on a large number of individuals, but that the frequency of these acts decreases as students who may succumb to being bullied and those who are resistant are identified (Perry et al., 1990, cited in Harachi et al., 1999).

Stage 2: testing the waters

If, after stage 1, a child is perceived as being a potential victim, the next move is for the bully to activate the bullying in a minor way. He may walk past the potential victim's desk and knock off a pencil case. This is a small but symbolic act that tests the child's response. If his reaction is weak, he gives the message that he is a potential victim. (If he retaliates successfully, he may move out of the potential victim group and be accepted by the main group.)

Stage 3: something more substantial occurs

Stage 2 confirms the existence of a potential victim. When he arrives at school the next day, four boys walk very close to him and jostle him, one grabs his bag and then they throw it around. He runs from boy to boy, feeling panicky, and they laugh. A teacher comes over and asks what is going on. 'Just having fun', the leader says. The victimized boy does not contradict him. He hopes that if he says nothing he will be seen as cool.

Stage 4: the bullying escalates

More often than not, the bullying goes unchecked and gets worse because there is nothing to stop it. If the boys see they can get away with their behaviour, they may beat up their victim or degrade him. They can also subject him to bullying outside school and orchestrate a campaign of intimidation. The peer group does nothing, but watches passively, united in their complicity.

Stage 5: the bullying becomes fully established

The boy who is being bullied is losing confidence, failing academically, truanting and, in a worst case scenario, may eventually attempt suicide. Those who are bullying get an unrealistic sense of their power and, as they get older, commit other antisocial acts that are not tolerated by the adult world. Crime and imprisonment can be the results. The bystanders are now immobilized by their inaction and have a sense of the world as an unsafe and frightening place in which they are essentially powerless.

Figure 3.2 illustrates what is occurring for the bully, the victim and the bystanders. This process is represented as a downward spiral because, as the bullying becomes worse, so do the consequences for everyone. Further, even if the bullying is halted then a person who has been victimized over a long period of time and has truanted to avoid his tormentors will not automatically recover. He may have lost his confidence and be performing poorly academically. All these areas of his life are now in deficit and need to be thoughtfully and supportively rebuilt. It is not an easy process.

The bullying iceberg

Even in the face of excessive bullying, children tend not to report being bullied.

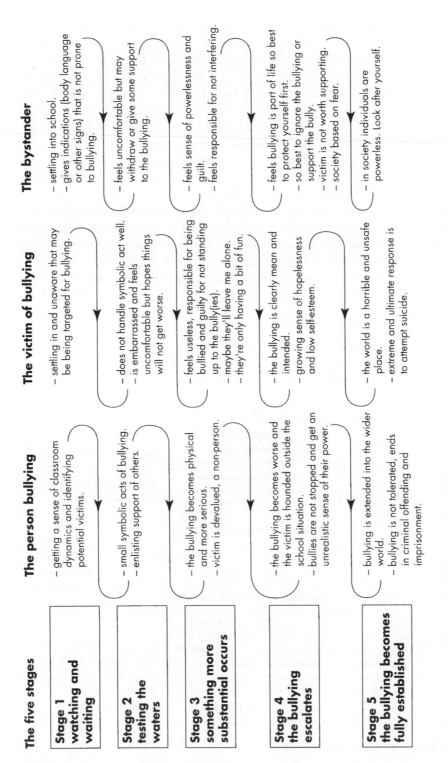

The five stages	The person bullying	The victim of bullying	The bystander
Stage 1 watching and waiting	– getting a sense of classroom dynamics and identifying potential victims.	– settling in and unaware that may be being targeted for bullying.	– settling into school. – gives indications (body language or other signs) that is not prone to bullying.
Stage 2 testing the waters	– small symbolic acts of bullying. – enlisting support of others.	– does not handle symbolic act well. – is embarrassed and feels uncomfortable but hopes things will not get worse.	– feels uncomfortable but may withdraw or give some support to the bullying.
Stage 3 something more substantial occurs	– the bullying becomes physical and more serious. – victim is devalued, a non-person.	– feels useless, responsible for being bullied and guilty for not standing up to the bully(ies). – maybe they'll leave me alone. – they're only having a bit of fun.	– feels sense of powerlessness and guilt. – feels responsible for not interfering.
Stage 4 the bullying escalates	– the bullying becomes worse and the victim is hounded outside the school situation. – bullies are not stopped and get an unrealistic sense of their power.	– the bullying is clearly mean and intended. – growing sense of hopelessness and low self-esteem.	– feels bullying is part of life so best to protect yourself first. – so best to ignore the bullying or support the bully. – victim is not worth supporting. – society based on fear.
Stage 5 the bullying becomes fully established	– bullying is extended into the wider world. – bullying is not tolerated, ends in criminal offending and imprisonment.	– the world is a horrible and unsafe place. – extreme and ultimate response is to attempt suicide.	– in society individuals are powerless. Look after yourself.

Figure 3.2   The downward spirals of bullying

Adair et al.'s (2000) New Zealand-based study found that although 81 per cent had observed bullying, only 21 per cent had reported it to an adult. Research conducted in 25 secondary schools in the UK revealed that 8 per cent of pupils believed that if they reported bullying to a teacher they would be told to 'stop telling tales', and about 13 per cent believed that 'teachers would not be interested'. Overall, only 14 of 115 students interviewed thought there would be an improvement following intervention, and 41 thought that things would get worse 'because teachers would intimidate, embarrass or break confidentiality to the detriment of the victim. Whatever the source of evidence, there is concern that over 50 per cent of teacher interventions in the investigation overall are perceived as of limited effect' (Glover et al., 2000: 151–2).

Much of the research shows a discrepancy between pupils' and teachers' reports of the frequency of bullying and their estimations of the efficacy of intervention (Reid et al., 2004). Students generally lack confidence in their teachers' skills to intervene effectively, and so fail to report bullying (Craig et al., 2000).

In addition, the message from the peer group (particularly among adolescents) is that ratting is unacceptable, and there is a real danger that if anyone tells, the bullies will retaliate. Children tend to believe that bullying will occur no matter what, and that nothing can be done about it. This belief may spring from the sense of hopelessness that is one of the effects of being bullied.

Reports of bullying can be likened to an iceberg: the incidents reported account for the tip, but most incidents lie below the surface (Figure 3.3).

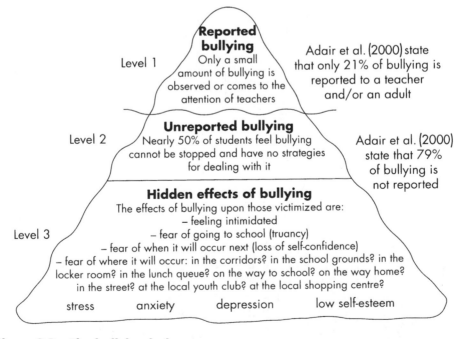

Figure 3.3   The bullying iceberg

Teachers need to be trained to encounter bullying in a careful way so that they do not add to the trauma of bullying but are part of the solution. This is more likely to occur when schools have well-developed and supported anti-bullying programmes and where openness, respect and empathy are upheld as part of the school culture (Smith, 1999).

References

Adair, V. (1999) 'No bullies at this school: creating safe schools', *Journal of Children's Issues Centre*, 3: 32–7.

Adair, V., Dixon, R.S., Moore, D.W. and Sutherland, C.M. (2000) '"Ask your mother not to make yummy sandwiches": bullying in New Zealand secondary schools', *New Zealand Journal of Educational Studies*, 35(2): 207–21.

Arseneault, L., Walsh, E., Trzesniewski, K., Newcombe, R., Caspi, A. and Moffitt, T.E. (2006) 'Bullying victimization uniquely contributes to adjustment problems in young children: a nationally representative cohort study', *Pediatrics*, 118: 130–8.

Banks, R. (1997) *Bullying in Schools*. Report No. ED–407–154. Washington DC: ERIC Clearinghouse.

Batsche, G.M. and Knoff, H.M. (1994) 'Bullies and their victims: understanding a pervasive problem in the schools', *School Psychology Review*, 23(2): 165–74.

Benitez, J.L. and Justicia, F. (2006) *Bullying: Description and Analysis of the Phenomenon*. Granada: University of Granada, Department of Developmental and Educational Psychology.

Bowers, L., Smith, P.K. and Binney, V. (1992) 'Cohesion and power in the families of children involved in bully/victim problems at school', *Journal of Family Therapy*, 14: 371–87.

Bowes, L., Arseneault, L., Maughan, B., Taylor, A., Caspi, A. and Moffitt, T. (2009) 'School, neighborhood, and family factors are associated with children's bullying involvement: a nationally representative longitudinal study', *Journal of the American Academy of Child and Adolescent Psychiatry*, 48(5): 545–53.

Byrne, B. (1999) 'Ireland', in P.K. Smith, Y. Morita, J. Junger-Tas, D. Olweus, R. Catalano and P. Slee (eds), *The Nature of School Bullying: A Cross-national Perspective*. London: Routledge.

Campbell, M.L.C. and Morrison, A.P. (2007) 'The relationship between bullying, psychotic-like experiences and appraisals in 14-year-olds', *Behavior Research and Therapy*, 45: 1579–91.

Carney, A.G. and Merrell, K.W. (2001) 'Bullying in schools: perspectives on understanding and preventing an international problem', *School Psychology International*, 22(3): 364–82.

Cowie, H. and Sharp, S. (1994) 'Empowering pupils to take positive action against bullying', in P.K. Smith and S. Sharp (eds), *School Bullying: Insights and Perspectives*. London: Routledge.

Craig, W., Pepler, D. and Atlas, R. (2000) 'Observations of bullying in the playground and in the classroom', *School Psychology International*, 21(1): 22–36.

Craig, W.M. and Pepler, D.J. (1995) 'Peer processes in bullying and victimisation: an observational study', *Exceptional Education Canada*, 5: 81–95.

Cullingford, C. and Morrison, J. (1995) 'Bullying as a formative influence: the relationship between the experience of school and criminality', *British Educational Research Journal*, 21(5): 547–60.

Dautenhahn, K., Woods, S. and Kaori, C. (2007) 'Bullying behaviour, empathy and imitation: an attempted synthesis', in C.L. Nehaniv and K. Dautenhahn (eds), *Imitation and Social Learning in Robots, Humans and Animals: Behavioural, Social and Communication Dimensions.* Cambridge: Cambridge University Press.

Delfabbro, P., Winefield, T., Trainor, S., Dollard, M., Anderson, S., Metzer, J. et al. (2006) 'Peer and teacher bullying/victimization of South Australian secondary school students: prevalence and psychosocial profiles', *British Journal of Educational Psychology*, 76: 71–90.

Drake, J., Price, J., Telljohann, S. and Funk, J. (2003) 'Teacher perceptions and practices regarding school bullying prevention', *Journal of School Health*, 74(9): 347–55.

Eron, L.D., Huesmann, R.L., Dubow, E., Romanoff, R. and Yarnel, P.W. (1987) 'Childhood aggression and its correlates over 22 years', in David H. Cravell, Ian M. Evans and Clifford R. O'Donnell (eds), *Childhood Aggression and Violence.* New York: Plenum.

Espelage, D.L. and Swearer, S.M. (2004) *Bullying in American Schools: A Social-Ecological Perspective on Prevention and Intervention.* Mahwah, NJ: Erlbaum.

Espelage, D.L., Bosworth, K. and Simon, T.S. (2001) 'Short-term stability and change of bullying in middle school students: an examination of demographic, psychosocial, and environmental correlates', *Violence and Victims*, 16(4): 411–26.

Fabre-Cornali, D. (1999) 'France', in P.K. Smith, Y. Morita, J. Junger-Tas, D. Olweus, R. Catalano and P. Slee (eds), *The Nature of School Bullying: A Cross-national Perspective.* London: Routledge.

Farrington, D.P. (1993) 'Understanding and preventing bullying', in M. Tonry and N. Norris (eds), *Crime and Justice, Volume 17.* Chicago: University of Chicago Press.

Fosse, G.K. and Holen, A. (2007) 'Reported maltreatment in childhood in relation to the personality features of Norwegian adult psychiatric outpatients', *Journal of Nervous and Mental Disease*, 195(1): 79–82.

Garbarino, James and deLara, Ellen (2003) *And Words Can Hurt Forever: How to Protect Adolescents from Bullying, Harassment, and Emotional Violence.* New York: Free Press.

Glover, D., Gough, G. and Johnson, M. with Cartwright, N. (2000) 'Bullying in 25 secondary schools: incidence, impact and intervention', *Educational Research*, 42(2): 141–56.

Griffin, R. and Gross, A. (2004) 'Childhood bullying: current empirical findings and future directions for research', *Aggressive and Violent Behaviour*, 9: 379–400.

Harachi, T., Catalano, R. and Hawkins, J. (1999) 'United States', in P.K. Smith, Y. Morita, J. Junger-Tas, D. Olweus, R. Catalano and P. Slee (eds), *The Nature of School Bullying: A Cross-national Perspective.* London: Routledge.

Kaltiala-Heino, R., Rimpelä, M., Marttunen, M., Rimpelä, A. and Rantanen, P. (1999) 'Bullying, depression, and suicidal ideation in Finnish adolescents: school survey', *British Medical Journal*, 319 (7 August): 348–51.

Kaltiala-Heino, R., Rimpelä, M., Rantanen, P. and Rimpelä, A. (2000) 'Bullying at school – an indicator of adolescents at risk for mental disorders', *Journal of Adolescence*, 23: 661–74.

Kim, Y.S. and Leventhal, B. (2008) 'Bullying and suicide. A review', *International Journal of Adolescent Medicine and Health*, 20: 133–54.

Klomek, A.B., Marrocco, F., Kleinman, M., Schonfeld, I.S. and Gould, M.S. (2007) 'Bullying, depression, and suicidality in adolescents', *Journal of the American Academy of Child and Adolescent Psychiatry*, 46(1): 40–49.

Klomek, A.B., Sourander, A., Niemelä, S., Kumpulainen, K., Piha, J., Tamminen, T., Almqvist, F. and Gould, M.S. (2009) 'Childhood bullying behaviors as a risk for suicide attempts and completed suicides: a population-based birth cohort study', *Journal of the American Academy of Child and Adolescent Psychiatry*, 48(3): 254–61.

Kupersmidt, J.B., Coie, J.D. and Dodge, K.A. (1990) 'The role of peer relationships in the development of disorder', in S.R. Asher and J.D. Coie (eds), *Peer Rejection in Childhood*. Cambridge: Cambridge University Press.

Lösel, F. and Bleisener, T. (1999) 'Germany', in P.K. Smith, Y. Morita, J. Junger-Tas, D. Olweus, R. Catalano and P. Slee (eds), *The Nature of School Bullying: A Cross-national Perspective*. London: Routledge.

Lumsden, L. (2002) *Preventing Bullying*. Report No. EDO-EA-02–02. Eugene, OR: University of Oregon.

Maines, B. and Robinson, G. (1998) *All for Alex: A Circle of Friends*. Bristol: Lucky Duck Publishing.

Maslow, A. (1970) *Motivation and Personality*. 2nd edn. New York: Harper & Row.

Maxwell, G. and Carroll-Lind, J. (1997) *The Impact of Bullying on Children*. Wellington: Office of the Commissioner for Children Occasional Paper No. 6.

Mellor, A. (1999) 'Scotland', in P.K. Smith, Y. Morita, J. Junger-Tas, D. Olweus, R. Catalano and P. Slee (eds), *The Nature of School Bullying: A Cross-national Perspective*. London: Routledge.

Nansel, T.R., Overpeck, M., Pilla, R.S., Ruan, W.J., Simons-Morton, B. and Scheidt, P. (2001) 'Bullying behaviors among US youth: prevalence and association with psychosocial adjustment', *Journal of the American Medical Association*, 285: 2094–100.

Newman, K. (2004) *Rampage: The Social Roots of School Shootings*. New York: Basic Books.

Olweus, D. (1978) *Aggression in the Schools: Bullies and Whipping Boys*. London: Wiley, Halsted Press.

Olweus, D. (1984) 'Aggressors and their victims: bullying at School', in N. Frude and G. Gault (eds), *Disruptive Behaviour in Schools*. New York: John Wiley.

Olweus, D. (1991) 'Bully/victim problems among schoolchildren: basic facts and effects of a school-based intervention programme', in D. Pepler and K. Rubin (eds), *The Development and Treatment of Childhood Aggression*. Hillsdale, NJ: Erlbaum.

Olweus, D. (1993) *Bullying at School: What We Know and What We Can Do*. Oxford: Blackwell.

Olweus, D. (1994) 'Bullying at school: long term outcomes for the victims and an effective school-based intervention programme', in R. Huesmann (ed.), *Aggressive Behavior: Current Perspectives*. New York: Plenum Press.

Olweus, D. (1999) 'Norway', in P.K. Smith, Y. Morita, J. Junger-Tas, D. Olweus, R. Catalano and P. Slee (eds), *The Nature of School Bullying: A Cross-national Perspective*. London: Routledge.

Owens, L. (1996) 'Sticks and stones and sugar and spice: girls' and boys' aggression in schools', *Australian Journal of Guidance and Counselling*, 6: 45–57.

Owens, L. and MacMullin, C. (1995) 'Gender differences in aggression in children and adolescents in South Australian schools', *International Journal of Adolescence and Youth*, 6: 21–35.

Reid, P., Monsen, J. and Rivers, I. (2004) 'Psychology's contribution to understanding and managing bullying within schools', *Educational Psychology in Practice*, 20: 241–58.

Rigby, K. (1994) 'Family influence, peer-relations and health effects among school children', in K. Oxenberry, K. Rigby and P.T. Slee (eds), *Children's Peer Relations: Conference Proceedings*. Adelaide: Institute of Social Research, University of South Australia.

Rigby, K. (2002) *New Perspectives on Bullying*. London: Jessica Kingsley.

Rigby, K. (2007) *Children and Bullying: How Parents and Teachers Can Reduce Bullying*. Oxford: Blackwell.

Rigby, K. and Cox, I.H. (1996) 'The contributions of bullying at school and low self esteem to acts of delinquency among Australian teenagers', *Personality and Individual Differences*, 21: 609–12.

Ross, D.M. (2003) *Childhood Bullying, Teasing, and Violence: What School Personnel, Other Professionals, and Parents Can Do*. 2nd edn. Alexandria, VA: American Counseling Association.

Salmivalli, C. (2010) 'Bullying and the peer group: a review', *Aggression and Violent Behavior*, 15(2): 112–20.

Salmivalli, C., Kaukiainen, A. and Lagerspetz, K. (1998) 'Aggression in the social relations of school aged girls and boys', in P. Slee and K. Rigby (eds), *Children's Peer Relations*. London: Routledge. pp. 60–75.

Sanders, C.E. and Phye, G.D. (eds) (2004) *Bullying: Implications for the Classroom*. San Diego, CA: Academic Press/Elsevier.

Saufler, C. and Gagne, C. (2000) *Maine Project against Bullying. Final Report*. Augusta, ME: Maine State Department of Education.

Sharp, S. (1996) 'Self-esteem, response style and victimisation: possible ways of preventing victimisation through parenting and school-based training programmes', *School Psychology International*, 17: 347–57.

Sharp, S. and Thompson, D. (1992) 'Sources of stress: a contrast between pupil perspectives and pastoral teachers' perspectives', *School Psychology International*, 13: 229–42.

Smith, P.K. (1999) 'England and Wales', in P.K. Smith, Y. Morita, J. Junger-Tas, D. Olweus, R. Catalano and P. Slee (eds), *The Nature of School Bullying: A Cross-national Perspective*. London: Routledge.

Smith, P.K. and S. Sharp (eds) (1994) *School Bullying: Insights and Perspectives*. London: Routledge.

Sourander, A., Jensen, P., Rönning, J.A., Niemelä, S., Helenius, H., Sillanmäki, L., Kumpulainen, K., Piha, J., Tamminen, T., Moilanen, I. and Almqvist, F. (2007) 'What is the early adulthood outcome of boys who bully or are bullied in childhood? The Finnish "From a Boy to a Man" Study', *Pediatrics*, 120(2): 397–404.

Sourander, A., Rönning, J., Brunstein-Klomek, A., Gyllenberg, D., Kumpulainen, K., Niemelä, S., Helenius, H., Sillanmäki, L., Ristkari, T., Tamminen, T., Moilanen, I., Piha, J. and Almqvist, F. (2009) 'Childhood bullying behavior and later psychiatric hospital and psychopharmacologic treatment: findings from the Finnish 1981 Birth Cohort Study', *Archives of General Psychiatry*, 66(9): 1005–12.

Stephenson, P. and Smith, D. (1989) 'Bullying in the junior school', in D.P. Tattum and D.A. Lane (eds), *Bullying in Schools*. Stoke-on-Trent: Trentham Books.

Swearer, S.M., Espelage, D.L. and Napolitano, S.A. (2009) *Bullying Prevention and Intervention: Realistic Strategies for Schools*. New York: Guilford.

Tehrani, N. (2004) 'Bullying: a source of chronic post traumatic stress?', *British Journal of Guidance and Counselling*, 32(3): 357–66.

Veenstra, R., Lindenberg, S., Oldehinkel, A.J., De Winter, A.F., Verhulst, F.C. and Ormel, J. (2005) 'Bullying and victimization in elementary schools: a comparison of bullies, victims, bully/victims, and uninvolved preadolescents', *Developmental Psychology*, 41(4): 672–82.

Vettenburg, N. (1999) 'Belgium', in P.K. Smith, Y. Morita, J. Junger-Tas, D. Olweus, R. Catalano and P. Slee (eds), *The Nature of School Bullying: A Cross-national Perspective*. London: Routledge.

Whitted, K.S. (2005) 'Student reports of physical and psychological maltreatment in schools: an under-explored aspect of student victimization in schools', University of Tennessee.

Whitted, K.S. and Dupper, D.R. (2008) 'Do teachers bully students? Findings from a survey of students in an alternative education setting', *Education and Urban Society*, 40(3): 329–41.

Williams T., Connolly J., Pepler D. and Craig W. (2005) 'Peer victimization, social support, and psychosocial adjustment of sexual minority adolescents', *Journal of Youth and Adolescence*, 34(5): 471–82.

CHAPTER 4

TYPES OF BULLYING 1: RACIST BULLYING, BULLYING OF SPECIAL EDUCATIONAL NEEDS CHILDREN, HOMOPHOBIC BULLYING AND SEXUAL BULLYING

Introduction: when bullying finds a target

Bullying can happen to anyone at any time, but some children and young people are victimized because of particular characteristics that identify them as different or set them apart from their peers. Of particular concern is bullying that occurs because of being culturally and physically different (racist bullying), of needing extra and different educational support (bullying of special educational needs, or SEN, children), and because of an actual or perceived non-heterosexual sexual orientation (homophobic bullying).

A major concern is also bullying of a sexual nature in which the target is not necessarily someone who is different but who for various reasons becomes the focus of unwanted sexual attention. This type of bullying is called sexual bullying.

When students are bullied because they are seen as different, their humanity is to some extent dismissed and denied; when students are sexually bullied, they also become objects to their tormentors.

Racist bullying

As a result of being incessantly insulted and harassed by a 15-year-old British National Party supporter, a 14-year-old girl of mixed white English and black African parentage attempted suicide by taking an overdose of stress pills and painkillers. When the girl was found, she was rushed to hospital and then spent two months in a psychiatric clinic. She has continued to receive psychiatric treatment and she and her family have moved to another part of England (Wardrop, 2009). In July 2009, the boy became the first English school pupil to be convicted of the racially aggravated harassment of a fellow pupil. Following a trial, he was sentenced to six months' supervision, made to pay £500 compensation to the girl and instructed to carry out 10 hours of indirect reparation, the equivalent of community service (Allen, 2009).

Racist bullying is where racism and bullying meet. It can be identified by the fact that the person is attacked not as an individual but as the representative of a family, group or community, and by the racist motivation of the bully and the language used. It occurs in all countries and is usually aimed at members of minority groups.

Racism has been the cause of untold misery, brutality and murder in the history of humankind. Racist insults and behaviour are devastating expressions of personal animosity and social malaise. Those who are targeted often feel that not only they as individuals but also their families and communities are under attack. Racist words and behaviour are experienced as onslaughts on the fundamental values, beliefs and self-worth of the victims. They are also attacks on a person's very identity.

Racism frequently results in the coining or redefinition of words that are used as slurs and insults, such as coon, nigger, Paki, coconut and wog. It also frequently leads to neologisms such as Islamophobia that is now common in the UK – a phenomenon that occurs when particular groups become the butt of prejudice, hatred and fear.

A 2009 UK Teachers' TV survey found that 55.1 per cent of 802 respondents were aware of race-related bullying against pupils, and more than 10 per cent stated it was also often directed against teachers as well (Bloom, 2009). While it was linked to religion and religious intolerance generally, Muslim pupils and teachers were specifically targeted. Patrick Nash, chief executive of the Teacher Support Network, stated that high numbers of black and ethnic-minority teachers regularly call its helpline to discuss racist harassment at school. Andrew Bethell, chief executive of Teachers TV, said that 'Racist bullying is the unspoken curse of schools at the moment. Racism is an issue that schools have been trying to address for 30 years now. Lip service has been paid at the highest policy level, but we haven't changed the landscape very much during that time' (BBC News, 23 April 2009).

The Anti-Bullying Network (2006) states that racist bullying in schools can range from ill-considered remarks not intended to be hurtful to deliberate physical attacks causing serious injury. In the UK, following the Race Relations Amendment Act 2000, a general duty was placed on many public authorities to promote race equality, through giving emphasis to the need to eliminate unlawful racial discrimination, support equality of opportunity and promote good relations between people of different racial groups (http://www.antibullying.net/racistinfo3.htm). Schools have a statutory duty to record all incidents of racist bullying and report them to the local authority, and schools must ensure that all pupils feel safe. However, many news items and articles suggest that, while the legislation is thorough, well thought-out and comprehensive, practice in schools is patchy and often quite inadequate (Pilgrim and Scourfield, 2007).

Experience has been similar elsewhere in the world. For example, in the USA several states have explicit legislation against racist bullying, but school practice (and clearly the climate in pockets of the wider society) is often at odds with the legislation. The Assist Beginning Teachers web pages co-sponsored by Michigan State University and the Michigan State Education Board recommend that 'Racist bullying must be explicitly discussed in the classroom and there must be clear school guidelines for dealing with incidents' (http://assist.educ.msu.edu/assist/school/principal/workbegintchrs/toolformsofbully2.htm). However, incidents of racist bullying still continue to be reported, and may (as with the bullying iceberg, see Chapter 3) be only a fraction of those that actually occur.

Clearly, victims of racist bullying can do nothing about what it is that has made them a target. They are who they are. It is only the behaviour of the bullies that can change and, it is to be hoped, the wider tolerance and humanitarianism of societies. As the British Children's Minister Delyth Morgan said, racism in schools is 'completely unacceptable'. 'Children are not born racist and we must work hard to ensure they are educated to be tolerant of difference, and stop bigoted views from outside schools spilling over into the playground' (*BBC News*, 23 April 2009).

Bullying of special educational needs children

Carter and Spencer's (2006) analysis of the findings from 11 studies published from 1989 to 2003 concluded that students with disabilities, both visible and non-visible, experienced bullying more than their non-disabled peers. Whitney et al. (1994) found that when matched with non-SEN children of the same age, ethnicity, gender and year, SEN children are two or three times more at risk of being bullied and are also more likely to bully. They identified three reasons for this:

1. Learning difficulties or other disabilities make them a target.
2. They tend to be less well integrated into their class.
3. Some children with behavioural problems act out in aggressive ways and, as a result, are susceptible to becoming provocative victims, that is, both aggressor and victim.

Other studies have been able to refine some of these conclusions. A data analysis of over 100,000 US households measured associations between having a special health-care need and being a victim of bullying, bullying other children and being a bully/victim in children and adolescents aged 6 to 17. Using five screening questions, the study concluded that children with special health-care needs were associated with being bullied but not with bullying or being a bully/victim. Having a chronic behavioural, emotional or developmental problem (the fifth screening question) was associated with bullying others and with being a bully/victim (Van Cleave and Davis, 2006).

Luciano and Savage's study (2007) similarly found that students with learning difficulties are bullied significantly more often than those without, and that children with attention deficit hyperactivity disorder (ADHD) are both more likely than other children to be bullied and somewhat more likely to bully their peers.

Bullying of SEN children is an extremely harmful and discriminatory practice. Children suffering from medical conditions that affect their appearance (such as cerebral palsy, paralysis and spina bifida), from Asperger's syndrome and autism, from conditions such as obesity, diabetes and stuttering, and from developmental and behavioural difficulties are already at a disadvantage. When their difference makes them the target of bullying as well, they are likely to go backwards academically, socially and behaviourally (the downward spirals of bullying, see Chapter 3).

A Medical University of South Carolina-led study in 2009 (see www. HealthNewsDigest.com) found SEN children were more often the targets of bullying than their non-SEN counterparts, and this included being ostracized or purposely ignored more frequently. The researchers were concerned about serious negative effects this could have in terms of self-esteem, sense of belonging, being in control and having a sense of meaningfulness; they ascertained that this could ultimately result in impaired coping skills, social withdrawal and mental health problems (http://collegeofdirectsupport.blogspot.com/2009/05/special-needs-children-left-out-bullied.html).

The Commons Select Committee on Education in the UK in 2007 placed serious emphasis on bullying in British schools, and heard that a separate survey of more than 100 families for the National Autistic Society Scotland had shown that 38 per cent of autistic children were bullied at school. The Children's Commissioner referred specifically to the bullying of children with Asperger's syndrome and autism (Richard Garner and Andy McSmith, *Independent*, 26 March 2007).

In the US, the bullying of SEN children may cross the line to become 'disability harassment', which is illegal under Section 504 of the Americans with Disabilities Act 1990.

All schools ultimately exist to provide a place where children can reach their potential. They can do this only if schools are safe and positive environments where difference is embraced and abilities are shepherded and encouraged to grow. Embedding anti-bullying practices and philosophies in schools in relation to *all* children, and especially those with SEN and disabilities, is a clear application of human rights and non-discriminatory values (Department for Children, Schools and Families, 2008).

Homophobic bullying

Within a social context that enforces normative identity and behaviour standards through threats, taunts and physical attacks, young people who are lesbian, gay, bisexual or transgendered (LGBT), or who look as if they may be LGBT, or who may be questioning their sexual orientation, are at special risk of being bullied, with the accompanying threats to their academic, psychological and physical well-being (Basile et al., 2009; Birkett et al., 2009; Poteat, 2008; Rivers, 2001; Sears, forthcoming; Swearer et al., 2008).

There are widespread reports internationally of homophobic bullying, which can be defined as follows:

> any form of physical (e.g. hitting or kicking), emotional (e.g. spreading rumors or teasing), or social (e.g. being ignored) aggression perpetrated against an individual because of her or his actual or perceived sexual orientation, or because that individual's behaviour is not typical of her or his sex. Homophobic bullying can be hard to identify. Name-calling is perhaps most frequently associated with it: names such as gay, fag, queer, dyke, and homo are the most often cited as a means of identification, though physical harm or emotional abuse (social isolation and rumor mongering) are also common. (Rivers et al., 2007: 71)

In addition to the range of behaviours described above, there are many reported cases of students being seriously sexually assaulted and raped when they have become a target of homophobic bullying, and of some who attempt or commit suicide. More rarely, some students have been murdered. A boy of 13 from Ajax, Ontario, hanged himself after being relentlessly bullied by his classmates. He had told a friend he was gay and the friend told everyone else. A few days before he died, the boy was stuffed into a rubbish bin by some of his classmates. In Oxnard, California, on 12 February 2008, Lawrence (Larry) King, a gay 15-year-old, was shot twice in the head by a 14-year-old classmate in front of his class and teacher. Larry was a child who had been bullied incessantly for years because of his obvious homosexuality: he had apparently tried to fight back by being flamboyant (Setoodeh, 2008).

A paper published by Rivers in 2001 reported on a three-year study of a sample of 190 lesbians, gay men, and bisexual men and women who were bullied at school and the long-term impact it had on their lives. In the survey of psychosocial correlates and long-term effects, over 50 per cent of a subsample of 119 participants reported thinking about self-harm or suicide, with 40 per cent making one or more attempts. As adults, they still had some of the negative symptoms.

Awareness of homophobic bullying has led to a lot of research about rates and distribution (for example, Douglas et al., 1999; Guasp, 2009; Hunt and Jensen, 2007). In the UK, the Stonewall report (Hunt and Jensen, 2007) found that almost 65 per cent of young LGBT students had experienced direct bullying, with the number increasing to 75 per cent at religious schools. Over 97 per cent of all students heard insulting homophobic phrases and remarks used frequently, and 35 per cent of gay pupils did not feel safe or accepted at school. The National School Climate Survey, conducted in 2005 by the Gay, Lesbian and Straight Education Network (GLSEN) in the USA, found that three-quarters of the high school students surveyed heard derogatory and homophobic remarks 'frequently' or 'often' at school, and that 90 per cent heard the term 'gay' used generally to imply that someone is stupid or something is worthless (Kosciw and Diaz, 2006). Among students who self-identified as LGBT, 90 per cent had been bullied in the past year. Of these, 66 per cent had been verbally abused, 16 per cent physically harassed and 8 per cent assaulted (http://www.stopbullyingnow.hrsa.gov/HHS_PSA/pdfs/SBN_Facsheet_GLBT.pdf). Where lesbian and bisexual girls were more likely to recall being shunned and taunted, boys were more often attacked, pushed around or jostled (Rivers, 2001).

An article in the *Calgary Herald* (30 January 2008) on the suicide of the 13-year-old from Ajax concludes with the following point:

> The schoolyard seems to be the only place where people are allowed to torment others with impunity, to the point where those who are victimized become suicidal. If this sort of thing were happening in an adult workplace, it wouldn't be tolerated … School as a safe place. Now there's a radical idea.

There are many regional and national government documents that relate to homophobic bullying. Most define what it is, give an idea of its frequency and suggest ways schools and students can tackle it. For example, the Alberta Cross-Ministry for the Prevention of Bullying urges students to 'break the silence' and 'take a stand against homophobia' by telling someone, knowing their rights, staying safe, writing everything down, remaining calm and finding support in the community, if they or someone they know is the victim of homophobic bullying (www.child.alberta.ca). In Ireland, an initiative against homophobic bullying in schools was launched in October 2006, and Niall Crowley of the Equality Authority made the point that a student subject to homophobic bullying may be able to take a case under the Equal Status Acts, which prohibit harassment on a number of grounds including sexual orientation (www.equality.ie).

Clearly, homophobic bullying is a threat to individual health and safety and also to the health of schools, communities and societies. It is, like all bullying, a human rights issue, and one that can have devastating effects upon a person's identity and ability to live safely within their own community.

Sexual bullying

Sexual bullying is the term used to describe bullying of a sexual nature. It was formerly referred to as sexual harassment, but since this phrase has wider application, sexually motivated bullying is better referred to by this term. (The Australian Centre for the Study of Sexual Assault calls it 'sexualized bullying'.)

Sexual bullying consists of unwanted sexual attention that makes the recipient feel uncomfortable, demeaned or humiliated. It is usually directed against females (Shute et al., 2008) but can also be against males, and it is usually cross-gender but can also be boy–boy and girl–girl (Craig et al., 2000; Rigby, 2003). Sexual bullying includes obscene gestures or communication, remarks about a person's body, sexual demands, suggestive statements or remarks, and taunting or teasing. It also includes offences such as unwanted sexual touching, assault and rape that can be pursued as criminal offences. Other forms of bullying can have sexual dimensions too. Clearly, unwelcome conduct of a sexual nature can affect a student's ability to participate in or benefit from an education programme or activity, and create an intimidating, threatening or abusive educational environment.

A recent Canadian study (Chiodo et al., 2009) of 1734 students from 23 high schools found that:

- 44.1 per cent of girls and 42.4 per cent of boys were victims of sexual harassment.
- The victimized girls were subjected to more sexual jokes, unwanted comments, gestures and touch than boys.
- The victimized boys were subjected to homosexual slurs and being shown or given unwanted sexual pictures, photographs, messages or notes.
- A significant number of both boys and girls reported being subjected to all types of sexual harassment.
- Sexual harassment that occurs at the beginning of high school is a strong predictor of future sexual harassment by peers and dating partners.
- When victimization in girls is severe, they may be at risk of dysfunctional and abusive relationships in adulthood, in part because they come to expect demeaning behaviours as normal in heterosexual relationships.
- For girls who had been sexually harassed, there was a twofold to sixfold increase in risk factors in terms of suicidal thoughts, self-harm, maladaptive dieting, early dating, substance use and school safety.
- For boys who had been sexually harassed, there was an increased risk factor in terms of suicidal thoughts, early dating, substance use and school safety, although to a lesser degree than for girls.
- Boys and girls who reported sexual harassment victimization in grade 9 were 2.5 to three times as likely to report it again 2.5 years later.

These findings support the view that once started, sexual abuse tends to continue.

Based on their findings, the authors argue convincingly that greater prevention and intervention strategies are needed to address sexual harassment in schools. Their concerns are echoed in other countries. For instance, the American Association of University Women (AAUW, 2001) found that 81 per cent of females reported experiencing sexual harassment at least once in a while at school, while 27 per cent reported being frequent victims. In relation to Australia, Rigby (2003) reported that a study of 613 year 9 students found 33 per cent of girls and 19 per cent of boys were targets of unwanted sexual remarks.

In the UK, following a *Panorama* programme called 'Kids Behaving Badly', the BBC reported that government figures showed that in 2006–07 there were 3,500 fixed period exclusions and 140 expulsions from schools in England for sexual misconduct (anything from explicit graffiti to rape). Of these, 280 expulsions were from primary schools and in 20 cases the child responsible was 5 years old (*BBC News*, 5 January 2009). *Panorama* conducted a survey of 273 children with the charity Young Voice, and found that one in 10 children aged 11–19 said they had been forced to take part in sex acts (Jessica Shepherd, *Guardian*, 5 January 2009).

The *Guardian* article also refers to a high incidence of sexual bullying of teachers and of criminal sexual behaviour in schools. Research has been done on possible links between sexual bullying and other gender-based violence such as rape that is 'implicitly based on the expectation that bullying and sexual violation are similar behaviors or have similar risk factors' (Basile et al., 2009: 336).

Clearly, the effects of sexual bullying can be extreme and devastating. Gruber and Fineran (2008), for instance, found that when girls are sexually harassed they are likely to experience academic difficulty, physical symptoms (such as headaches), and interpersonal relationship and sexual difficulties. These effects can be exacerbated by the fact that schools do not always respond when a student reports an incident of sexual bullying or assault. For example, in Victoria, Australia, a 15-year-old girl was held down in the playground and had her breasts exposed and touched by a male student. When she went to the principal and asked to see the school counsellor, the principal told her that the counsellor 'did not have time for such petty things' (Quadara, 2008: 4). It is crucial that school staff have the expertise and training to handle such reports appropriately: first, to listen; second, to take care of the victim; third, to take action – by making referrals to counselling, medical and/or legal authorities, and by alerting parents and school boards.

Sexual bullying and sexualized behaviour are likely to cause serious damage to victims and also, in the process, to dehumanize and desensitize those responsible for it.

References

Allen, N. (2009) 'Schoolgirl victim of racist bullying says tormentor's sentence is "pants"', *Daily Telegraph*, 20 August.

American Association of University Women (AAUW) (2001) *Hostile Hallways: Bullying, Teasing, and Sexual Harassment in School.* Washington, DC: AAUW.

Basile, K.C., Espelage, D.L., Rivers, I., McMahon, P.M. and Simon, T.R. (2009) 'The theoretical and empirical links between bullying behavior and male sexual violence perpetration', *Aggression and Violent Behavior*, 14(5): 336–47.

Birkett, M., Espelage, D.L. and Koenig, B. (2009) 'LGB and questioning students in schools: moderating effects of homophobic bullying and school climate on negative outcomes', *Journal of Youth and Adolescence*, 38(7): 989–1000.

Bloom, A. (2009) 'Racist bullying rife in (British) schools', *Times Educational Supplement*, 24 April.

Calgary Herald (2008) 'Homophobic bullying in schools can and does kill', *Calgary Herald*, 30 January.

Carter, B.B. and Spencer, V.G. (2006) 'The fear factor: bullying and students with disabilities', *International Journal of Special Education*, 21(1): 11–24.

Chiodo, D., Wolfe, D.A., Crooks, C., Hughes, R. and Jaffe, P. (2009) 'Impact of sexual harassment victimization by peers on subsequent adolescent victimization and adjustment: a longitudinal study', *Journal of Adolescent Health*, 45(3): 246–52.

Craig, W.M., Henderson, K. and Murphy, J.G. (2000) 'Prospective teachers' attitudes toward bullying and victimization', *School Psychology International*, 21(1): 5–21.

Department for Children, Schools and Families (2008) *Bullying Involving Children with Special Educational Needs and Disabilities*. Nottingham: Department for Children, Schools and Families.

Douglas, N., Warwick, I., Whitty, G., Aggleton, P. and Kemp, S. (1999) 'Homophobic bullying in secondary schools in England and Wales – teachers' experiences', *Health Education*, 99(2): 53–60.

Garner, R. and McSmith, A. (2007) 'School bullies targeting children with special needs', *Independent*, 26 March.

Gruber, J.E. and Fineran, S. (2008) 'Comparing the impact of bullying and sexual harassment victimization on the mental and physical health of adolescents', *Sex Roles*, 59(1–2): 1–13.

Guasp, A. (2009) 'The teachers' report: homophobic bullying in Britain's primary and secondary schools', Stonewall (UK) (www.stonewall.org.uk/educationforall).

Hunt, R. and Jensen, J. (2007) 'The school report: the experiences of young gay people in Britain's schools', Stonewall (UK) (www.stonewall.org.uk/educationforall).

Kosciw, J.G. and Diaz, E.M. (2006) *The 2005 National School Climate Survey: The Experiences of Gay, Lesbian, Bisexual and Transgender Youth in Our Nation's Schools*. New York: GLSEN.

Luciano, S. and Savage, R.S. (2007) 'Bullying risk in children with learning difficulties in inclusive educational settings', *Canadian Journal of School Psychology*, 22(1): 14–31.

Pilgrim, A.N. and Scourfield, J. (2007) 'Racist bullying as it affects children in Wales: a scoping study', *Contemporary Wales*, 20(1): 144–58.

Poteat, V.P. (2008) 'Contextual and moderating effects of the peer group climate on use of homophobic epithets', *School Psychology Review*, 37: 188–201.

Quadara, A. (2008) *Responding to Young People Disclosing Sexual Assault: A Resource for Schools*. Australian Centre for the Study of Sexual Assault Wrap No. 6. Melbourne: Australian Institute of Family Studies.

Rigby, K. (2003) *Stop the Bullying: A Handbook for Schools*. Melbourne: Australian Council for Education.

Rivers, I. (2001) 'The bullying of sexual minorities at school: its nature and long-term correlates', *Educational and Child Psychology*, 18(1): 32–46.

Rivers, I., Duncan, N. and Besag, V.E. (2007) *Bullying: A Handbook for Educators and Parents*. Westport, CT: Greenwood.

Sears, J. (ed.) (forthcoming) *Homophobic Bullying*. London: Routledge Sociology.

Setoodeh, R. (2008) 'Young, gay and murdered', *Newsweek*, 19 July (http://www.newsweek.com/id/147790&GT1=43002).

Shepherd, J. (2009) '3,500 pupils suspended for sexual bullying', *Guardian*, 5 January.

Shute, R., Owens, L. and Slee, P. (2008) 'Everyday victimization of adolescent girls by boys: sexual harassment, bullying or aggression?', *Sex Roles*, 58(7–8): 477–89.

Swearer, S.M., Espelage, D.L. and Napolitano, S.A. (2008) *Bullying Prevention and Intervention: Realistic Strategies for Schools*. New York: Guilford.

Van Cleave, J. and Davis, M.M. (2006) 'Bullying and peer victimization among children with special health care needs', *Pediatrics*, 118: 1212–19.

Wardrop, M. (2009) '"Racist bullying destroyed family", mother of suicidal schoolgirl says', *Daily Telegraph*, 23 July.

Whitney, I., Smith, P.K. and Thompson, D. (1994) 'Bullying and children with special educational needs', in P.K. Smith and S. Sharp (eds), *School Bullying: Insights and Perspectives*. London: Routledge.

CHAPTER 5

TYPES OF BULLYING 2: CYBERBULLYING

Introduction: the complexion of bullying in cyberspace

In terms of public responses to acts of bullying, cyberbullying is the area currently of most concern. It is a relatively new phenomenon that has received wide publicity and appears to be growing in frequency, range and seriousness. Once initiated, an act of cyberbullying can irreversibly speed through the ether with instantaneous and devastating effect. This sense of its treacherousness is strengthened by the fact that there have been several well-publicized incidents of young people committing suicide after having been cyberbullied.

What we know about cyberbullying

Defining cyberbullying

Cyberbullying is the deliberate, malicious and repeated use of information and computer technologies (ICT) to hurt, humiliate and/or manipulate and/or exclude another person or persons. In school settings, cyberbullying is often a form of relational aggression that is intended to hurt someone by damaging their relationships with their peers (Berger, 2007, cited in Johnson, 2009). Further:

> Cyber bullying is … [unlike] other more traditional forms of bullying because of the perpetrator's anonymity and ability to harass their victim 24 hours a day. Anonymity inherent in many electronic communications modes … reduces social accountability, making it easier for users to engage in hostile, aggressive acts … This new technology [also] allows victims to be attacked at anytime, and in any place … The invincibility and anonymity of

cyber bullies makes [cyberbullying] difficult to manage within the school system and opens the door for more youth to take part in this type of behavior. (Johnson, 2009: 1)

It is clearly not only the use of ICT that makes an event an act of cyberbullying. It is also its context, that is, whether it is part of an ongoing bullying campaign; its complexion, that is, whether it occurs between equals; and its specific content and effect, that is, whether it involves intimidating and/or criminal behaviour and has a life-threatening outcome.

Single acts of cyber-aggression are not necessarily bullying. The power of bullying comes not from one aggressive act but from repeated incidents; and it is this ongoing, unpredictable and seemingly relentless process that has the power to wear down a victim's sense of confidence, happiness and safety. However, it is important to find out whether one-off acts of cyber-aggression are in fact components of a larger multi-type bullying campaign.

When two equals vociferously and repeatedly attack each other in cyberspace (behaviour known as flaming), this is an act of cyber-aggression rather than cyberbullying as there is no imbalance of power.

A recent phenomenon, named happy slapping in England, can be part of the cyberbullying complex. Happy slapping is a nasty aggressive act in which a targeted individual(s) is physically assaulted while the act is recorded via mobile phone and then sent to others for their amusement.

A recent case of cyberbullying

On 12 July 2009, 18-year-old Keeley Houghton posted the following message on her Facebook home page: 'Keeley is going to murder the bitch. She is an actress. What a fucking liberty. Emily Fuckhead Moore.' As a result of the threat to murder, Houghton was prosecuted, found guilty and became the first British citizen jailed for cyberbullying. During her trial, she denied any malicious intent and argued, on the one hand, that she had been drunk and could not recall posting the message, on the other, that she had posted it late at night. Her 'cyber-fingerprint', however, showed it was done at 4 o'clock in the afternoon. The contradictory evidence and suggestion of dishonesty would probably have counted for less had this not been the culmination of four years of continuous bullying and harassment. Ms Houghton had already been expelled from school for assaulting Ms Moore and convicted of causing criminal damage to her home. On 21 August, she was sentenced to three months at a youth offenders' institution for threatening to murder and issued with a five-year restraining order prohibiting contact or making comments about Emily on any social networking system or website. In summing up the case, District Court Judge Morgan stated:

> Since Emily Moore was 14 you have waged compelling threats and violent abuse towards her. Bullies are by their nature cowards, in school and society. The evil, odious effects of being bullied stay with you for life. On this day you did an act of gratuitous nastiness to satisfy your own twisted nature. (Carter, 2009)

This act of cyber-aggression was a one-off incident but was part of a process of bullying consisting of ongoing acts of physical and psychological bullying in real space and time. It fitted the criteria of bullying in that it was repetitive, abusive, manipulative, and based on an assumption of power and invulnerability. It differed from the in-school bullying of Emily in one main respect, however. When Keeley beat up Emily on her way home, there were probably a few people who saw what happened. Parents, teachers and other students would have heard about the incident, and several people in the community would have known about it. When Keeley posted her threatening comment on Facebook, it had the potential to reach a far larger audience. It could be viewed every time the page was visited and for as long as she chose to leave it there. This dimension in fact constituted a perpetual threat of violence against Ms Moore.

The incident embodies three features that are typical of adolescent cyberbullying:

1. When cyberbullying occurs, it is usually accompanied by in-school bullying.
2. There is a sense of invulnerability in the attack in the apparent limitlessness of reach, audience and durability.
3. The technology involved is a double-edged sword that provides the means both to commit the act and also to entrap the perpetrator.

While anonymity was clearly not an issue in this instance, the sense of invincibility that comes with anonymity definitely was.

This case shows what can happen when any form of bullying becomes criminal activity, when sanctions and discipline fail to change aggression and antisocial behaviour, and such activity finally moves outside the jurisdiction of the school and comes within the ambit of the criminal justice system. Although schools and parents do not have the legal authority of a judge, they do have the right and responsibility to create a set of rules, regulations and procedures about what is appropriate behaviour in school populations, and what the consequences are if the rules and regulations are ignored or broken.

In most cases, in-school anti-bullying policies and programmes will support and enhance prosocial behaviour and healthy peer relationships so that breakdowns in peer relations do not become criminal in motivation and/or outcome. The Houghton case at least shows that proactive responses to cyberbullying can halt the behaviour and, more importantly, underline its unacceptability and seriousness and create a precedent (in this case, legal) for its handling.

How cyberbullying works

The decision to carry out a cyberbullying attack is a conscious act with malicious intent. Figure 5.1 shows that it entails a five-step process, which is comprised of three steps where selections are made and two decision-points.

Step 1: decision to initiate cyberbullying

An aggressor(s) decides to initiate an act of bullying in cyberspace.

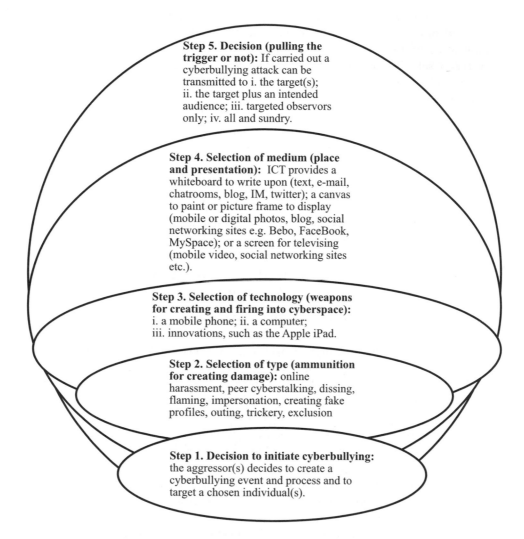

Step 5. Decision (pulling the trigger or not): If carried out a cyberbullying attack can be transmitted to i. the target(s); ii. the target plus an intended audience; iii. targeted observors only; iv. all and sundry.

Step 4. Selection of medium (place and presentation): ICT provides a whiteboard to write upon (text, e-mail, chatrooms, blog, IM, twitter); a canvas to paint or picture frame to display (mobile or digital photos, blog, social networking sites e.g. Bebo, FaceBook, MySpace); or a screen for televising (mobile video, social networking sites etc.).

Step 3. Selection of technology (weapons for creating and firing into cyberspace): i. a mobile phone; ii. a computer; iii. innovations, such as the Apple iPad.

Step 2. Selection of type (ammunition for creating damage): online harassment, peer cyberstalking, dissing, flaming, impersonation, creating fake profiles, outing, trickery, exclusion

Step 1. Decision to initiate cyberbullying: the aggressor(s) decides to create a cyberbullying event and process and to target a chosen individual(s).

Figure 5.1   The five steps taken to initiate, prepare and launch a cyberbullying attack

Note: Steps 2, 3 and 4 are interrelated choices that are made in the preparation of a cyber-attack. They are presented here as sequential but can occur in a different order or as part of a single process.

Step 2: selection of type (ammunition for creating damage)

The aggressor(s) chooses a type of ammunition and develops it in order to embarrass, humiliate, intimidate or exclude the targeted person(s). The following is an overview of common types.

- **Online harassment** is one-on-one cyberbullying and consists of unpleasant texts, email messages or other forms of posting being sent to an intended victim and/or others.
- **Peer cyberstalking** is similar to online harassment but is more severe. It involves the use of ICT to stalk a chosen victim, not only to harass but also to threaten and create a sense of fear and impending danger through an ongoing and intense campaign of cyber-attacks. It can include accusations, threats of harm, and the communication of 'dirt' for harassment and intimidation purposes. *Note:* The term 'cyberstalking' refers to the predatory practice of adults who use the Internet to contact and attempt to meet up with vulnerable minors, usually in order to solicit sex.
- **Dissing** is the sending or posting of harmful, untrue or cruel information to third parties, and sometimes informing the chosen victim(s) as well. It can include making nasty and false accusations and/or posting material online with the intention of damaging friendships and reputations.

> **Comment**: Online harassment, peer cyberstalking and dissing are similar in that they are forms of direct attacks on a chosen victim(s). Online harassment and peer cyberstalking both involve cyberbullying by one person against another. Dissing consists of direct attacks on a victim and orchestrating a wider campaign to include third parties, either as observers or contributors.

- **Flaming** is hostile and insulting interaction between Internet users. Flaming usually occurs when people are involved in discussion boards, Internet Relay Chat (IRC), or email or video-sharing websites. It is usually the result of discussion about real-world issues like politics, religion and philosophy, or of issues that polarize subpopulations (for example, debate over electronic games or rock bands). Flaming can be considered cyberbullying if it is carried out relentlessly by someone or if it is orchestrated so that a group of people make a joint attack against another.
- **Impersonation** is when someone humiliates another by pretending to be that person, either through hacking into their email account, or otherwise assuming their identity, and sending messages on social networking sites that make the sender appear hostile, offensive or stupid.
- **Creating fake profiles** involves spreading false, malicious and untrue information to embarrass, humiliate and attack a person's credibility through creating a website or blog.
- **Outing** occurs when sensitive, private or embarrassing information about someone is sent to others through texts or photographic transmission by mobile phone, email or social network postings in order to embarrass or humiliate them. It can involve exposure of a person's sexual orientation.
- **Trickery** is when outing is done through obtaining information by devious means, such as pretending to be a friend and then sending confidences to others.

Because of the two steps involved, it entails both deceit and humiliation, and is, in effect, an act of double bullying.

• **Exclusion** is the mean-minded and purposeful exclusion of individuals from an online group. This is made worse by ensuring that everyone knows about the exclusion, demeaning the victim even further.

Step 3: selection of technology (weapons for creating and firing into cyberspace)

A mobile phone or computer can be used both to generate and then launch an act of cyberbullying. The nature of the ammunition will decide what technology to use to propel it into cyberspace. Until recently, the computer was clearly the weapon of choice, but the development of smartphones has increased flexibility of use and the range of facilities available. The advantage computers have in their larger screens is balanced and sometimes outweighed by the portability of mobile phones and smartphones.

Step 4: selection of medium (place and presentation)

Aggressors can use virtual whiteboards, a canvas, frame or screen, accessing many types of technologies and media. There are six main means for developing and posting cyberbullying creations, the first five specified on the American website CyberBully   (http://www.cyberbullyalert.com/blog/2008/08/top-5-technologies-used-to-cyberbully/):

1. **Social networking sites** are very popular among teenagers, for example, MySpace, Facebook and Bebo. The social networking carried out there is similar to what is done in real life, but the downside is that they also provide cyberbullying opportunities. Individuals can choose to post hurtful and humiliating items, to wage a campaign against a targeted person, and to steal user IDs and passwords, with malicious postings being made by those who pose as the person whose cyber-identity has been stolen.
2. **Instant messaging (IM)** is a staple of major Internet companies such as AOL, Yahoo, Google (through its Gmail service) and MSN. It is made up of a collection of technologies that allow text-based real-time communication to occur between two or more recipients. Instant messaging differs from chat rooms in that, rather than cyber-talking with a large and often anonymous web-based group, individuals can be chosen from lists of known friends and contacts. Instant messaging facilitates immediate contact and also involves access to webcams and limited file transfer. Unfortunately, it is also used as a means of harassment. With IM, cyberbullies can adopt fake screen names and 'ping' chosen individuals with profanities and threats of violence.
3. **Email** is a relatively anonymous medium, especially if a person hacks into an email account or uses a disguise. Threatening messages, rumours, lies and cruel images have been sent via email, sometimes using false or stolen identities.
4. **Photoshop** allows the transformation of harmless and attractive photographic images into insulting or pornographic ones that can be sent via mobile phone or

computer. Perpetrators can also secretly take embarrassing pictures and then transmit them so as to humiliate and expose.

5. **Blogs**. Many teenagers have created Internet blogs with the aim of dissing rivals or enemies and inviting others to participate in this process. Because blogs are easy to set up and creators hard to identify, this can result in the existence of destructive, hurtful and permanent spaces.

6. **Twitter** is the latest craze. It serves the purpose of social reporting and allows people to discuss activities, provide regular postings, and make comment on contemporary events and the activities of others. There have been an increasing number of nasty and hurtful messages about individuals that are sent 'via Tweet'.

Step 5: decision (pulling the trigger or not)

Cyberspace lacks boundaries, in terms of observers/participants (all of whom can potentially witness the bullying materials) and time (a cyberbullying act can be played and re-played as new observers arrive, and others alerted to its existence). If a decision is made to pull the trigger, a cyberbullying attack can be sent to the target(s), the target plus an intended audience, an intended audience excluding the target, or all and sundry.

What contemporary research tells us about cyberbullying

Research on cyberbullying provides information that can be used to assist schools in the development of policy and practice for confronting and handling this type of bullying. There is a huge amount of material available (both in print and electronically) that can be overwhelming in its detail. The following therefore provides an overview of the most useful research findings.

How young people use ICT

A large percentage of young people are cyber-literate. They spend much of their time learning about and using ICT in both their social and school-based activities. Generally, their experience and knowledge are far greater than that of parents and teachers (NCPC, 2007).

The extent of cyberbullying

Rates of cyberbullying recorded in recent research surveys have been very variable, but indicate that it is both a well-known and common form of bullying.

Wang et al. (2009) carried out a study of the experiences of bullying of 7,182 grades 6 to 10 American adolescents during the two months prior to the survey. The findings indicate that although the rate of cyberbullying is significant, when compared to in-school bullying it was considerably less:

- 13.6 per cent had been cyberbullied.
- 8 per cent had received harassing computer pictures or messages.

- 6 per cent were bullied by mobile phone.

But:

- 53.6 per cent were victims of verbal bullying.
- 51.4 per cent were victims of relational bullying/social exclusion.
- 20.8 per cent had been either perpetrators or victims of physical bullying.

Juvonen and Gross's (2008) survey of 1,454 12- to 17-year-old Americans, which focused specifically on cyberbullying over a 12-month period, found that a larger percentage of cyberbullying was experienced:

- 72 per cent had experienced cyber-aggression at least once.
- 41 per cent reported being subjected to between one and three incidents.
- 13 per cent reported four to six incidents.
- 19 per cent reported seven or more incidents.

In Campbell and Gardner's Australian study (cited in Campbell, 2005):

- 11 per cent of respondents identified themselves as cyberbullies.
- nearly 14 per cent identified themselves as targets.

This is similar to a New Zealand study, in which 11 per cent of 1,169 15-year-olds said they had been text-bullied, and 7 per cent said they had text-bullied others (Marsh et al., forthcoming).

Generally, it appears that boys cyberbully slightly more than girls, and that girls are cyberbullied more often than boys, especially in their mid-teens (Li, 2006; Wang et al., 2009).

Correlation between online and in-school bullying

Of the 72 per cent of 12- to 17-year-olds who had experienced cyber-aggression at least once in Juvonen and Gross's (2008) study, 85 per cent were also bullied in school.

O'Neil's (2008) Canadian study of pre-teen and teenage girls found that cyber-bullying was an extension of relational-aggression attacks, similarly occurring in school.

Comment: Students being bullied online are likely also to be bullied in school. For many pre-teens and teens, cyberspace is part of their everyday social environment. Just as bullying occurs in real time and place, so it occurs in cyberspace.

Student responses to cyberbullying

When a large group of American students were surveyed (NCPC, 2007), they reported various emotional responses to cyberbullying:

- 56 per cent reported feeling angry.
- 33 per cent said they were hurt.
- 32 per cent reported being embarrassed.
- 13 per cent said they felt scared.
- Many (percentage not provided) claimed it did not bother them.

In the same survey, students thought people cyberbully for one (or more) of the following reasons:

- They think it is funny (81 per cent).
- They do not like the person (64 per cent).
- They see the victim as a loser (45 per cent).
- They probably do not see cyberbullying as a big deal (58 per cent).
- They do not expect there will be any tangible consequences (47 per cent).
- They do not think they will get caught (45 per cent).

While anonymity is usually an initial feature of cyberbullying, about three out of four targeted students said they could eventually figure out who the culprit was. In three-quarters of these cases, it was a friend or someone they knew (from school or elsewhere) (NCPC, 2007). Other studies (for example, Li, 2007) suggest that as many as half do not know who their tormentor is.

The role of social networking sites in the lives of young people

A study of cyberbullying links it to the entire world that children live in:

> Bullying on the Internet looks similar to what kids do face-to-face in school. The Internet is not functioning as a separate environment but is connected with the social lives of kids in school. Our findings suggest that especially among heavy users of the Internet, cyber-bullying is a common experience, and the forms of online and in-school bullying are more alike than different. (Wolpert, 2008)

In Boyd's American research (2007b) into teenagers and Internet-based social networks, she found 87 per cent of 12- to 17-year-olds used the Internet, and 55 per cent had created MySpace profiles (64 per cent for the 15–17 subgroup). Among those who had not joined, it was either because parents had banned them from social networking or the teenagers had taken an ideological stand against the corporate ownership of MySpace. Boyd asks (2007b: 119):

> Why do teenagers flock to these sites? What are they expressing on them? How do these sites fit into their lives? What are they learning from their participation? Are these online activities like face-to-face friendships or are they different, or complementary? ... While particular systems may come and go, how youth engage through social network sites today provides long-lasting insights into identity formation, status negotiation, and peer-to-peer sociality.

The 'life cycle' of cyberbullying

Williams and Guerra's (2007) study of prevalence and predictors of Internet bully-ing among school students in Colorado found that although rates were lower than for physical and verbal bullying, they followed the same trend, that is, having a low rate at fifth grade, peaking at eighth grade, and having fallen off by eleventh grade.

> **Comment**: The life cycle of bullying across the school years appears to be the same as it is for in-school bullying, and adds strength to the perspective that cyberbullying and in-school bullying are 'in league' together.

The importance of healthy school atmosphere and parental support

Juvonen and Gross (2008) found that:

- only 10 per cent of students reported cyberbullying experiences to their parents or other adults;
- 31 per cent said they did not tell because they were concerned their parents might restrict their Internet access;
- this concern was especially common among girls between the ages of 12 and 14 (46 per cent of these girls feared restrictions as compared with 27 per cent of boys in the same age group);
- one-third of 12- to 14-year-olds reported they did not tell an adult because they were afraid they would get into trouble with their parents.

Li's Canadian study (2006) found that:

- the majority of victims did not report the cyberbullying;
- girls were more likely to report cyberbullying than boys.

At least one reason why students do not report cyberbullying to adults is different from the reasons why much in-school bullying is not reported: students fear restric-tions being placed on their access to the world across the space and time horizon.

However, research suggests that there are three main circumstances in which stu-dents are more likely to report Internet bullying: when they feel more connected to their schools in a trusting, fair and pleasant climate; when they regard their peers as caring and helpful, and there are good perceived friendship rates; and when parental support is high (Juvonen and Gross, 2008; Wang et al., 2009; and Williams and Guerra, 2007).

In fact, students who were surveyed showed a keen awareness of issues that cre-ate healthy environments, including concern about the fact that many parents are not familiar enough with ICT, and are often unaware of what their children are accessing. The NCPC findings (2007) suggest that while parents were generally vigilant in rela-tion to younger children's time spent online, teens were largely unsupervised.

Summary of what we know

The main facts we know are that:

- cyberbullying is a growing problem, with a large percentage of ICT users being aggressed against;
- in most cases, students who are cyberbullied are also being bullied in the physical world;
- cyberbullying occurs in a world about which adults tend to be more ignorant than children and teens.

The characteristics of cyberbullying are that:

- it is often carried out by people known to the victim;
- it is carried out using mobile phones and/or computers;
- students sometimes use mobile phones to bully during school hours;
- it is often accompanied by physical and/or psychological bullying carried out at school;
- although done anonymously, students are sometimes able to figure out who is doing it;
- it follows the same patterns as normal bullying, peaking during the middle school/junior high years;
- although cyberbullying affects students' lives in school, it often happens outside of school hours;
- students are reluctant to tell adults, either teachers or parents;
- girls are more prepared to tell adults than boys.

How to deal with cyberbullying

It is essential to understand the world of ICT and cyberspace in attempting to understand and tackle cyberbullying. Just as researchers and practitioners have examined the psychology, sociology and anthropology of school and peer cultures, and the philosophical, physical and emotional environments of classrooms and school playgrounds in their efforts to understand in-school bullying, researchers and practitioners need to understand the new cyberworld beyond the frontiers of time and space.

Boyd (2007a: 1) argues that in order to deal with students' new social reality, it is essential that the adult world understands and embraces the new social technologies so as to be able to advise and guide young people through these murky waters. She sensibly suggests that 'as youth are far more adept at navigating the technologies through which these changes are taking place, we must learn from our students in order to help them work through the challenges that they face'.

Comment: From the point of view of dealing effectively with cyberbullying, any policy and practice would clearly benefit from a partnership between the experienced (parents and teachers/counsellors/administrators) and the cyber-literate (the students).

Creating a policy and plan to deal with cyberbullying

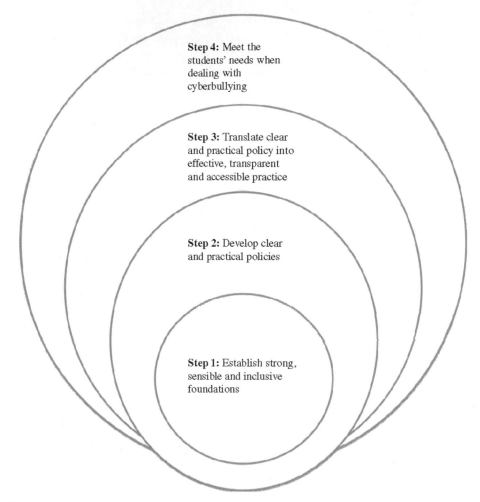

Figure 5.2   Developing a school's foundations, policy, practice and outreach for dealing effectively with cyberbullying

Step 1: establish strong, sensible and inclusive foundations

The policies and procedures used by the school for dealing with bullying should provide the foundations for dealing with cyberbullying.

In combination with these, it is important also to refer to contemporary research to help us respond effectively to the issues and problems that are:

- similar to in-school bullying;
- distinctive to cyberbullying.

Because students are usually much more literate about the technological aspects of ICT than adults, and tend to understand the dynamics of cyberbullying, they need to be involved in plans to tackle it in their schools. Consequently, a partnership between the school, students, parents and community should be set up when confronting the problem of cyberbullying.

It is also useful to gather together a cyberbullying resource kit, with a small collection of books, articles and DVDs for general reference and problem-solving, for example, Bauman, 2011; Bisonette, 2009; Schrock and Boyd, 2008. Websites are also useful, for example, www.cyberbullying.ca, www.stopcyberbullying.org, www.cyberbullying.us and http://netsafe. org.nz/.

Step 2: develop clear and practical policies

In order to be effective, policies need to be clear and easy to use. As with the foundations, policies for addressing cyberbullying should be linked to and grow out of the established policies for dealing with bullying, for example, making it clear that bullying of all types will not be tolerated; that all acts of cyber-aggression and cyberbullying will be thoroughly investigated; that the process will be fair, transparent and dealt with as quickly as possible; and that solutions and consequences will range along a continuum from benign to disciplinary and, in worst cases, to criminal prosecution.

The incident(s) will be placed within the broader context of physical and psychological intimidation and bullying that may have been occurring, with an understanding that the effects of bullying, in any form, are both damaging and long term.

Step 3: translate clear and practical policy into effective, transparent and accessible practice

Although schools are increasingly becoming aware of the damage that cyberbullying can cause, it can be very difficult to track down and deal with perpetrators as they often hide behind pseudonyms and their anonymity is hard to penetrate. Web pages are difficult to take down and ICT is in a stage of rapid and ongoing innovations within a context of few and largely ineffective controls. What is also true, however, is that any new frontier throws up issues and anomalies that lead to the development of rules and regulations. Because of the particular nature and complexion of instances of cyber-aggression, legislation and processes for prosecuting individuals for abuse on the Internet are being created and enacted.

Key responses to cyberbullying include:

- talking and gathering information;
- providing emotional and psychological support;
- discovering the identity of the cyberbully.

The cloak of anonymity can be thrown open by:

- saving evidence of cyber-aggression and cyberbullying by downloading and

printing the images or text involved;
- taking screenshots of bullying websites;
- contacting the victim's ISP (Internet service provider);
- speaking with a lawyer or, if a crime has occurred, contacting the police.

Some tactics for proceeding include:

- telling the cyberbully to stop in a non-emotional, assertive message;
- informing cyberbullies that threatening messages posted online can be traced through the nine-digit ISP attached to the computer from which the message is sent;
- ignoring or blocking the cyberbully;
- changing the victim's screen name or email address;
- avoiding the website where the victim has been attacked;
- filing a complaint on the offending website or mobile phone network. This may be particularly effective since cyberbullying is a violation of the 'terms of use' of most mobile phone companies, ISPs and websites.

Step 4: meeting the student's needs when dealing with cyberbullying

When assisting a student who has been cyberbullied (and in-school bullied as well), it is important to deal with the situation humanely and clearly, using whatever counselling and listening skills are appropriate, as in any case of bullying.

References

Bauman, S. (2011) *Cyberbullying: What Counselors Need to Know.* Alexandria, VA: American Counseling Association.

Bisonette, A. (2009) *Cyber Law: Maximizing Safety and Minimizing Risk in Classroom.* London: Sage.

Boyd, D. (2007a) 'Social network sites: public, private, or what?', *Knowledge Tree*, 13: 1–7 (http://kt.flexiblelearning.net.au/tkt2007/?page_id=28).

Boyd, D. (2007b) 'Why youth ♥ social network sites: the role of networked publics in teenage social life', in D. Buckingham (ed.), *Youth, Identity, and Digital Media.* MacArthur Foundation Series on Digital Learning. Cambridge, MA: MIT Press.

Campbell, M.A. (2005) 'Cyber bullying: an old problem in a new guise?', *Australian Journal of Guidance and Counselling*, 15(1): 68–76.

Carter, H. (2009) 'British teen is country's first jailed for Facebook bullying', *Guardian*, 21 August.

Johnson, J.M. (2009) 'The impact of cyber bullying: a new type of relational aggression', paper based on a programme presented at the American Counseling Association Annual Conference and Exposition, Charlotte, NC.

Juvonen, J. and Gross, E. (2008) 'Extending the school grounds? Bullying experiences in cyberspace', *Journal of School Health*, 78(9): 496–505.

Li, Q. (2006) 'Cyberbullying in schools: a research of gender differences', *School Psychology*

International, 27(2): 157–70.

Li, Q. (2007) 'Bullying in the new playground: a research into cyberbullying and cyber victimization', *Australasian Journal of Educational Technology*, 23(4): 435–54.

Marsh, L., McGee, R., Nada-Raja, S. and Williams, S. (forthcoming) 'Brief report: text bullying and traditional bullying among New Zealand secondary school students', *Journal of Adolescence*.

National Crime Prevention Council (NCPC) (2007) *Teens and Cyberbullying*. Arlington, VA: National Crime Prevention Council.

O'Neil, S. (2008) *Bullying by Tween and Teen Girls: A Literature, Policy and Resource Review.* Edmonton: The Society for Safe and Caring Schools & Communities.

Schrock, A. and Boyd, D. (2008) 'Online threats to youth: solicitation, harassment, and problematic content'. Literature review prepared for the Internet Safety Technical Task Force. Berkman Center for Internet and Society, Cambridge, MA: Harvard University (http://cyber.law.harvard.edu/sites/cyber.law.harvard.edu/files/ISTTF_Final_Report-APPENDIX_C_Lit_Review_121808.pdf).

Wang, J., Iannotti, R.J. and Nansel., T.R. (2009) 'School bullying among adolescents in the United States: physical, verbal, relational, and cyber', *Journal of Adolescent Health*, 45(4): 368–75.

Williams, K.R. and Guerra, N.G. (2007) 'Prevalence and predictors of internet bullying', *Journal of Adolescent Health*, 41(6): 14–21.

Wolpert, S. (2008) 'Bullying of teenagers online is common, UCLA psychologists report', UCLA Newsroom, 2 October (http://newsroom.ucla.edu/portal/ucla/bullying-of-teenagers-online-is-64265.aspx).

PART 2

PHILOSOPHY, PLANNING AND POLICY

CHAPTER 6

HOW TO CREATE AN ANTI-BULLYING INITIATIVE

Introduction: adopting a whole-school approach

Once a school has decided to tackle bullying, it should clarify its philosophy, examine its strengths and weaknesses, and survey the nature and extent of the problem. It then needs to write an anti-bullying policy, and implement and maintain an anti-bullying initiative.

Research has found that when a school wants to create an anti-bullying initiative, a whole-school approach produces the best results. Philosophically, the underpinnings of a whole-school approach are the notions of inclusivity, ownership and agreement.

Inclusivity

Although the person most affected by bullying is the victim, a number of other people are affected. It is important to include representatives of all groups in the development and implementation of an anti-bullying initiative (see 'Who else is affected by bullying?', in Chapter 3).

Ownership

Those who are involved in developing an anti-bullying programme are likely to feel that it is theirs. They will be loyal to it and interested in making sure it is well implemented.

Agreement

If schools fully embrace the processes of inclusivity and ownership through discussion, then eventually decisions can be made. The more opportunities people have to discuss ideas, the more chance there is of their arriving at an early consensus and beginning to work on the harder issues of philosophy, policies and programmes.

Summary

A whole-school approach is socio-ecological. One entity – in this case, bullying – is looked at not in isolation but in terms of its environment (Figure 6.1). It is approached consistently throughout the school, by staff and students, and their actions are supported and acknowledged by the wider community of families, community groups and social services. A whole-school approach to bullying may also lead to a decrease in other antisocial and problematic behaviour such as drug abuse and truanting.

The six-step anti-bullying plan

I have developed a six-step plan to help schools put an anti-bullying initiative in place. Central to this plan is the idea of having both a 'loose' and 'tight' approach. The loose aspect is that everyone who is interested is encouraged to participate and that ideas flow freely. The 'tight' aspect is that each step must be monitored and meet specific goals. The procedure involves planning, developing policies and programmes, implementing the initiative and maintaining it.

Planning

Step 1: preliminary explorations

Defining the philosophy and getting started

Step 1 is preparatory. At this point the school should examine its philosophy and response to bullying. The philosophy is the foundation for all policy and practice in the school (see Chapter 7). This can be done through a meeting of staff and boards of trustees (or their equivalents), focusing on the current school charter as well as identifying the school's underlying ethos and intentions, with the aim of clarifying beliefs, goals and values into a conscious philosophy.

A meeting of the entire school community should be organized to discuss the philosophy and the school's attitude to bullying. Every family, as well as school administrators and auxiliary staff, school trustees/governors and people from relevant community agencies (for example, religious leaders, community police officers and social workers), should receive a written invitation. An agenda for the meeting should be drawn up.

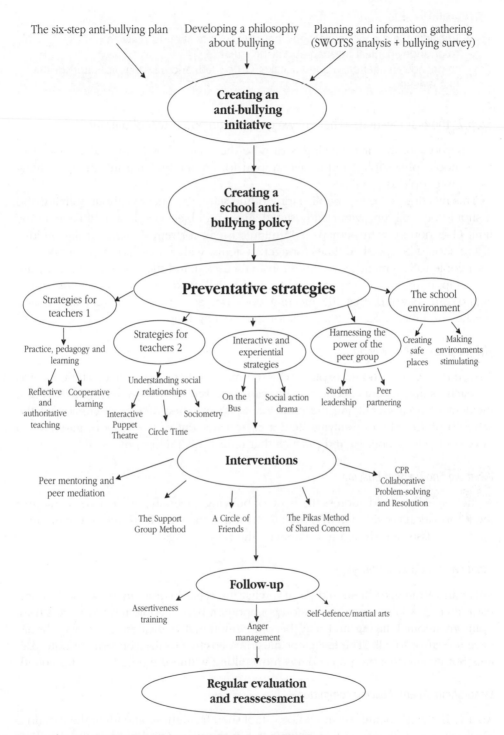

Figure 6.1 A whole-school anti-bullying initiative

The aims of step 1 are:
- to clarify the school's philosophy, particularly in relation to bullying;
- to arrange an initial meeting about the initiative;
- to provide an agenda, a guest speaker (if decided) and a skilled facilitator for the first meeting.

Step 2: the first meeting, 'What are we going to do about school bullying?'

The purpose of the first meeting is to raise the issue of bullying in the context of the school's philosophy, and to get support for an anti-bullying initiative involving as many people as possible.

This meeting is the first public airing of the school's concerns about bullying and it should be well run, with clearly stated aims and objectives. It should have a time limit (1–2 hours), with perhaps a 15-minute break for refreshments in the middle. There should be specified times for agenda items, with reasonable gaps in between for people to comment or ask questions. Discussion and the exchange of ideas are very important, and an experienced facilitator will make sure that the items on the agenda are covered, that the meeting does not go off on a tangent and that it finishes on time. A possible agenda for the meeting follows.

The purpose of the meeting

First, the facilitator should explain why the meeting has been called. The concerns of teachers and parents about bullying can be raised, perhaps referring to a recent incident without identifying the participants. There should be a discussion of the school's philosophy on bullying, and a clear statement of the school's intention to develop bullying policies and practice that reflect this philosophy.

What we know about bullying

A guest speaker could address the issue of bullying generally, or a teacher could use the information provided in this book to set the scene. This is meant as a brief introduction to issues; it should not dominate the proceedings.

What we can do about bullying

This part of the agenda should discuss what the school community can do to combat bullying. A fairly open discussion is important here. People tend to have strong opinions about bullying and may become emotional or heated. Everyone should have a chance to talk. The facilitator must be sensitive to the concerns of irate parents but ensure that the proceedings move along within the time frame prescribed.

Establishing an anti-bullying committee

An anti-bullying committee should be established from those attending the meeting. The purpose of the anti-bullying committee is to oversee and support the development of an anti-bullying policy and programme, to gather information about bullying, to liaise with community members, and to decide how to monitor and evaluate the implementation of anti-bullying strategies.

Part of its task is to find out about bullying, the approaches other schools are using and who in the local community may want to be involved.

Establishing terms of reference

The anti-bullying initiatives must have clear and concise terms of reference, for example:

- to find out what the school's strengths are and what resources are already in place;
- to find out the school's weaknesses and whether more careful monitoring of bullying is needed (see 'Adapting the SWOT Analysis', in Chapter 8);
- to find out the extent and kind of bullying in the school (see 'Survey and questionnaire', in Chapter 8);
- to develop an anti-bullying policy that is appropriate for the school;
- to suggest approaches that can be adopted in order to anticipate bullying and to make the school a safe place;
- to investigate what anti-bullying programmes are available, how much they cost and whether they work;
- to investigate what other resources (books, videos, reports) may be worth acquiring;
- to make recommendations about the various schemes;
- to consult widely and form small groups where appropriate for getting specific information (for example, on the anti-bullying initiatives of other schools);
- to provide a preliminary report and make a set of recommendations for policy and programme development.

It is also important for the school to determine a budget for the purchase of resources and training packages.

Deciding on a time frame

A reasonable time frame for the various steps needs to be drafted and presented to the meeting. Typically, the whole process may take from 12 to 18 months.

> The aims of step 2 are:
> - to introduce the topic with clarity and enthusiasm;
> - to provide opportunities for all to participate;
> - to form an anti-bullying committee and develop its terms of reference;
> - to draft a preliminary plan that will include a draft policy statement and a programme for dealing with bullying, plus a timeline.

Developing policies and programmes

Step 3: the anti-bullying committee gets to work

This stage is probably the most intensive and productive. A few individuals work together to develop a clearer picture of the school's strengths and weaknesses, and the nature and extent of bullying in the school. The aim is to draft an anti-bullying policy that addresses the needs of the school.

Carrying out a SWOTSS analysis

In most schools, some teachers and administrators will have already developed strategies for preventing or dealing with bullying. It is important at this point to evaluate current school policy and practice, to ask such questions as 'What has been done about bullying to date?', 'How effective has it been?', 'What good policy and practice exists?', 'What else needs to be done?' and 'What are the areas of deficiency?' In the business world, SWOT analyses are used to find a company's strengths and weaknesses. I have developed a variation termed a SWOTSS analysis that can be used in schools (see Chapter 8), which committee members can carry out to assess the current state of the school.

Completing a survey of bullying

So far, bullying has been discussed both theoretically and anecdotally. Carrying out a survey will provide concrete information about the nature and extent of bullying in the school. I have created a straightforward bullying questionnaire that will help this process (see Chapter 8).

Writing a draft anti-bullying policy

Now it is time to begin writing an anti-bullying policy and to select appropriate strategies for putting the policy into practice. An anti-bullying policy should be based on the following considerations:

- the policy should reflect the philosophy of the school;
- it should take into account information about school bullying that has been gathered by the committee;
- it should address the legal requirements that the school must meet according to any legislation or binding regulations;
- the policy should be clearly stated, straightforward and achievable.

An example of a school anti-bullying policy is provided in Appendix 1.

Developing strategies for dealing with bullying

Various strategies can be used to make a school safe. Some of these are preventative, others are interventions and still others are mixtures of the two.

Within the classroom itself, it is crucial for teachers to develop specific pedagogic practices and styles to support these strategies (see Chapter 10), and to be familiar with the social make-up of their classes (see Chapter 11). Teachers can then more readily introduce programmes and strategies to raise pupils' awareness of the dynamics of bullying, help them understand the various roles in the bullying scenario and suggest solutions. Examples of such strategies are 'On the Bus' and the use of social action drama (see Chapter 12).

The harnessing and development of healthy peer relationships can also be a focus of a whole-school approach. Within the peer community of the school, three main types of strategy can be used: peer partnering, peer mentoring and peer mediation. The least interventionist of these is peer partnering, and the most is peer mediation. These can be initiated, guided into place and supported by teachers, but they are student-centred and are run by students (see Chapters 13 and 15).

It is also crucial to create an interesting and safe physical environment (see Chapter 14). There are numerous anti-bullying interventions that can be introduced to the school (see Part 4).

In the case of particular and relatively recent forms of bullying that involve the use of computers, the Internet and mobile phones, different information and strategies are required (see Chapter 5).

Schools should investigate the range of what is available and make their own selection. Using the Internet is a good way to check resources and to find out what other schools are doing.

Consolidating findings

The anti-bullying committee should put together a short report providing an overview of its considerations and making a series of recommendations. This is intended to report findings and clarify and consolidate information. The report is also a means of sharing this with the wider community and for defining a clear set of directives.

The aims of step 3 are:
- to examine the issues surrounding bullying and come up with an action plan for developing an anti-bullying policy in line with the school's philosophy;
- to report on the school's strengths and weaknesses in relation to dealing with bullying (a SWOTSS analysis, Chapter 8);
- to provide a survey of bullying in the school (Chapter 8);
- to write a draft anti-bullying policy (Chapter 9);
- to make recommendations about what programmes to adopt (preventative and interventionist) and practices to initiate (Parts 3 and 4);
- to recommend what other resources, such as videos, books and reports, the school should acquire (short-listed so that a selection can be made according to financial resources available);
- to provide a short report containing this information.

Step 4: presenting a plan to the school

The report of the anti-bullying committee (see step 3) can provide the basis for a discussion about the best course of action for the school. It is essential to debate the report as part of a refining process. For instance, some suggestions may be too costly or complex to put in place. Committee members may want to have the policy ratified and the programme implemented right away, but the school authorities may urge a slower, more considered approach. Such issues must be debated. It is essential to be realistic and selective about goals.

After the report has been discussed, it is important to decide what will be implemented, how this will be monitored, and who will be responsible for the programme as a whole and for the individual components. When staff become part of the implementation process, this work must be properly acknowledged as being part of an individual's workload.

The aims of step 4 are:

- to consider the plan and its recommendations;
- to debate the document;
- to consolidate the policy;
- to plan for the implementation of the programme.

Implementing the initiative

Step 5: the initiative is put in place

Disseminate the policy widely

Parents must be informed in writing about what the school intends to do. Alternatively or additionally, a public meeting could be held to provide information and to answer questions and discuss issues. (The communication styles of relevant cultural and ethnic groups need to be taken into account. In New Zealand, for example, Maori and Pacific Island people are much more receptive to an oral rather than a written interchange.) The policy needs to be widely disseminated.

This policy, in effect, becomes the school's contract with parents and pupils about school bullying. The school's obligations are to administer and support the policy and to carry out the letter of it. It is equally important that parents and children support the spirit of the policy. The policy should also be announced and talked about at a school assembly and in classrooms. The anti-bullying programmes that have been selected should be introduced and described. It should also be explained how they reflect the anti-bullying philosophy and policy of the school.

Establish the practice

It is vital, now, to put the policy into practice, particularly in relation to already identified cases of bullying. Some pupils may 'push the boundaries' to test the policy and see if the school means what it says. Uniformity of response must be maintained across the staff. This period will be challenging, but if the school is consistent, the policy will retain its integrity.

> The aims of step 5 are:
> * to establish the policy and programme in practice;
> * to let people know that this is happening.

Maintenance of the initiative

Step 6: evaluation and maintenance of the initiative

Although, after a bullying initiative has been put in place, it may seem that the work has been done and it is time to move on, it is essential to maintain rigorous support for the programme. If not, the same old problems will recur. If a programme is maintained, it will continue to work well, even when staff and pupils leave; each new cohort of pupils and teachers will need to be introduced to the school's anti-bullying philosophy, policy and programmes.

Within the cycle of school management tasks, there should be regular evaluation of the extent of bullying and of the anti-bullying programme to ensure that the former is abating and the latter is working. Major evaluations should be carried out after 18 months and after three years.

It is worth noting that introducing an anti-bullying initiative raises people's awareness of bullying in all its forms. As it becomes safe to report instances of bullying and people understand it better, a survey can give the impression that the rate of bullying has in fact increased. This impression is probably incorrect.

Research has shown that the full process of consolidation, development and implementation can be long, and that monitoring provides useful feedback on the success of the implementation (see Macklem, 2003; Thompson et al., 2002).

> The aims of step 6 are:
> * to maintain and modify the programme as appropriate on a regular basis;
> * to make sure that the school's anti-bullying initiative is explained to new pupils and teachers.

References

Macklem, G.L. (2003) *Bullying and Teasing: Social Power in Children's Groups*. New York: Springer.

Thompson, D., Arora, T. and Sharp, S. (2002) *Bullying: Effective Strategies for Long-term Improvement*. London: Routledge.

CHAPTER 7

DEVELOPING A PHILOSOPHY ABOUT BULLYING

Introduction: making the ethos explicit

Every school has a philosophy about the purpose of education and how to go about delivering it. Often, however, the philosophy is implied rather than stated, and is expressed in the atmosphere, or ethos, of the school. It is crucial to bring important philosophical issues to the surface and to make them explicit, through debate and discussion.

The nature of this philosophy will determine the school's attitude towards bullying. In setting up an anti-bullying initiative, visiting or revisiting the school's philosophy is the essential first step. In the same way that a house must have strong foundations before the rest of the structure can be erected, a school must clarify its philosophy so that initiatives and policies can be built on this philosophy.

In developing a school philosophy on bullying, it is useful to look both inwards and outwards. Looking inwards means appraising and discussing the school's existing philosophy, and clarifying it into a general statement or charter. Looking outwards means examining what other schools have done and seeing what anti-bullying researchers and programme developers have to offer. This means learning from others' experiences but making decisions that fit the culture of a particular school.

In deciding to undertake these inward and outward journeys, it is useful to consider two models. The first relates specifically to the *ethos* of the school and is a continuum: at one end is the dysfunctional school, at the other the safe school and in the middle what I call the conflicted school. This model illuminates the relationship between the school's ethos and its approach to bullying. The second model depicts three different philosophical *perspectives* on bullying behaviour: the punishment approach, the consequences approach and the feelings approach.

The school ethos: identifying and developing the school's philosophy

When a school decides to deal with bullying, it needs to be clear about its founda-tions – the values or beliefs of the school, its academic and educational aspirations, the nature of the personal relationships it fosters, and the societal attitudes and responsibilities modelled and taught at the school. When its foundations are clear, then its philosophies can be made explicit. And when the philosophy is explicit, then it can more easily be refined, maintained and monitored.

Recent bullying research has made a link between the adoption of a whole-school policy, the school's attitude towards bullying and the successful implementation of effective anti-bullying programmes. In the Sheffield project in England, for instance, it was found that the successful schools stood out because the attitudes, processes and programmes within them were consistent, positive, thorough and well maintained.

In a follow-up study, Eslea and Smith (1998) revisited four primary schools from the original study. In two of the project schools, bullying had reduced further since the project had formally ceased; in one school, things had remained virtually the same; and in the fourth school, bullying had become worse. In a still more recent study, Smith et al. (2004) concluded that the schools where bullying had continued to decrease were those where the policies and programmes had been maintained and had even developed beyond the schools' initial involvement in the project.

So what is meant by school ethos? It is the feeling of the school – its atmosphere. Inwardly, it is the school's sense of itself as a community of educators, learners and parents. Outwardly, this is manifested as the policies and programmes of the school, which, in turn, are grounded in the school's philosophy, its attitudes, beliefs and values, and its vision of what it hopes to achieve.

The ethos of the school is usually set by its leadership: the principal, adminis-trative staff, governors/board of trustees members and senior teachers. It is also determined by the nature of the school community. Examining a school's philoso-phy is a useful exercise for a school to go through so that attitudes, expectations and values are clarified. Without this process, misunderstandings and contradictions are likely to occur. For instance, if a teacher and principal give different explana-tions of the rules of the school to a pupil or a parent, this is not only confusing but also undermining. It suggests that the school is disorganized and lacks cohesion. It suggests a philosophical void rather than an ethical strength.

Having a school philosophy does not mean that everyone has to think the same or that rules become inflexible and discretion an anathema. What it does mean is that the participants in the school culture agree to play the same game, and that rules can be articulated into anti-bullying policy. When the school's thinking is clear, then internal processes can be constructed and external programmes and strategies chosen. The resultant philosophy and anti-bullying policies are consistent. As the processes prove successful, what happens every day in the school will also be founded on the philosophical foundations, policies and programmes. The ethos will inform the ethics, and each will reinforce the other.

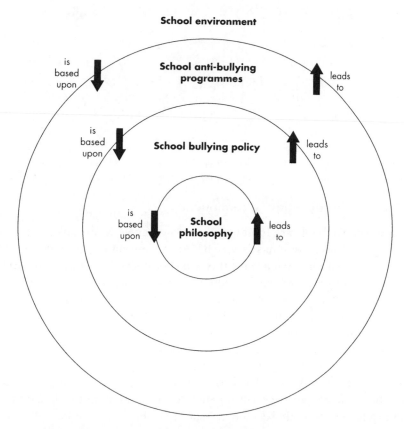

Figure 7.1   The relationship between a school's philosophy, its anti-bullying policy and programmes, and the school environment

A school's ethos is a fundamental determinant for the rate of bullying, truancy and general disruptive behaviour. Its clearest expression is in the adoption of a whole-school policy that is necessarily cogent and explicit.

Looking inwards: the school ethos and its relationship to bullying

The following description of three hypothetical types of school ethos provides an insight into some of the issues schools face when they start to deal with a difficult and complex problem such as bullying.

The dysfunctional school: the do-little/do-nothing approach

The school's philosophy

At the negative end of the continuum is the dysfunctional school. A school may be classified as dysfunctional because of a number of characteristics. Research tends to

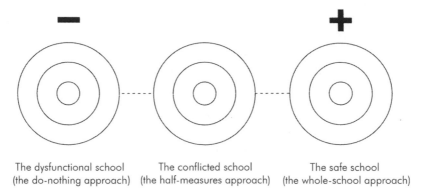

The dysfunctional school   The conflicted school   The safe school
(the do-nothing approach)   (the half-measures approach)   (the whole-school approach)

Figure 7.2   The school ethos: a continuum

suggest that such schools are located in run-down areas where the social and economic malaise of the community is matched by the malaise of the school. Although
a school in any area may win against the odds because of its philosophy and vision
and the commitment of its staff, when it is poorly administered and lacking in
morale, it is less likely to remain healthy and more likely to mirror any social problems that are part of the culture surrounding the school.

There may be alcohol or drug abuse and high unemployment in the community,
and criminal activity among family members, including some of those still at school.
Bullying may occur frequently, but it may be only one of an array of problems. For
instance, the school may be subject to a high incidence of physical attacks upon
teachers, theft, truancy and vandalism. Such a school may find it difficult to attract
and retain teachers, and those who do stay may have low morale. Even young,
committed teachers who have chosen this hard posting for idealistic reasons may
find that so much of their time is taken up with crisis intervention that they cannot
implement any proper change or follow it through.

If challenged, such a school would vilify bullying, but in fact it is dominated by
a range of antisocial behaviours that are dealt with haphazardly or not at all. There
is no coherent philosophy, and little commitment to developing one.

Developing a school anti-bullying policy

If such a school were to struggle towards defining its philosophy, it might find that
staff are simply not available when they are needed. For instance, a meeting is called
and the guidance counsellor cannot attend because there is a crisis elsewhere that
she has to handle. Most long-term members of staff have become cynical in their
outlook, and are not prepared to try another 'do-good' effort; or they are simply too
overloaded and have low morale. In addition, there is very little will among parents
to get involved in the school.

Choosing and implementing an anti-bullying programme

The school has been assessed by government as needing extra support because of

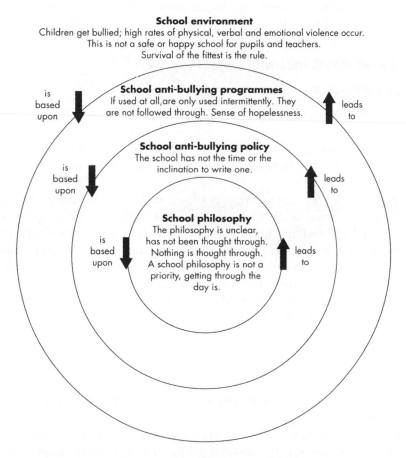

Figure 7.3   The dysfunctional school (the do-nothing approach)

its location and the social problems of its population, so some extra funding for running an anti-bullying programme has been provided. The school buys a programme but, although parents and staff are invited to a meeting to introduce it, attendance is poor and ongoing meetings are only sporadically supported. Against the odds, the programme works well for the first three months, then loses impetus and eventually fails. Its failure proves to staff, parents and students that there is little point in trying to do things differently.

The school environment

For the top dogs, school is tolerable. It is a place where they can exert power. The situation for everyone else is essentially survival of the fittest. Children are bullied on a regular basis, most often to extort food, money and personal possessions, but students are also subjected to emotional and verbal abuse. Some children who have been badly bullied start truanting on a regular basis and eventually drop out.

Teachers are disaffected, disrespected and in despair. This school is an unsafe place for both pupils and teachers.

The conflicted school: the half-measures approach

The school's philosophy

Conflicted schools take two forms.

1. Different staff members in the school take conflicting positions.
2. What the school says it believes in and what it does are contradictory.

In the first instance, the principal may not think there is a bullying problem in the school. This is because essentially he believes that learning to stand up to bullying is character-building and that a little 'rough play' is normal. He therefore concludes that a preoccupation with bullying is unnecessary, and that if he waits, any misplaced concern will disappear.

Several of the teachers think there is a bullying problem in the school, however, and want to do something about it. The principal, reluctantly bending to pressure from the teachers, allows an investigation and the development of an anti-bullying policy.

In this situation, anti-bullying initiatives could be undermined in the following ways.

- The principal could allow insufficient resources to be allocated to bullying so the job will not be done properly.
- He could allow meetings to be arranged to set up a bullying policy, but make them voluntary and out of teaching hours, not committing himself or other administrative staff to attending. This would give the message to the rest of the staff that the initiative is not important.
- In handling bullying, he could use different strategies than those decided by the anti-bullying team or suggested in the adopted anti-bullying programme.

In the second instance, an anti-bullying stance is taken that is supported by policy, but contradicted by practice. Some conflicted schools rely very much on their academic or socio-economic standing and, while paying lip-service to innovations and staff development, prefer to keep their culture intact. Staff in such a school may handle bullying incidents when they arise in a piecemeal, unreferenced and often ineffective manner but, if challenged about their interpretation of the event or their handling of it, will close ranks and write off the challengers (usually parents) as interfering, ignorant or overprotective.

Such a school exhibits the following belief syndrome. *Ideologically*, the school does not approve of violence or cruelty in any form. *And because of this*, there is no bullying in the school. Redefinition of the event denies the existence of the phenomenon. Bullying only exists 'out there', in 'bad' schools.

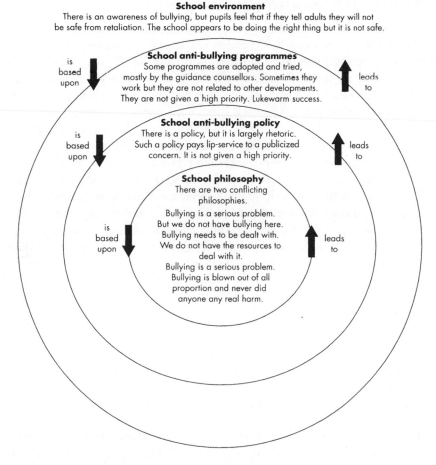

School environment
There is an awareness of bullying, but pupils feel that if they tell adults they will not
be safe from retaliation. The school appears to be doing the right thing but it is not safe.

is based upon

leads to

School anti-bullying programmes
Some programmes are adopted and tried,
mostly by the guidance counsellors. Sometimes they
work but they are not related to other developments.
They are not given a high priority. Lukewarm success.

is based upon

leads to

School anti-bullying policy
There is a policy, but it is largely rhetoric.
Such a policy pays lip-service to a publicized
concern. It is not given a high priority.

is based upon

leads to

School philosophy
There are two conflicting
philosophies.

Bullying is a serious problem.
But we do not have bullying here.
Bullying needs to be dealt with.
We do not have the resources to
deal with it.
Bullying is a serious problem.
Bullying is blown out of all
proportion and never did
anyone any real harm.

Figure 7.4   The conflicted school (the half-measures approach)

Developing a school anti-bullying policy

In the first instance, the school may go through the motions of developing an anti-bullying policy, and this process may be driven by one or two people who see bullying as an important issue. Here, the job of coordinating the initiative may be regarded as a voluntary activity, and in this way the school hierarchy signals that the initiative is not a priority. Teachers who in other circumstances might have become involved do not do so because school leadership does not place enough value on the process. It is also difficult for teachers to fit it into their busy schedule. Such a policy is not fully embraced by the school.

In the second instance, the school may fully support the idea of developing an anti-bullying policy and involve the school community in doing so. It may appear to pick up the idea and embrace it wholeheartedly, producing a viable policy. The question is then whether the policy can be accepted and implemented.

Choosing and implementing an anti-bullying programme

In the first instance, the principal may provide money for staff training or the purchase of an anti-bullying programme but perhaps not enough to develop the programme fully. It will eventually fall to the guidance counsellor, the head of school discipline (HSD) or a teacher to handle all cases of bullying, and they may become overwhelmed and unable to act effectively because of other demands on their time. The bullying programme may lose support because it is not considered important in light of other developments. If the guidance counsellor asks for more bullying resources the following year, she may be told, 'We did bullying last year and will be working on truancy this coming year'. Pupils may be encouraged to report incidents of bullying and begin to do so, but then find that the bullying is not handled properly and the bullies retaliate. In other words, if there is no thoroughly developed and implemented programme for dealing with bullying, the initiative will probably fail in the long term.

In the second and third instances, while an anti-bullying programme may be adopted, when bullying occurs, it is usually ignored, misinterpreted or handled badly. Only extreme cases of physical bullying are treated seriously. There is no cohesive holistic approach: policy is not able to be implemented.

The school environment

An outsider looking into these schools may see institutions that seem to be performing well. They may be located in affluent middle-class areas and, by the perceived important criterion, academic success, they do very well. There may be no immediately obvious signs of bullying, but physical and verbal bullying and bullying by exclusion are occurring just below the surface. Such schools collude in pretending this is not the case.

Pupils know that, more often than not, teachers will dismiss reports of bullying. As a result, most students do not tell. They feel that, if they report an incident of bullying, it will probably not be resolved and the bullies will get back at them. Despite appearances to the contrary, for some pupils such schools are not safe places.

Some staff may feel disaffected because their extra work in the bullying programme has not been appreciated or supported. Others may feel confused, defensive and uneasy.

In some ways, a conflicted school is worse than a dysfunctional school because it makes the right noises and appears to be doing the right thing. Not only is the school's philosophy mixed and uncertain, but so are the messages, the policies and the safety of pupils.

The safe school: the whole-school approach

The school philosophy

The safe school is one that has adopted a whole-school policy based on the philosophy of creating a school that is safe from bullying and supporting the development of each person towards their potential. Research indicates that, when a school takes the issue of bullying seriously and develops a thorough and inclusive anti-bullying initiative, it is most successful in combating bullying. In the whole-school approach, everyone in the extended school (administrators, teachers, students, parents and the community) is involved in all processes, from the early discussions, and through the development, consolidation and implementation stages. Everyone knows what the rules are because they have participated in generating them and so own and feel responsible towards them.

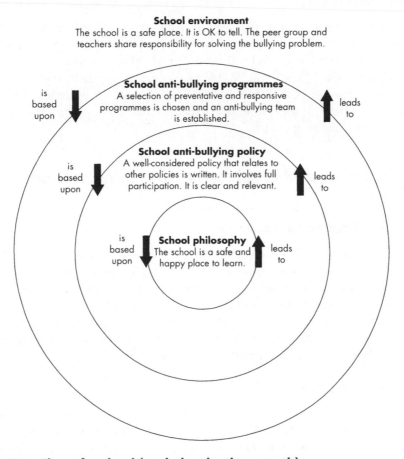

Figure 7.5   The safe school (a whole-school approach)

Developing a school anti-bullying policy

An anti-bullying policy is a realistic set of understandings and expectations flowing directly and logically from the school philosophy. The policy will be clearly written and will relate, in its tone and intentions, to policies designed for other areas that put people at risk, such as alcohol and drug use, disruptive behaviour and fighting, and truancy. In other words, school policies will be integrated.

Choosing and implementing an anti-bullying programme

Once the policy is clear, then it is logical for the school to develop and choose a set of preventative and intervention strategies to implement. These programmes should reflect the values and beliefs of the school community and the policies of the school.

The school environment

As a result of having a carefully prepared, consolidated and implemented policy, the school will be safe from bullying. It will be bully-proof. The teaching staff and pupils will know what the rules are and will not be afraid either to intervene or to get help when bullying occurs. Pupils will be able to concentrate on their work without fear of being intimidated or bullied and there will be a culture of awareness. The school will understand that it is acceptable and expected that students can either intervene or tell an adult if bullying occurs.

Looking outwards: what approaches to bullying have been developed?

Three ways of dealing with bullying

Essentially, three distinctive ways of dealing with bullying have been developed in recent years: the punishment approach, the consequences approach and the feelings response. The first two derive from a deficit perspective, which seeks to change behaviour rather than systems, and the third is an example of a constructivist perspective, which instead attempts to alter the ecology of the bullying environment and rid the system of the bullying dynamic. I will describe each of them and discuss their advantages and disadvantages.

The punishment approach

The punishment approach as a response to bullying reflects the criminal justice system. In the latter, if an offence is committed and the person is found guilty, he or she is punished by doing community service, paying a fine or going to prison. The equivalent punishments in a school context are detention, extra homework, tasks around the school and, if the behaviour persists, suspension and expulsion.

Bullying courts are an example of a punishment-based approach. Whereas in most of these approaches it is the school that metes out the punishment, in this case the peer group is put in the position of judge. The bully court concept was introduced in the UK by Robert Laslett (1980, 1982), and brought to prominence by Michele Elliott, director of Kidscape, a London-based anti-bullying organization (Elliott, 2002). In the bully courts, perpetrators of bullying are brought before a panel of their peers (with some teacher representation) and 'put on trial', as in a court of law. If they are judged to be guilty of bullying, a sentence is passed, for example, staying in for an hour after school every day for a week and picking up litter in the school grounds. The intention is to let the bully know that, if they choose to bully, they will not get away with it. This could be described as a short, sharp shock approach.

The consequences approach

When I spoke with Delwyn Tattum of the Cardiff Institute of Higher Education's Countering Bullying Unit, he described an approach to bullying that he calls crisis care (see Tattum et al., 2003). This is typical of what could be termed the consequences approach: if a student chooses to bully, then there have to be consequences. The distinction Tattum made between this approach and punishment-based responses is that consequences should be educative rather than punitive. In other words, rather than just listening to the circumstances surrounding a bullying incident and then punishing the bully, the intention is to talk to the victim, offer support and let the bully know that there will be consequences (which may or may not be specified) if the bullying does not stop.

The feelings response

A third way of dealing with bullying can be termed the feelings response. The philosophy here is that, rather than punishing or providing consequences for bullying, it is more effective to appeal to the better nature of the bullies and to alter the bullying system. One of the characteristics of bullying is that those who bully usually see their victims as worthless, as non-people, a picture that the victims, in their despair, probably share. With a feelings approach, a major concern is to 'rehumanize' the situation. This means not only stopping the bullying but also aiming to change the behaviour of the perpetrator so that they empathize with the victim, have a sense of remorse and come to the realization that it is wrong to bully. This change comes about not because of a fear of punishment or a wish to avoid inconvenient consequences, but because humanity is restored to the relationship.

Another important dimension of this approach is that tapping into feelings often extends to the peer group. It is not left solely to the one doing the bullying to learn how to empathize, but the supporters, reinforcers and larger peer group are also drawn into the process of change (the Support Group Method, Chapter 16, is an example of this).

The philosophies behind the three ways

I considered the above descriptions and thought, if I were a member of a group in a school whose job it was to decide how to develop an anti-bullying initiative, what questions would I ask? How would I try to align the details of the initiative and the programme choice with my emerging sense of my school's ethos and philosophy? First, I thought about the underlying characteristics of each approach.

The punishment approach

1. The bully must be punished for bullying, by detention, suspension or expulsion (also known as exclusion) from the school, or by some other form of punishment.
2. The punishment is meted out by someone with power.
3. The victim of bullying does not have any role to play.
4. The intention of this approach is to make bullies stop bullying because they will be punished in an escalating fashion if they do not.

The consequences approach

1. The bullies must be made to change their behaviour or face the consequences, which could include a written record of the bullying and other punitive responses.
2. The consequences are meted out by an adult with power.
3. The victim of bullying is rescued by the adult running the programme.
4. The intention of this approach is to make bullies stop bullying because there will be escalating consequences if they do not.

The feelings response

1. The victim of bullying is encouraged to describe how it feels to be bullied.
2. A group of peers including the bully is helped to understand how it feels to be bullied.
3. The emphasis is on finding a solution, not attributing blame.
4. The intention of this approach is to make the bully stop bullying because the peer group suddenly understands what has been happening and learns to empathize with the victim. The dynamics of the situation change so that it is no longer easy or acceptable for the perpetrator to victimize others.

Clearly, there are differences between these three approaches, philosophically and fundamentally, and also in terms of the ethos or atmosphere they create and the outcomes they produce.

The punishment approach relies on an authoritarian figure upbraiding a bully and meting out punishment for the crime of bullying. Laying down the law may be a clear way to teach right from wrong, but it could be argued that this approach is essentially the same as the act of bullying itself: it involves a person in power in some way of hurting a person with less power.

The consequences approach also gives a clear message about the unacceptability of a certain type of behaviour. It is less authoritarian than the punitive approach, but is similarly static. Someone in power has to deal with bullying as one more form of disruptive behaviour in which the perpetrator must be sorted out.

Both these approaches are essentially behaviouristic, that is, they take a gamble on the chance that bullies will give up their antisocial behaviour because they know if they do not they will be punished, in the first instance, and face consequences, in the second instance.

The only real difference between the two is one of degree: punishment is immutable; consequences may be later removed from the record. In the first, the victim is avenged; in the second, the bully may be redeemed. In both, behaviour is controlled through threats and manipulation.

If there is punishment or there are consequences for an incident of bullying, it is arguably only the symptom of the bullying rather than the bullying itself that is being addressed. These types of responses also expose bullied children to retaliation and revenge.

The feelings approach gives bullies a chance to understand what the effects of bullying are, to empathize and to personalize. It also involves the onlookers, and makes it clear to them that they have the choice to support, to counter or to do nothing. If the purpose of bullying someone is to gain peer approval, then the withdrawal of this approval will immediately undermine the bully.

In effect, the first two approaches deal with the events in isolation from the overall context. They take the situation as given and then attempt to change the behaviour of the bullies. The feelings approach is essentially a systems approach. The underlying intention is to change the dynamics of the situation, to raise awareness of the participants about bullying and to support the peer group in taking responsibility for the bullying.

The feelings approach is potentially empowering, and presents what, to me, is a better paradigm of social interaction and the type of society I would like to live in than fear-based approaches. It has also produced many more useful anti-bullying materials than the punitive and consequences approaches.

References

Elliott, M. (2002) *Bullying: A Practical Guide to Coping for Schools*. 3rd edn. London: Pearson Education.

Eslea, M. and Smith, P.K. (1998) 'The long-term effectiveness of anti-bullying work in primary schools', *Educational Research*, 40: 203–18.

Laslett, R. (1980) 'Bullies: a children's court in a day school for maladjusted children', *Journal of Special Education*, 4: 391–7.

Laslett, R. (1982) 'A children's court for bullies', *Special Education: Forward Trends*, 9(1): 9–11.

Smith, P.K., Sharp, S., Eslea, M. and Thompson, D. (2004) 'England: the Sheffield project', in P.K. Smith, D. Pepler and K. Rigby (eds), *Bullying in Schools: How Successful Can Interventions Be?* Cambridge: Cambridge University Press.

Tattum, D., Tattum, E. and Herbert, G. (2003) *Bullying: A Positive Response*. Cardiff: University of Wales Institute Cardiff, Countering Bullying Unit.

CHAPTER 8

PLANNING AND INFORMATION GATHERING

Introduction: expediting development and planning

The school can expedite the process of developing and planning policy, first, by examining its strengths and weaknesses, and gaining a clear picture of itself; and second, by gathering information about the nature and extent of bullying that occurs in the school. It can achieve the first of these aims by running the educational equivalent of a SWOT analysis, and the second by administering a questionnaire throughout the school.

Adapting the SWOT analysis for planning and policy in schools

A SWOT analysis is a useful business tool that has been developed for strategic planning (see, for example, Bradford et al., 2000) so that a company can examine itself closely in order to improve its competitive edge. Using the SWOT analysis process, a company can ascertain its strengths and weaknesses, and develop a strategy to minimize or change the weaknesses, and to build on and extend its areas of strength.

SWOT stands for strengths (S), weaknesses (W), opportunities (O) and threats (T). SWOT analyses not only focus on the characteristics of the company but also on the environment in which it functions. Strengths and weaknesses are internal characteristics that, when fully recognized and strategically altered, can improve the company's competitive advantage. An opportunity is an aspect of the surrounding environment that, if harnessed, can enhance the company's strategic planning and improve its performance. In a school, the competitive aspects of the environmental setting are less significant than in the business world, but the identification of opportunities nevertheless remains a valid perspective in the sense of renewal and resourcefulness. A threat is a condition or characteristic of the larger environment that can work to undermine the business's potential.

An adapted SWOT analysis gives a school an objective picture of itself and helps it to identify its areas of strength and weakness. The school can then plan to build on its areas of strength and to correct its weaknesses. Because it is an empirical analysis, it can, for example, be used to look specifically at the physical environment of the school, the creative use of space both in buildings and in playgrounds (see Chapter 14), and the ratio of staff to students. And because it is also an impressionistic analysis, it gives access to such aspects as a sense of the character of relationships between peers and others in the school, the morale of teachers and the role of parents.

In schools, a SWOT analysis can be usefully adapted to plan for the future, either on a large scale or, in this particular instance, in deciding how best to prepare for an anti-bullying initiative. For these purposes, I have added a step to the SWOT process that focuses on providing strategies and solutions (SS), which then makes it a SWOTSS analysis.

A SWOTSS analysis can be carried out in schools either by an individual or by an anti-bullying committee.

A case study of a SWOTSS analysis

Here is an example of a SWOTSS analysis used to develop an anti-bullying initiative.

Benburn School (a fictional name) stands on hilly farmland on the outskirts of a medium-sized city in New South Wales. It is an area school with a population of approximately 300 students, 14 full-time teachers and three administrative staff. The school has a small kindergarten and full primary and secondary sections. Although the school does not appear to have a bad bullying problem, the teachers are aware that bullying occurs in all schools and that it is often not reported. There is a particular worry about the school's special needs children, some of whom are being bullied. The school has decided to find ways of improving its systems so as to create an environment that is not conducive to bullying, and to find better ways of detecting and monitoring bullying.

For the purpose of this SWOTSS analysis, I have included the greater school community, parents as well as teachers and students, in the school's internal environment. The external environment is the wider community, both social and political.

Strengths: internal and potential internal strengths

The school population is small and spans the years from the start of early childhood until the end of secondary school. From the perspective of developing an anti-bullying initiative, the following strengths were identified:

* There is a positive school ethos. Students are taught responsibility with kindness, which means many older students take care of and have good relationships with younger children.

- There is an interesting and friendly school environment, with many diverse spaces and mini-environments in the school.
- The teachers are largely devoted to the children's well-being, have good intentions and are committed to their work.
- Several of the teachers have demonstrated skills in dealing with difficult issues such as bullying and are well liked by the students.
- The classes are smaller than the national average (22 rather than 30 students).
- The school structure minimizes stress for students at transition points: entering the early childhood sector, entering primary school, beginning intermediate school and starting secondary school. At these times children can be vulnerable and at risk of being bullied. Having all sectors in one school largely removes the stress.
- Some teachers at the school use cooperative learning. By working together in a cooperative fashion, children learn to appreciate diversity.
- The school can afford to purchase anti-bullying resources. The school has an annual fair that raises money to support in-school developments. Some of this money could be used to buy anti-bullying resources.
- The teachers are involved in the school's democratic decision-making processes. Tasks are shared out among staff in an equitable way.
- There is strong support from parents, many whom are involved in the school on a voluntary basis, and can be called on to help monitor the playground and provide specialist resources to the school, for example, acting, dance, music, photography classes and sports training.

Weaknesses: current and potential internal weaknesses

- The school is hard to patrol. It is spread out over a large area of varied terrain, and there are a lot of potential blind areas, nooks and crannies, with many buildings. This means that there are many places where bullying could take place.
- The staff are not trained to deal specifically with bullying.
- Because there is no policy on bullying, it is difficult for teachers to be sure about the school's stance in relation to bullying, how to handle it, who is 'in charge' and what to do about contacting parents.
- The kindergarten, primary and secondary sectors of the school are largely independent, making it hard to coordinate efforts.
- There are a large number of competing demands on teachers' time.
- The school has good intentions but is often slow at getting things in place. This is partly a result of the school's democratic nature.
- Special needs children are bullied behind the teachers' backs.

Opportunities: current and potential external opportunities

- Some funding may be available to support the development of an anti-bullying initiative from the New South Wales Department of Education and Training, and grants can be applied for from charities (such as the Australian Lottery Board). These could be investigated.

- Several parents are skilled in anger management training, assertiveness training and counselling, and have contact with social agencies. They have been approached by the school and are willing to help develop an anti-bullying plan.
- There is a growing awareness of bullying in the greater school community. Partly because of recent media attention, most parents are aware that bullying is occurring in all schools. It is therefore an opportune time to develop an anti-bullying initiative and any efforts are likely to receive parental support.
- A lot of time, effort and money have gone into research about bullying and to develop anti-bullying programmes for schools. Using money from the school budget selectively to purchase books on bullying and anti-bullying kits would provide a useful resource base for the school.

Threats: potential external threats

This dimension is the least relevant of the four because, unlike businesses, schools are only minimally in competition with each other. However, one external issue was identified:

- If the school addresses bullying, it could be regarded as having a bullying problem. Rather than being seen as proactive and responsible, the school could be labelled a 'bullying school'. Since funding is directly related to the number of students in the school, bad publicity could have a detrimental economic effect if parents choose to send their children to other schools.

Strategies and solutions

Preventative measures

- Peer support. A class-to-class buddy system could be developed using the wide age range of the children within the school. For example, Class 5 could develop a caring relationship (buddying) with Class 1. This would be a beneficial and learning process for the children in both classes, and would mean that a younger child who was being bullied would have someone they could turn to for advice (see Chapter 13, 'Harnessing the Power of the Peer Group').
- School policy on bullying. Clearly, it is important to develop and write a whole-school bullying policy that outlines how to make the school a safe environment for all its members, and identifies the rights and responsibilities of the various groups.
- More teachers in the playground. To make sure that the opportunities for bullying are minimized, it is important for teachers to be more visible and involved with children out of the classroom. Because the school grounds are spread out, teachers need to patrol widely so that potential danger spots are not overlooked.
- Monitor system in the playground. It was suggested that selected senior students be given responsibilities for playground and classroom supervision of younger children. This could operate in a similar fashion to bus monitors, which is already

a success. Bus monitors record and report misbehaviour and reinforce good behaviour.

- More combined outing activities. There was a suggestion that more activities be arranged in which different classes go out and do activities together, such as river outings, sports days and walks. This concept is already in place but could be greatly expanded.
- Allocate funds for an in-service course in cooperative learning. It was suggested that teachers with cooperative learning experience share this with other teachers and that the possibility of in-service training in cooperative learning be explored.
- Parent involvement in lunchtime activities. Parents could become involved with generating and running interesting activities, such as teaching children games and taking small groups for various indoors and outdoors activities. It would be important to consider what and who is appropriate.
- Address the anti-bullying requirements of the special needs children. There should be a consciously constructed programme for teaching and demonstrating to children how to behave with people with disabilities. This could be done in class or through assemblies. It would also be useful to invite visitors who have struggled to overcome a disability to speak to an assembly.
- Create foundations of mutual support with the parents. Early networking and discussion could prevent later problems with issues such as bullying.

Interventions

- Adopting the Support Group Method. The written and audio-visual resources of this anti-bullying programme have been made available to the teachers and have been discussed (see Chapter 16). It will be recommended that the school adopts this as a major strategy. Even though it is an overseas programme, the school regards it as its first choice after having considered several others. There was some concern that the programme would be too old for kindergarten children and that another programme should be found for them (perhaps Circle of Friends, see Chapter 17).

Conclusion

A number of strategies and solutions have been suggested as a result of using the SWOTSS process. At this point an important consideration is how best to continue. Is it better to plan to introduce a number of strategies over a specified period of time, or to adopt only one strategy and do it thoroughly and well, before moving on to another?

Survey and questionnaire

As well as a clearer picture of its strengths and weaknesses, a school needs to have some idea of the nature and extent of its bullying before it can plan for appropriate policies and initiatives. The results of a questionnaire, once collated, are an important record of the state of the school at a particular time, and can also be used to support the argument for a whole-school policy and an anti-bullying initiative. Once an initiative is implemented, the collated first survey can be used for comparative purposes.

A questionnaire should be designed not only to elicit information about who bullies, where it happens, when it happens and how often, but also to outline the types of bullying there are and therefore to educate children about what is and is not bullying. A questionnaire must be clear and simple for ease of understanding by those taking the survey; for ease of generating statistics, for those who have to add everything up; and for ease of interpreting, when the information is presented to parents, staff, students and trustees/governors.

The following questionnaire was written with secondary students in mind, and can be altered and adapted for younger age groups as necessary. Once the questionnaire has been completed, the same basic form can be used to record the total responses to each question for statistical purposes.

Reference

Bradford, R.W. and Duncan, J.P. with Tarcy, B. (2000) *Simplified Strategic Planning: A No-Nonsense Guide for Busy People Who Want Results Fast!* Worcester, MA: Chandler House Press

Questionnaire about school bullying class/form/grade

Introduction: This school takes bullying very seriously and we wish to know how much bullying is taking place in the school. Bullying can be hitting, kicking or the use of force in any way. It can be teasing, making rude gestures, name-calling or leaving you out. It can involve nasty texts being distributed or cruel messages being posted about you on Facebook, via email, and in other Internet and computer-generated communication systems.

Bullying means that these things happened more than once and were done by the same person or persons. Bullying means to hurt, either physically or so that you feel very bad.

This is an anonymous questionnaire. This means that you can answer the questions but you don't have to let us know who you are. There is a blank for your name, however, if you want to tell us who you are. All information received will be dealt with in a confidential and sensitive manner.

Name:_____
(give your name only if you wish)

First of all, please answer these questions:
1. Are you a boy or a girl?
2. How old are you?
3. Which class/form/grade are you in?

The following are statements about bullying. Please mark up your responses for us:

4. Since I have been at school, I have been bullied (circle one of the following):
never   once in a while   about once a week   more than once a week
5. I have been bullied in the following ways (tick √ for yes or cross x for no for each category):
- hitting (punching, kicking, shoving)   Yes   No
- a knife or a gun or some kind of weapon was used on me
- mean teasing
- purposely left out of things
- had my things damaged or stolen
- was horribly sworn at
- had offensive sexual suggestions made to me
- had a nasty racial remark made to me
- received nasty (poisonous) letter(s)
- someone said nasty things to make others dislike me
- had untrue and mean gossip spread about me
- had mean texts sent out about me/to me
- had nasty things said about me via computer/on Facebook etc.
- I was threatened
- had rude gestures or mean faces made at me
- anything else (write it in here) _____
6. Since I have been at school, I have bullied someone (circle one of the following):
never   once in a while   about once a week   more than once a week
7. I have bullied someone in the following ways (tick √ for yes or cross x for no for each category):
- hitting (punching, kicking, shoving)   Yes   No
- use of a knife or a gun or some kind of weapon on someone
- mean teasing

- purposely left someone out of things
- damaged or stole someone's possessions
- swore at someone
- made offensive sexual suggestions to someone
- made a nasty racial remark about someone
- sent nasty (poisonous) letter(s)
- said nasty things to make others dislike someone
- made up and spread untrue and mean gossip about someone
- sent mean texts about/to someone
- sent nasty messages about someone via computer/on Facebook etc.
- I threatened someone
- made rude gestures or mean faces at someone
  anything else (write it in here) _____

8. Since I have been at school, I have seen bullying take place (circle one of the following):
   never   once in a while   about once a week   more than once a week

9. I have watched or have heard about the following types of bullying (tick √ for yes or
   cross x for no for each category):
- hitting (punching, kicking, shoving)   Yes   No
- use of a knife or a gun or some kind of weapon on someone
- mean teasing
- someone purposely being left out of things
- someone having their things damaged or stolen
- someone being horribly sworn at
- someone having offensive sexual suggestions made to them
- someone having a nasty racial remark made to them
- someone receiving nasty (poisonous) letter(s)
- someone having nasty things said to make others dislike them
- someone having untrue and mean gossip spread about them
- someone being sent cruel texts
- someone having nasty things said about them via computer/on Facebook etc.
- someone being threatened
- someone having rude gestures or mean faces made at them
- anything else (write it in here)

10. Tick (√) all places where you have been bullied or have seen bullying take place:
- in the playground
- in the corridors
- in the classroom
- in the cafeteria
- in the library
- in the locker room
- in the toilets
- on the way to school
- on the way home from school
- on the bus/train
- anywhere else (write it in here)

11. Where are the 'danger spots' where most bullying takes place? Please list these:
   i
   ii
   iii
   iv
   v

CHAPTER 9

CREATING A SCHOOL ANTI-BULLYING POLICY

Introduction: focusing on policy

After a school has clarified its philosophy and gathered information about itself and the bullying that occurs in the school, the next step is to create a school policy on bullying. A written anti-bullying policy is a very important document, the school's equivalent of a bill of rights. It states the school's intentions and how it will enforce and uphold its rules and processes; what teachers', students' and parents' rights and responsibilities are; and what procedures are in place. It is, in effect, a contract between the school and its community.

Before such a policy can be written, consultation and discussion need to occur. Once the policy is written, the stages of implementation, monitoring and maintenance will follow.

In this chapter, I will discuss how to go about creating a school policy, what and who should be included in the various stages, and the steps that follow its creation. An example of a school anti-bullying policy is given in Appendix 1.

The stages: writing policy, putting it in place and maintaining it

Stage 1: consultation

In order to work, the policy has to be a whole-school policy. All groups and individuals who will be affected should be consulted (students, teachers, parents and the greater school community). Policy development is the time and place for parent and community input, while the implementing, running and maintaining of the school's anti-bullying initiative will largely be the responsibility of the teachers (and, in the case of peer programmes, the students with support from teachers). Consultation can be done through group meetings, interviewing individuals, surveys and through carrying out brainstorming sessions in focus groups. Part of the consultation process should be to educate people about bullying so that the suggestions and advice are based on a good understanding of what bullying is.

The students

Students do not report most of the bullying that occurs, so, if they are asked to contribute to the development of a bullying policy, it shows them that the school is serious about stopping bullying and that their input is valued.

Students can be asked, in classes or smaller groups, to discuss and think about bullying. This can be done through self-selected or nominated groups, structured sessions or the use of questionnaires. Ideas and issues that arise can be used to keep the momentum of discussion going. It is important (perhaps through school assemblies) to keep the whole student population informed of the process. There should be several helpful outcomes:

- The students, who know most about bullying, can contribute to the process.
- A clear message that the school really cares is the first step in creating a safer environment.
- Some very useful ideas and information are likely to come out of this process.

The teachers

Teachers' input is as crucial as that of the students, for several reasons. Teachers will be generally responsible (the classroom teachers) and specifically responsible (the counsellor/psychologist and the head of school discipline/deputy principal) for dealing with bullying when it occurs, and for running any anti-bullying programmes adopted by the school. They will be making sure that the school policy is implemented, and constructively and consistently supported. They have a good knowledge about bullying in general and where it is likely to occur. They understand how students interact and have specific knowledge about the relationships among their student population. They often know who is likely to bully or be bullied. They are also familiar with the school's regulations and requirements.

The administrators and governors

The people who run the school, either as part of the management team or as a member of the board, are ultimately responsible for the school meeting its responsibilities to its community and to government. In particular, their expertise should be used to consider the legal implications of a bullying policy. It is also their job to make sure the school has the resources to put any programme in place. By being involved in the development process, this very important group is better able to support and understand the intentions of the policy.

People who are elected to boards usually have prestige and status in a particular area (accountancy, law, medicine or public administration, for instance), but in educational terms they tend to be generalists. Although they are valued for the specific skills they bring to the school, their role as overseers of school policies is even more valuable. They can make sure there is consistency with other school attitudes and responses when initiatives such as an anti-bullying policy are introduced, or when they are consulted on specific incidents of bullying.

The parents

Parents must be involved in the process from the start. In the ripple effect of bullying, they are described as secondary victims of bullying (see Chapter 3). They are usually willing to become involved in making suggestions if their child has been bullied, but it is better that their involvement occurs more neutrally, when policy is being developed. In a multi-ethnic school, parents can also present perspectives from each cultural point of view.

The wider community

Within the wider community, there may be experts who can contribute their knowledge to the policy-making process, which may help build bridges between school and community. In addition, if the community knows that the school is handling bullying in a positive and proactive way, this can improve social harmony and the way the school and its students are regarded in the community. Community involvement may also be of help to agencies outside the school who may be dealing with bullies who get into trouble elsewhere.

In a multicultural school, representatives of the different cultures may want to be involved. In New Zealand, a *kaumatua* (elder) from a Maori student's tribe may be willing to help with a bullying problem. (A similar process of tribal involvement and responsibility has been introduced in the criminal justice sector.) In many Pacific Island communities, if one person transgresses then the whole family takes responsibility for the misdeed. The involvement of such people and their presence as resources for the school are critical. In a multicultural setting, building on cultural knowledge is both helpful and essential.

Stage 2: discussion

The anti-bullying committee can discuss the various perspectives and results that come out of consultation. They can also refer to the work of various government agencies and departments (for example, the Michigan State Board of Education Model Anti-Bullying Program; the New Zealand Post Primary Teachers' Association School Anti-Violence Toolkit; the schoolnet website of the UK Department for Education); particular school anti-bullying policies (for example, Bailey Road Primary and Intermediate School, Auckland; Broward County Public School, Florida; St Ivo School, St Ives, Cambridgeshire; St Patrick's Primary School, Tuam, Co.

Galway); and theoretical work from other sources (see Chapters 2 and 3). The school may already have a policy on bullying that needs revision or a related policy on disruptive behaviour. All relevant matters should be thoroughly discussed before moving to the next stage. This can be done by an anti-bullying committee (or individuals given this task).

Stage 3: writing an anti-bullying policy

Once all the information has been gathered, it is possible to write a clear, straightforward and useable policy document. The policy can include:

- a clear definition of bullying;
- how staff, students and parents should respond if they see or become aware of bullying;
- encouragement to speak up, with suggestions of who to approach when bullying occurs;
- procedures for contacting parents;
- ways of making sure the policy is working.

Possible themes within the policy may be:

- a belief that bullying can be stopped;
- a culture in which all students feel able to tell if they are being bullied;
- the fact that everyone needs to share responsibility to help stop bullying behaviour;
- the fact that the problem is the bullying behaviour rather than the victim's behaviour.

The policy also needs to list points of contact for students:

- use of email alerts and anonymous concern boxes;
- students who are part of a peer support network;
- senior students who are part of the anti-bullying team;
- staff who are also part of the anti-bullying team.

The policy should be based on the two following procedural principles.

1. All staff need to be committed to a common response to bullying when it does happen. Their immediate intervention is crucial.
2. Clear procedures must be used when a case of bullying is discovered.

An example of a school anti-bullying policy is given in Appendix 1.

Stage 4: implementation

School anti-bullying policies need to be completely practical, based on common sense, logical, flexible, easy to understand and straightforward in application. They also need to be designed to lay down a paper trail so events are not forgotten, redefined or 'swept under the carpet'. In addition, they must attend to all those involved: parents, students and teachers.

1. When a parent approaches a school staff member with a complaint about bullying, they must be listened to and their complaint dealt with in a problem-solving manner, and they must be taken into the anti-bullying system so they are part of the solution.
2. When a student tells a teacher they are being bullied, or that they know someone else is being bullied, they must be listened to and be in no doubt that their concerns are being attended to.
3. Teachers must be fully familiar with the anti-bullying procedures of the school. The procedural steps can be printed on small laminated cards and given to all staff so they are all card-carrying supporters of the school's anti-bullying policy.

The steps provide a procedural continuum for dealing with bullying.

Bullying incident: immediate response

Step 1 Become aware of a bullying incident.
Step 2 Make sure the victim is safe.
Step 3 Take no immediate action against the perpetrators. Be dispassionate and considered.
Step 4 Tell the anti-bullying coordinator about the incident.
Step 5 Put the event on record. Fill in Part 1 of the Bully Incident Report Form.

Once these steps have been taken, the anti-bullying team takes over. The steps they need to take are as follows:

Bullying incident: handover response

Step 1 Decide who is going to work on the case (preferably two people).
Step 2 Snapshot/diagnosis: where does the incident fall on the bullying checklist?
Step 3 Action plan: match the response to the incident.
Step 4 Fill in Part 2 of the Bully Incident Report Form.

Any school that has an effective anti-bullying policy will have identified its team of bullying experts. These are people who have recognized knowledge, and who have the concrete functions of implementing procedures, supporting teachers, and helping create, develop and uphold a safe environment. Any bullying incident should be assigned to at least two members of this team so that no one has to work alone. This is both for protection and for safety.

The point of the 'Bullying incident: handover response' steps 2 and 3 is not to provide ammunition to attribute blame but to institute a system that supports a safety culture. Once the bullying incident has been fully described and a prognosis of treatment has been made, the ways to handle it can be identified. The form thus embodies an incident trail. If a procedure does not work and the bullying recurs, the dynamics become more complex. The form allows interventions to be reconsidered and the whole incident to be looked at again.

Here is an example of a bully incident report form.

Bullying incident report form

Part 1

Incident reported by: When:

Came to my attention by:

Where did the incident happen?

When did the incident happen?

Students actively involved (circle victim):

Names of bystanders (list ALL who were present):

Brief description of incident:

Referred to: (List Anti-Bullying Team members)

Part 2

Assessment: (Comment on the situation. Is it one-off or part of an ongoing relationship? Have the individuals been involved in similar incidents previously? Is it typical/atypical for this group of students?)

The participants: (Comment on history, background, previous incidents for perpetrator and victim. Comment on any bystanders.)

Action plan: (Identify the type of intervention that will be used, by whom, when and the type of communication/follow-through that will result.)

Stage 5: monitoring and maintenance

Policies are developed and written on the basis of information available at the time. When they are being implemented, changes will need to be made to accommodate unforeseen circumstances and dynamics. A policy should be a living document, that is, refined and updated on a regular basis. If a policy and programme have been well thought through and are seen to be working, this momentum will keep them going; however, it is also important to maintain and support them, and to continue the process of monitoring and evaluation.

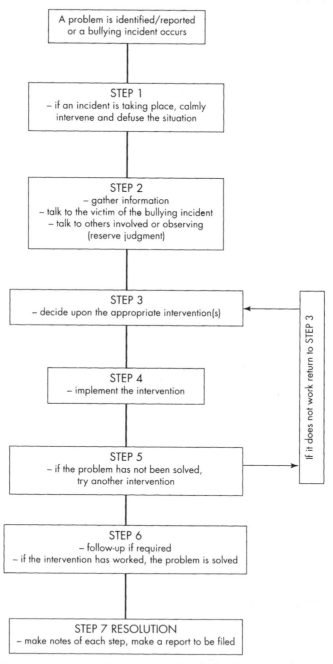

Figure 9.1   A step-by-step guide to handling a bullying incident

PART 3

PREVENTATIVE STRATEGIES

CHAPTER 10

STRATEGIES FOR TEACHERS: PRACTICE, PEDAGOGY AND LEARNING

Introduction: how teachers can help or hinder a bullying culture

This chapter focuses on teaching style and classroom and learning practices that can create an anti-bullying bedrock. First, it discusses the ways in which teachers can contribute to a bullying culture (as ineffective practitioners), and the means by which they can be central to creating a safe and proactive culture (as reflective practitioners). It suggests that there are approaches to managing a classroom that are less likely to allow bullying to breed, involving teaching style, the teacher as role model, and the encouragement of healthy and cooperative learning practices. It therefore specifically examines the strategies of authoritative teaching and cooperative learning.

Ineffective practitioner/reflective practitioner

Several international studies show that the great majority of bullying is not noticed by teachers, is ignored by them or is not dealt with by them. A Canadian study which videotaped children playing at school (Craig and Pepler, 1995; Pepler and Craig, 1995) indicated that duty teachers were aware of only a small percentage (17 per cent) of the playground bullying observed by the researchers. What is more, for the incidents they did witness, teachers chose to intervene only 23 per cent of the time. This means that, overall, teachers attended to only 3.9 per cent of the bullying. These observations are supported by evidence from another Canadian study (Bentley and Li, 1995) in which 31.5 per cent of children who were victims of bullying reported that teachers almost never tried to stop it. On top of this is the fact that in many schools bullying is not reported to teachers, usually because children do not believe anything will be done about it, and that the reporting will in fact expose them to more bullying.

As a first step, it must be clear that the school will intervene and that it has strategies for dealing with bullying. It is crucial that teachers know what to do and are supported by their schools in doing it. It is not helpful if teachers and schools do not respond when bullying occurs, or if teachers completely ignore instances of bullying and say they 'don't want to know', or if they respond to those who have sought help by telling them to sort things out themselves. If a bullying culture is allowed to flourish in the school, it will in fact create a breeding ground for pervasive bullying that may be partially hidden or extremely overt.

Sometimes, when teachers do intervene, the outcome is not successful. There are many reasons for this, some of which are the responsibility of the teacher.

Failure is most frequent when teachers respond irresolutely and half-heartedly to a problem that needs to be thoroughly followed through. This may be because they do not fully understand what bullying is, or are swayed by the deceit and lies that are part of the bullying culture.

In one case, a 14-year-old girl, whom we shall call Tania, was harassed every afternoon on the school bus by two younger boys, Benji and Rainer aged 11 and 12. They made lewd remarks and gestures that grew more obscene every day, until eventually she lost her temper and swore at them. Tania was very upset and told her parents what had been happening. They contacted the boys' teacher who said that Tania must have identified the wrong boys, that Benji in particular was very well behaved and always pleasant and would never indulge in such rudeness. The teacher also stated that, because Tania had sworn at the boys, she was a guilty party and had to accept some blame.

Tania's parents pointed out that, whatever their daughter had done, she was not to blame for the incident on the bus. They decided to go to the principal to get the incident properly dealt with, but he also said that Tania must have made a mistake: Benji would never behave like this. Her parents insisted that she had not made a mistake and asked the principal to follow it up. He did, with the two boys, and the boys' parents, who were very upset with Tania's mother and father for involving the school. The boys did not trouble Tania again.

Six months later, an incident occurred in the school playground when Benji viciously attacked a younger boy. He was dealt with severely by the duty teacher. Several other children then came forward to say he had been bullying them. Soon afterwards his parents removed him from the school.

In this case, the victim was not believed because the boy she accused of bullying had convinced all the teachers at the school that he was a 'good boy'. Tania was also held responsible for the unpleasant nature of the incident and its escalation because she had sworn at the boys. It was only because her parents fully supported her that the school took action, but the situation was not really resolved until the bullying occurred again (with other victims). Once it became overt, the incident involving Tania was reframed and redefined by the school.

Some of the dynamic problems of bullying are clear in this example: in this case, the school espoused an intolerance of bullying, and some teachers went so far as to say that there was no bullying in the school. This allowed them to overlook and deny Tania's parents' report of bullying.

Sometimes teachers contribute directly to the bullying dynamic themselves, in two main ways. They misunderstand the symptoms exhibited by bullied children and treat them as annoying or wilful; or they blame the bullied children for their victimization and thus expose them to further victimization.

A common occurrence, especially in girls' bullying, is that certain children are systematically isolated from the group. Such children are not only most at risk of being bullied at school but are also most likely to be misunderstood by their teachers. Besag (1989: 117) states: 'The shyness or confusion of such children can lead to them being thought of as stupid or, in some cases, disobedient.' These children are then the victims of both the social world of their peer group, and of their teachers. If teachers choose to ignore such children or treat them as stupid or disobedient, they reinforce the behaviour of the peer group and the bullying of that child.

Sometimes teachers believe that a child is at least partly to blame for his or her victimization and that the onus is on the child to behave differently and thus to bring an end to the bullying. If the teacher models this attitude to the pupils, the bullying is likely to escalate. In addition, teachers who use their greater verbal and intimidatory skills to victimize certain children may appear to condone and be complicit in bullying.

In these cases, the teacher is contributing to the harm done by bullying and allowing a bullying culture to exist. This is the antithesis of the proper role of the teacher, which is to help in the creation of a safe environment for everyone at the school.

Central to education today is the concept of the teacher as reflective practitioner (see Dymoke and Harrison, 2008; Schon, 1996). This means that, when teachers are faced with small or large problems (both in learning and children's peer relations), they call on their problem-solving skills, reflect on their teaching experiences (or refer to a more experienced colleague), and use current educational research that focuses on the problem area. By using reflective practice, teachers can manage their classrooms in such a way that they anticipate and prevent bullying, or deal with it effectively when it does occur. In the case study of a bullied child in a New Zealand school (see Sullivan, 1998), the 9-year-old passive victim of bullying (Sarah) was found to be systematically isolated and ridiculed by her peer group, and either patronized or rejected by her teacher. When her parents spoke to the principal, he called a meeting with them, the class teacher and the deputy principal. Together they closed ranks and said that Sarah had been a worry to all her teachers since she was a new entrant, and that it was a psychological rather than an educational problem. The school put what was an act of bullying by a group of 9- and 10-year-old girls in the too-hard basket. They called in an educational psychologist who observed Sarah's isolation and unhappiness, and the principal told her parents that the case was outside the school's spectrum of expertise and therefore not its responsibility. They also reframed the concerted and long-standing bullying of Sarah as caused by the victim herself. Supported by the educational psychologist, the parents decided to move her to another school.

A reflective practitioner may have handled this differently. She may have decided first to find out whether Sarah's bullying could be seen as an academic classroom-based problem, rather than as a psychological problem. She may have seen how Sarah could be supported first in the classroom, respected, encouraged, and praised for good work or positive interactions. She may have decided to watch carefully her own affirmative role-modelling and to take it up a notch in her classroom management. She may have decided to call on the experience of colleagues and the outcomes of certain bullying research in order to address the problem of bullying. She may have considered and tried appropriate anti-bullying strategies.

Authoritative teaching

Most teachers enter the profession because they want to make a difference to society, they relate well to children and they love learning. Teaching is a complex job, at any level. In order for teachers to teach well, they have to be able to create stability in their classrooms, be organized and put their lessons into meaningful contexts.

Many aspects of the work are outside of the teacher's control:

- the changing landscape of teachers' and students' daily routines;
- the make-up of classes;
- the variable levels of maturity and ability of the students in any one class;
- the daily variables of whether the students are hungry, grumpy, sad or tired;
- the state in which the various students arrive in the classroom, whether from home (in the case of elementary schools, and the first class of the day in secondary schools) or from a previous class (in the case mainly of secondary schools).

In addition, because of assessment and curriculum requirements:

- teachers may have to concentrate on knowledge acquisition rather than on teaching the students how to think;
- the emphasis may be on teaching the subject, not the child.

Some teaching styles are more effective than others and are more likely to contribute to a positive and safe learning environment. When a teacher is authoritative, they lead by example, they are clear about what is acceptable and what is not, there is consistency and follow-up, they pay attention to each student, and they never use ridicule or sarcasm as a classroom management device. When a teacher is authoritarian, they rule by commands and threats, they show little or no respect for individual students, and they are likely to resort to verbal put-downs and aggression in order to control their classes. A neglectful/cynical teacher, on the other hand, tends to be inconsistent and unfair, to be unclear about what is and is not acceptable, and not to follow up when things go wrong. A permissive teacher wants to be liked by everyone and therefore does not provide clear and appropriate boundaries. Through 'trying too hard' he or she will end up being 'walked over' and have an out-of-control class.

These styles are illustrated in the four following teacher responses when Sean walks late into class.

The authoritative teacher: says, 'Sean, there's a desk over there. Please go and sit down. How can we get you here on time?'
There is minimum disruption to the lesson and the teacher makes sure Sean is included as quickly as possible, and later speaks to him privately.
The authoritarian teacher says: 'If you're late one more time, you can stay home. I'm sick of your lazy attitude. Now, don't you dare cross me again today.'
This is a public and arbitrary response. No effort is made to find out why he is late. The teacher moves from annoyance at Sean's lateness to a comment on his attitude. There is huge potential for escalation.
The neglectful/cynical teacher says: 'Well, got here finally did we? Seamus, is it? Now, let's get on with it.'
The teacher is not sure of Sean's name, is sarcastic and doesn't really care. There is no follow-up.
The permissive teacher says 'Seamus you are late again. You poor old thing! You must be really tired and stressed. Don't worry, it's ok. You do what you need to.'
The teacher condones the behaviour and doesn't check later to see if all is well, nor to stress the importance of being on time.

The foundations of authoritative teaching

Authoritative teachers recognize the need not only to be effective in their teaching but also to practise the values that underpin the school's anti-bullying approach. They should be prepared to deal with each student as an individual as well as attending to the class as a whole. Authoritative teachers:

- are well organized, have clear lesson plans and share these objectives with the class;
- are able to teach in ways that meet the different learning abilities and styles within the class;
- are flexible and able to deal with issues and crises that arise in the classroom;
- are interested in and knowledgeable about what they are teaching, and communicate this with passion;
- are in control and are vigilant for antisocial behaviour;
- are fair and do not have favourites;
- are always looking to give praise and support (often privately);
- are never sarcastic and never put down their students;
- do not play for attention;
- make their classrooms free from ridicule;
- have the expectation that every student can succeed, and have high expectations for all students;
- are non-confrontational and non-judgemental in style;
- use a good range of conflict resolution and problem-solving skills;
- are good communicators;
- give feedback that fosters enthusiasm for learning;
- encourage thinking and participation;
- strive to build connections between students;
- make sure their classroom is a sanctuary from social turbulence;
- are aware of peer relationships;

- are aware of cognitive, physical, psychological and social development;
- use discipline authoritatively and sparingly, with clear guidelines and consequences;
- role-model prosocial behaviour;
- actively support the vulnerable and consciously prop up the weak to increase their status and develop their skills.

See Figure 10.1 for characteristics of authoritative teachers.

Effective teachers recognize that safe classrooms create better learning environments. It takes time to achieve this, and this time is an investment. Once a healthy climate is established, teaching becomes easier and learning more productive. The teacher becomes the guardian of the class, and provides a framework in which it can function to its maximum ability.

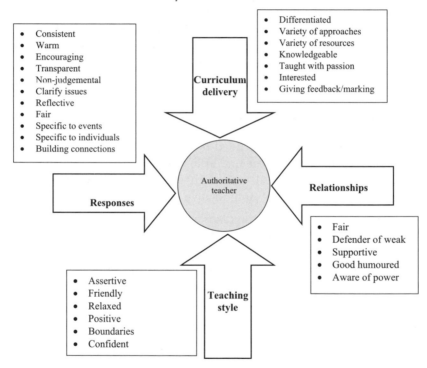

Figure 10.1   Characteristics of authoritative teachers

Cooperative learning

Cooperative learning is a well-constructed process in which the success of the group depends on the true cooperation of its members. In normal classroom situations, some children who are isolated and prone to bullying are dismissed by most of the class as dumb, unattractive or worthless. In a cooperative learning situation, hidden talents emerge and class members learn to value diversity and to be more accepting and supportive of their peers in general.

There are three basic types of learning: competitive, individualistic and cooperative. Competitive learning is when students in a class compete against each other through tests, examinations and answering questions, with an understanding that only a few will get high marks. The logical corollary is that those who do best will succeed not only in school but also afterwards in life. Individualistic learning is when students work by themselves to reach goals unrelated to others in the class. This is seen as more humanistic than competitive learning because it is criterion referenced: individuals are competing against themselves rather than against a norm. By competing against their past achievements, students can gain a sense of success rather than being failures compared with those who have outperformed them.

Cooperative learning is also criterion referenced but differs from individualistic learning in that its aims are group focused. If students work together on assignments but are still individually assessed, this is not cooperative learning. When information is gathered jointly and shared between the group but there is little motivation to teach each other what has been learned because of the emphasis on individual assessment, this, also, is not cooperative learning. In these cases, mutual help and sharing of information are minimal. Those who are conscientious put in a lot of effort whereas some are able to get by on the efforts of others and with minimal input themselves. In such situations, learning can be exploitative rather than cooperative.

The characteristics of cooperative learning groups

Cooperative learning groups are small (two or three people), and they aim to accomplish shared goals. They have the following five defining characteristics:

1. **Positive interdependence**. The efforts of each group member benefit both themselves and the group and maximize learning for all members. This creates a commitment to the success of others as well as oneself. If one fails, they all fail; if one succeeds, they all succeed.
2. **Individual and group accountability**. The group is responsible for meeting its goals and no one can expect a free ride. Each person honestly assesses their efforts and results and reports back to the group. Those who need help are given it by the group so that all members (each with different strengths and weaknesses) can benefit and, through group support, can perform better as individuals.
3. **Face-to-face promotive interaction**. Students provide support at both an academic and a personal level. When students explain how to carry out a procedure or argue against a proposition, they are accomplishing a cognitive and a social task and, through promoting each other's learning at a face-to-face level, also become more committed to supporting each other's learning.
4. **Teaching students interpersonal and small-group skills**. Cooperative learning is more complex than normal class work as it requires students both to learn the academic subject at hand and to develop skills to work effectively as part of a small group. This includes building trust, communicating well, dealing with conflict, learning how to lead, making decisions and being motivated.
5. **Group processing**. Cooperative learning is regarded as a social growth process

that has an evaluative component that makes sure things are working well. The group needs to have effective ways of monitoring and adjusting its work, checking how well goals are being achieved and maintaining personal relationships. The group must be objective about which actions are helpful and which are not. A careful analysis of the group's processes helps to improve working relationships and academic outcomes.

The group becomes greater than the sum of its parts, everyone performs better academically than they would if they worked alone; their social intelligence is increased in the process.

In addition, it is argued that cooperative learning is a way of gaining a healthy understanding of conflict. Johnson and Johnson (1994) point out that, if a conflict situation is approached competitively, one of the parties in the conflict must win and the other lose, whereas cooperative learning stresses that what is important is solving the problem for the benefit of everyone. Having this ethos in a class provides the basis for dealing with conflicts and potential conflicts that may result in bullying.

> **Comment**: Cooperative learning is a well-planned and rigorous approach to learning. In an examination of cooperative learning, Slavin (1995) found that it increased students' self-esteem and feelings of happiness, and that children named more people (and were named more) as friends, felt more successful academically and actually achieved higher results.

References

Bentley, K.M. and Li, A.K. (1995) 'Bully and victim problems in elementary schools and students' beliefs about aggression', *Canadian Journal of School Psychology*, 11: 153–65.

Besag, V. (1989) *Bullies and Victims in Schools: A Guide to Understanding and Management*. Milton Keynes: Open University Press.

Craig, W.M. and Pepler, D.J. (1995) 'Peer processes in bullying and victimization: an observational study', *Exceptional Education Canada*, 5: 81–95.

Dymoke, S. and Harrison, J. (eds) (2008) *Reflective Teaching and Learning: A Guide to Professional Issues for Beginning Secondary Teachers*. London: Sage.

Johnson, D.W. and Johnson, R.T. (1994) 'Structuring academic controversy', in S. Sharan (ed.), *Handbook of Cooperative Learning Methods*. Westport, CT: Greenwood.

Pepler, D.M. and Craig, W.M. (1995) 'A peek behind the fence: naturalistic observations of aggressive children with remote audiovisual recording', *Developmental Psychology*, 31: 548–53.

Schon, D.A. (1996) *Educating the Reflective Practitioner: Toward a New Design for Teaching and Learning in the Professions*. San Francisco, CA: Jossey-Bass.

Slavin, R.E. (1995) *Cooperative Learning: Theory, Research and Practice*. Boston, MA: Allyn & Bacon.

Sullivan, K. (1998) 'Isolated children, bullying and peer group relations', in P.T. Slee and K. Rigby (eds), *Children's Peer Relations*. London and New York: Routledge.

CHAPTER 11

STRATEGIES FOR TEACHERS: UNDERSTANDING SOCIAL RELATIONSHIPS, CREATING SAFE CLASSROOMS

Introduction: what teachers can do

This chapter examines strategies teachers can use to help them understand the social relationships in their classrooms; to improve these social relationships and to encourage prosocial functioning at the individual, group and class level; and to find answers to problems that arise. The strategies discussed in this chapter are Interactive Puppet Theatre, Circle Time and sociometry, and are particularly suitable for primary schools. Sociometry can also be used in secondary schools.

Interactive Puppet Theatre

I have created Interactive Puppet Theatre as a mechanism to help early childhood and lower primary school-age children to learn about the nature of bullying. Parents, childcare workers and teachers can take part in the process as facilitators and observers so that strategies can be developed to teach appropriate behaviour to all participants: those doing the bullying, those targeted and those who observe. The way it works is as follows.

The seven steps of the Interactive Puppet Theatre process

Step 1: making the stage and the puppets (the actors)

The process of making the puppets can be a fun classroom activity involving both children and adults (teachers and sometimes parents). They can talk together about what the puppets should look like, and simple, generic wooden or cloth puppets can be made with removable hats, masks, faces and clothes that can be slipped on and off. The activity itself is likely to stimulate discussion about using the puppets, writing and performing short plays, and building a puppet theatre, thus creating a sense of ownership and a positive foundation upon which to address the issue of bullying.

Together the adults and children can plan a wooden structure with curtains so there is a stage and a place where the puppeteers can sit or stand to operate the puppets. In the early childhood setting it is most likely that adults will operate the puppets, but in the lower primary school some of the older children could learn to do so.

Step 2: choosing a theme or event and writing the puppet play

A short play can be created that draws the children in, engages their imaginations, seeks their help to find solutions, and teaches them about bullying and its effects. There may currently be a child who is being bullied by one or a number of children or another who is bullying others, and a solution is looked for without naming those involved. A short puppet play can be created around this or any other chosen scenario, with action that emphasizes the bullying, and a short dialogue that can be improvised or written down. The words can be chosen by the group working together so that the play is realistic and the children have helped create it.

Here are two possible scenarios for early childhood and primary school settings:

1. Michael gathers up all the toys he wants and will not let Bobby have any. This happens every day. He hits Bobby and pokes out his tongue. Bobby is miserable and tries to stay out of Michael's way, but he really wants to play.
2. Michelle, Ali and Candy are friends. They always play together and they are going through a trunk of dressing-up clothes. Maggie wants to join in but they tell her it is too crowded and there is no room for her. Things like this happen all the time.

Step 3: performing the play

The play is introduced by a narrator who describes what it is about. The puppets perform the play and the children are drawn into what is going on.

Step 4: interacting with the play

After the puppets have acted out the play, the children are full of enthusiasm and wish to comment and make suggestions about what happened, the rights and wrongs, and what they may have done differently. The narrator suggests that the play is acted out a second time so the children can tell the puppets what they could do and say to address the bullying problem that is being presented.

Step 5: interacting with the puppets the second time

Here is a snippet from the second scenario:

Puppet one (Michelle):	Maggie, you are a silly girl. You don't need to dress up – you already have funny clothes. Yuck!!
The other girls laugh:	Hah! Hah! Hah!
Puppet two (Maggie):	I don't feel good. That's not nice. What should I say?
Narrator to the children:	What do you think, children? Is this right? What could we do if we saw this happening? What could we say? What can Maggie do?

Step 6: playing it again with a new script

The children have changed the script. It is played again to see how it feels, and to see if they want to change anything else.

Step 7: following up

The teacher will check to see whether any of the children are upset by the puppet play, and will find a space during the day to talk to them individually, just to check what is wrong and what can be done to help them.

The aims of puppet theatre

The aims of using puppet theatre are:

- to teach children how to treat each other well and how to negotiate fairly with their peers;
- to include adults (teachers, childcare workers and parents) in generating and facilitating the process, so they learn with the children about bullying, its causes and how to create a culture where it is less likely to occur;
- to create short plays that are acted out by puppets based upon bullying that has been reported and/or observed;
- to have fun.

Ground rules for puppet theatre

- Keep it simple and short.
- Get everyone fully involved
- Make it fun.
- Encourage the children to work things out themselves with quiet guidance from the adults (both teachers and parents).
- Reinforce good behaviour after points have been made and the lesson learned.
- 'Again.' Small children enjoy repetition (when they have a book they like, they

want it read over and over). Several years ago, the children's television pro-gramme *Teletubbies* became extremely popular, and used this knowledge of chil-dren's need for repetition. When an enjoyable scene occurred, a young voice said 'Again', and the scene was repeated. The viewer then had both the pleasure of instantly re-experiencing a positive experience and had a learning experience reinforced.

- Avoid blame and, as with the Support Group Method (Chapter 16), focus on how being bullied makes the targeted child feel.

Concluding remarks

Using drama through puppet theatre with small children can enable them to under-stand how bullying works. They can be taught what is right and wrong, and how bullying can be stopped. For children in the early childhood and primary sectors, it can also be a useful vehicle to an understanding of boundaries, social interactions, and how to be fair and kind. Addressing bullying at this early stage can be very useful.

Circle Time

Circle Time (see Bliss and Tetley, 2006; Weatherhead, 2008; White, 2009) is a regular activity in which students and their teacher spend time together every week sitting in a circle participating in games and dealing with serious issues such as bullying. Its major purpose is to encourage the class to work as a team rather than being only an alliance of cliques. It means that a teacher and a class of students can get to know each other better. It is also a way of having fun as a group and of increasing mutual support, breaking down barriers and encouraging the group to deal with difficult issues. From the teacher's perspective, it provides an extra dimension to their rela-tionship with their students, and gives them a lot of information about the individuals in their class. For the students, it gives them a chance to develop and practise relationship and communications skills. It encourages tolerance.

Circle Time warms people up, deals with the issues that are central to the partic-ular session and then brings the session to a close. The following steps can be used to construct a Circle Time session.

Step 1: preparation for Circle Time

It is recommended that, if possible, Circle Time occurs in the classroom as it is important to connect the positive interactions with this environment. It can be run on a regular basis at the same time each week (15 to 25 minutes is recommended for younger children, and 30 to 40 minutes for older children). It is important to clear a space in an orderly fashion, to lay out seats in a circle and to invite the children to sit there. As with other classroom activities, the teacher will need to plan both the structure (sequencing) and content (what topics will be covered).

Step 2: starting the session

In starting the session, it is important to welcome the children and to state the ground rules for Circle Time:

- We listen to whoever is speaking and will also be listened to.
- We listen to what the person speaking has to say.
- We do not laugh, giggle or make comments.
- Everyone has the right to pass (although it is important to return to those who have passed when you have gone round the circle – usually people will then contribute but are under no obligation to do so).

An activity such as the naming game can be used to start off the circle. In the naming game, the student introduces the person to their right, then themselves, then the person to their left. Everyone is included.

Step 3: getting the group to feel comfortable

There are various ways to help the group cohere. A game can be played that is designed to get everyone to stand up and move around and to sit next to someone they do not usually have much contact with. This can be done two or three times by saying, for instance: 'All people with younger brothers stand up and change places.' If the group has been asked to number off, the even numbers can be asked to stand up and change places. Students can now be paired up with the person sitting next to them (say, on their left).

The teacher can ask the pairs to identify two common interests.

Step 4: getting the group to work together

Now is the time to strengthen the glue that bonds and reaffirms the group. Here are two ways to do this: a smile is passed around the circle; or everyone holds hands and a squeeze is passed around the circle.

The teacher can then lead a game that requires students to work together to carry out a set of instructions. An example is everyone making the noises of wind and rain and, through the loud stamping of feet, the sound of thunder.

Step 5: beginning to address serious issues

Potentially difficult matters can be handled during a well-established circle process. If a sense of safety and trust has been built up, then issues such as bullying can be probed using a variety of techniques, the most non-threatening of these being the silent statement.

This involves the teacher saying something like: 'Stand up and change places if you know bullying has taken place in this school.' This can be followed by: 'Stand up and change places if you know bullying has taken place in this class.' The number who get up and move gives an indication of the severity of the problem.

Once students are involved and realize they do not have to admit personally to being bullied or bullying, a more specific strategy can be introduced such as a sentence completion exercise, for example, 'A child who has been bullied might feel … ', 'A child who is a bully might feel … '.

Step 6: making positive statements about others and hearing positive statements about themselves

The final step is designed to emphasize the positive qualities of each student, even those who may normally have been dismissed as having few redeeming qualities. This can be done by encouraging partners to make a positive statement about the person they have been working with, by creating new pairs through random connections (everyone who is wearing green, say something good about everyone wearing any blue), and by inviting positive comments 'off the floor'.

Comment: Circle Time can be used to prevent bullying because it encourages children to get to know others outside their normal groups. It teaches children to value diversity, including those from minority groups, those with disabilities and anyone who is different in some way. It supports the development of self-esteem and mutual appreciation on a one-to-one basis. It encourages the class to have a positive sense of itself as a whole and of the individuals within it.

Sociometry

Sociometry was created by psychotherapist Jacob Moreno and can be defined as the measurement of social relationships. For teachers, it is a useful tool for mapping out the dynamics of relationships in a class and for providing answers to such fundamental questions as: 'Who is in?', 'What is the nature of the various groups (the cliques)?', 'Which clique is dominant?', 'Who is the most popular pupil?' and 'Which pupils are isolated?' Teachers can use sociometry to better understand the relationships in the class and can use this knowledge to anticipate potential problems and prevent bullying.

A number of researchers have used sociometry to better understand classroom group processes. For me, the early work of Hargreaves (1973) still stands out for its incisiveness and clarity. In this section, I will also refer to McLean's (1994) sociometric model, and to the creative use of sociometry in anti-bullying research in Finland (Salmivalli et al., 1997, 1998).

In the 1960s, Hargreaves carried out research with five fourth-form classes at a streamed male secondary school in the north of England in order to develop a better understanding of the social systems within schools. He created a map of the social relationships of the groups in each of the five classes, determined the status of each pupil, and provided an analysis of the values and norms of each class. He identified that each of the fourth form classes he studied had its own particular micro-culture, and that the norms and values varied from class to class, as did the norms and behaviours of the various cliques within each class.

The A-stream class most represented the aspirations of the school, and the boys in the class exhibited behaviour and took on norms that reflected mainstream and prosocial values. In the lower streams, on the other hand, the norms were almost reversed. Leaders there tended towards antisocial behaviour, were good fighters and maintained their status by their ability to control through bullying. In all classes there were several cliques, each of which shared values and behaviours and an agreed set of norms. The cliques were defined by those who were 'in', those 'on the periphery' and those who were isolated ('out').

Hargreaves mapped out the social relationships in the fourth form classes by using three measures: a friendship measure, a power and status measure, and the academic achievement measure of each pupil. He also gathered information through interviewing students and staff at the case study school. The academic status of each student was obtained by teachers ranking students according to past examination results. The information on friendship measurement and the informal status hierarchy was gathered in the following fashion:

- All students in a class were asked to name up to five children they went around with most when they were at school. If they went around with just one or two people, they were asked to name only these individuals. By compiling this information, Hargreaves created a sociometric diagram to show the friendship groupings: who was in which group, who was most popular, who was isolated, who was on the periphery of a group. Hargreaves also asked students to name up to two people they disliked, and to name the student they most disliked. They were also asked to identify the person who was their best friend.
- In order to develop an informal status hierarchy, students were given a list of all students in their class and asked to place the names in one of three boxes. In the top box, they were asked to write the names of all students who were leaders (those who others admired or followed, those who led, those who were the bosses). In the bottom box, they were asked to place the names of those who had the least leadership potential (those who did not get much attention, those who got teased and picked on, those who were unpopular, those who did not take the lead, those who followed what the others did). All other names were to be placed in the middle box. By assigning a mark to each box and adding up the numbers, the informal status hierarchy was created.

Hargreaves stressed that, when students put names in one of the three boxes, their choice should not be determined by whether or not they liked the person but by whether or not they were leaders. This is an attempt to measure power and influence rather than preference and popularity. If those with the greatest social power can be identified, then so can the norms that are dominant in each class.

Here is an example of a questionnaire that could be used to generate a sociogram:

CONFIDENTIAL

Name

Friendship question
1.   Which pupils in the class are your friends?
2.   Which pupils are the most likely to bully and hurt others (physically and emotionally)? You can name from 0 to 5 people.
3.   Which pupils are most likely to be picked on and hurt by others? You can name from 0 to 5 people.

Informal status question
4.   You have been provided with a list of the pupils in your class. Place each name within one of the three boxes below.

| Definitely a leader | | Part of a group | | On the outside of things |

Researchers today are very concerned about the ethics of asking questions about who is liked and disliked. Maines and Robinson (1998) warn that filling out sociometric questionnaires can label students and have unpleasant results. I would suggest that if teachers use such measures to anticipate and identify bullying, this is the greater good. If such measures *are* used, however, they should be administered with sensitivity, confidentiality and forethought so that harm is unlikely to result.

In order to demonstrate Hargreaves's method, I have provided a friendship analysis for an imaginary class, Class 7. In Figure 11.1, each person in the class is represented by a number and the friendship links are represented by lines. Solid lines indicate a reciprocated choice, broken lines an unreciprocated choice.

Class 7: an example of sociometry in use

Class 7 is a mixed class of 24 11- and 12-year-old children in a primary school in a middle-class Manchester suburb. The teacher, Mrs Wright, has given the class a friendship question, asking them to name up to five friends. She has also asked them to name their best friend and up to two people they do not get on with (or leave it blank) and to name the person they do not get on with most in the class (or leave it blank). She has asked the class to place everyone into one of three leadership classifications (leader, neutral, rejected). She has put together her marks for the mid-year assessments and has ranked the class academically. (The school does not emphasize academic differences but still tracks each child's academic progress. The children themselves are in no doubt about who the academic leaders are.) Mrs Wright has tabulated the results, and generated the sociogram in Figure 11.1. She has done a detailed analysis of her findings.

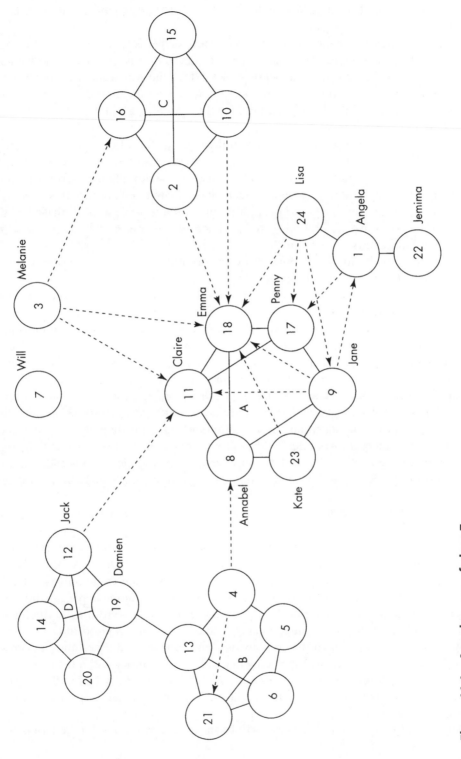

Figure 11.1   A sociogram of class 7

In terms of social relationships, Class 7 consists of four cliques, a pair, two isolated students and a new girl.

Clique A is the dominant clique of the class and it seems to set the norm for the class overall. Emma (child 18) is the dominant person in this group and the leader of the class. She has an informal status rank of 1, is the top student academically and has a very pleasant personality (although she can be mean to those who cross her). The average informal status ranking for the clique as a whole is 6.5 and academically the average is 5.

Emma was nominated the most times in the class as friend (nine times) but she nominated only three people as friends: Claire, Annabel and Penny. The two other girls in clique A, Kate and Jane, seem to be constantly seeking Emma's approval but she keeps them at a distance. When Emma makes negative remarks about someone, these two girls are the ones who make a point of being unpleasant to that person (Melanie has been isolated by this clique). This group works hard and also participates in school sports.

Clique B is made up of five boys. They are dominant among the prosocial boys in the class but are not as articulate as the girls in clique A.

Clique C is the academic clique of the class. It is made up of two pairs of children (2 and 10, 15 and 16).

Clique D is made up of four boys. They all chose each other in the friendship question and all chose Will as the person they most disliked in the class. Will used to hang out with the group but two of them, Damien and Jack (19 and 12), were caught stealing earlier in the term and they think Will told on them. The boys in the group are pleasant individually but together are becoming more and more disruptive. Although it has not been proved, they are thought to be responsible for the recent outbreak of vandalism and graffiti in the school, and they are suspected of intimidating some of the younger children from other classes. It seems that they are making things difficult for Will but it is unclear how. Academically, this clique fares the worst of all cliques: 18.5 is an average placing. They are about 12.5 in terms of their informal status placing.

Child 7 (Will) and child 3 (Melanie) are isolates. They have been chosen as friends by nobody in the class. Melanie (who wrote down three unreciprocated friendship choices) arrived from another school towards the end of the previous year. When she first arrived, she was adopted as a novelty by clique A. After about two weeks they stopped playing with her and they now make snide remarks about her clothes and her intelligence. Emma makes the most cutting remarks and the other girls follow her lead, particularly Jane and Kate. They were once challenged about this by the teacher but laughed and claimed it was all in good fun.

Will is very withdrawn. He has run away from home several times and performs very poorly academically. He has a tendency to lose his temper and most kids steer clear of him. Will was friends with 19 and 12 of clique D for a while at the beginning of the year, but after they were caught stealing from a local shop they blamed him for telling on them.

Angela and Jemima (1 and 22) have acted as a self-contained unit for the past three years and are not members of any cliques. They prefer it this way and consider themselves to be 'alternative'. They have been friends since they were small, but also have friendly and confident contact with many of the children. A new girl, Lisa, seems to be moving in on this relationship (and was also named by Angela as a friend). She has been spending a lot of time with Angela to the exclusion of Jemima.

So what use is this information?

This information is useful in several respects. It gives the teacher specific insights and allows her to see how the various cliques operate and how they perform a number of useful functions – they provide a sense of identity for their members and they solidify friendships. In terms of bullying and the potential for bullying, they suggest several areas of concern about the 'at-risk' condition or potential of at least three children in the class. For instance:

- Melanie cannot possibly keep up with the fashion demands of clique A. They accepted her into their ranks at first and then rejected her. The more she tries, the harder they make it for her, and she becomes increasingly isolated, low in self-esteem and a poor academic performer. The girls in clique A, however, are everyone's favourite pupils. They are the epitome of success, good-looking, articulate and well groomed, whereas Melanie is quiet, unsure of herself, shy and easy to ignore. Is this class a safe place for Melanie? No, it is not. What should and can the teacher do to make things better?
- Girl 24 (Lisa) has come from another school (from which she was excluded). She has a history of disruptive and antisocial behaviour and is very articulate and powerful. She seems to be breaking up the close relationship of Angela and Jemima. Should the teacher step in? Is it her business? What should be done?
- Will is surly and uncooperative. He appears to ask for trouble and is increasingly seen by the school as a troublemaker. A closer examination shows that he is disturbed and it is not clear exactly why (although there are rumours about abuse at home that should be referred to the school psychologist for investigation). He is being subjected to bullying by clique D, particularly by Damien (student 19). Whereas it first seemed that Will was the troublemaker, it is now apparent that he is being set up by Damien and other members of this clique (and a few boys from another class).

What sociometry tells us about social groups

Sociometry can be used creatively to understand the social relationships in a class, and to map out peer networks, children's participant roles and bully–victim relationships. Hargreaves provides the following useful information:

- Small groups (cliques) that interact regularly and frequently are united by common values and group norms. These define the criteria for membership and expected behaviour, and determine who is 'in' and 'out'.

- Cliques control their members by constantly exerting pressure to conform to central norms through punishing or rejecting those who deviate. A clique has less control over its members when the norms are weak.
- Cliques can influence a member's sense of identity, and control or regulate group behaviour. Members differ in the extent to which they conform with or deviate from the norms. Those who conform are more acceptable than those who deviate.
- Group members usually have different status that is dependent on length of membership, the esteem in which they are held, their assistance with group goals and the extent to which they conform. Within the group, leaders have high status and those with low prestige have low informal status.
- When groups form, similarities tend to develop between members in behaviour and communications, acceptance of group norms and expressions of the group's values. As each person's group membership indicates an acknowledgement of the norms, clique members can predict within reasonable limits the behaviour of their co-members.

As a cautionary note, Furlong (1984) argues that relationships are not as rigid as they appear in Hargreaves's model, and that students move in and out of what he calls interaction sets, which are determined by context. My sense is that both interpretations are right to a degree (and that interaction sets are probably a particularly useful measure for secondary schools as the number of groups individuals are part of tends to be much greater than in primary schools) and that both approaches can be useful if utilized sensibly and with caution.

References

Bliss, T. and Tetley, J. (2006) *Circle Time: A Resource Book for Infant, Junior and Secondary School.* London: Sage Publications – A Lucky Duck Book.

Furlong, V.J. (1984) 'Black resistance in the liberal comprehensive', in S. Delamont (ed.), *Readings in Classroom Interaction.* London: Methuen.

Hargreaves, D. (2002) *Social Relations in a Secondary School.* London: Routledge.

Maines, B. and Robinson, G. (1998) *All For Alex: A Circle of Friends.* London: Sage Publications – A Lucky Duck Book.

McLean, A. (1994) *Bullyproofing Our School: Promoting Positive Relationships.* Glasgow: Strathclyde Regional Council.

Salmivalli, C., Huttunen, A. and Lagerspetz, K. (1997) 'Peer networks and bullying in schools', *Scandinavian Journal of Psychology,* 38(4): 305–12.

Salmivalli, C., Kaukiainen, A. and Lagerspetz, K. (1998) 'Aggression in the social relations of school-aged girls and boys', in P. Slee and K. Rigby (eds), *Children's Peer Relations.* London: Routledge.

Weatherhead, Y. (2008) *Creative Circle Time Lessons for Early Years.* London: Sage Publications – A Lucky Duck Book.

White, M. (2009) *Magic Circles: Self-Esteem for Everyone in Circle Time.* 2nd edn. London: Sage Publications – A Lucky Duck Book.

CHAPTER 12

INTERACTIVE AND EXPERIENTIAL STRATEGIES

Introduction: understanding the dynamics of bullying

Once a school decides to adopt an anti-bullying initiative, it is useful for teachers to initiate classroom activities that give students a better understanding of the dynamics of bullying. Such activities place teachers in the role of facilitator as well as advocate of safe classrooms and healthy peer relationships. This chapter describes two specific programmes that are preventative as well as informative, which can be used as extensions of classroom learning and of the curriculum, particularly in secondary schools: 'On the Bus' and social action drama.

'On the Bus'

'On the Bus' is an action-based resource I developed with Mark Cleary, formerly a secondary school principal. This account is based on its use with a group of class 9 students at a New Zealand secondary school.

How it works: the eight steps

The eight steps of the programme are designed to give students a better understanding of the nature of bullying, leading to the development of solutions for the particular bullying scenario and a deeper knowledge of bullying in general. In this instance, students explore bullying on a school bus. This strategy can, of course, be used to examine other bullying scenarios (see Appendix 2).

Step 1: the teacher and students jointly choose a bullying scenario

The class was encouraged to discuss various types of bullying situations they had experienced or seen, and the type of bullying they felt most uncomfortable about. They decided to focus on bullying on the school bus.

Being subjected to bullying on a school bus can be very intimidating. Once a student is on the bus, he or she is trapped until their home stop or school.

> **Comment**: This first step is intended to start students thinking about bullying and to give it personal meaning.

Step 2: the scenario is extended

The students talked about the scenario they had created and elaborated on it so that it became real.

> **Scenario**: Kristy is called names and jostled every time she goes on the school bus. She does not tell anyone because she is afraid of retaliation. She cannot see any way out and feels more and more isolated.

Step 3: strategies and solutions are suggested

The students were asked, 'What should Kristy do?' They suggested she could:

- tell her parents;
- tell the principal;
- tell a teacher;
- tell the bus driver;
- sit with a friend;

- tell the bullies to stop calling her names;
- ignore them;
- catch another bus.

From the list of suggestions, three main strategies were identified: tell an adult, stand up to the bullies or avoid the bullies. In all three instances, the onus was on Kristy, the victim, to find a solution. This seemed an unsatisfactory conclusion.

> **Comment**: Having discussed the scenario, and called on their own experiences and observations of bullying, students suggest some possible solutions. These are written down and analysed.

Step 4: feedback and extra information are provided

In order to explore the scenario further and as a way to stimulate discussion, the class was told some statistics: for example, that recent New Zealand research revealed that only 20 per cent of students who had been bullied had sought some kind of help (Adair et al., 2000). This information caused the students to reconsider Kristy's position. They began to look more critically at the solutions they had suggested.

> **Comment**: The first set of solutions is a good start but it is now up to the teacher to take things further: providing extra information about bullying can help students address the underlying issues so that a deeper understanding is reached.

Step 5: the strategies are looked at again

The students were then encouraged to approach the problem from another direction. They knew that telling somebody about the bullying was fraught with difficulties and would not necessarily help Kristy anyway. They knew that catching another bus would only avoid the bullying, not stop it, and they could see that their conclusions side-stepped the bullying but did not confront or change it.

> **Comment**: The students now have a better understanding of Kristy's predicament and dismiss two of their original strategies.

Step 6: the students enter the bus

Another approach was used. Rather than providing more information, the teacher introduced visual stimulation. He drew a picture of the bus on the board to show where these acts of bullying were taking place. He wanted the students to think about the dynamics of the situation. He focused first on where the various actors in this scenario would be located.

Where would Kristy be sitting?

The group unanimously agreed that Kristy would be sitting at the front, close to the driver.

Where would the name-callers be sitting?

Everyone agreed that they would be sitting at the back of the bus.

Having established where people were sitting, discussion turned to the nature of the bullying.

What would happen to Kristy on the bus?

The students thought Kristy would be jostled and called names relentlessly, on the bus going home from school and in the morning on the way to school. They described how the bullies would push past her and make derogatory comments about her hair, her weight, her clothes, her intelligence, and so on.

- The group would consider these remarks 'a bit of fun', 'a good laugh'.
- The other students on the bus would be expected to join in and would, in fact, laugh along.
- Kristy would take her seat, dishevelled and humiliated.

These findings were explored further. Those who were the bystanders to the bullying, seen as sitting in the middle of the bus, were brought into the equation.

The teacher asks, 'So, what is happening here?'

For the one being bullied, Kristy?

Those who are close to the driver may feel they are under her mantle of protection, but her job is to transport children. She may choose to control as best she can what goes on in her bus, but her primary task is to drive safely. She does not see it as her role to protect children, understand the dynamics of peer relations or stop anyone from getting bullied. In fact, it would be dangerous for her to pay too much attention to what is going on, since she is driving.

If the back-seaters have chosen their victim well, Kristy will respond with more and more fear and will be clearly humiliated: her body language will reflect her passivity.

Those doing the bullying, the back-seaters, what's in it for them?

By sitting at the back of the bus, the bullies are locating themselves as far as possible from the adult in charge of the bus. This is where they are most likely to be able to be disruptive, to be objectionable or to bully, because the adult's main job is to drive the bus.

The back-seaters support each other in their abuse of Kristy. They are like a group of actors on a small stage (the back of the bus) who rely on the middle-seaters, their audience, to appreciate the play they are presenting. Their bullying is a demonstration of power over someone who is much less powerful than they are. Among the back-seaters, one student is probably the ringleader, initiating proceedings and controlling the group.

The back-seaters take the laughter and compliance of the others as an affirmation of their actions. It tells them that:

- everyone agrees that what they are doing is funny and fun;
- no one is really getting hurt;
- they are popular, cool and have lots of friends on this bus;
- they should keep doing it.

They act with confidence and bravado.

Those on the sidelines, what does this mean for them?

The middle-seaters are physically, and symbolically, in the middle of the conflict. Their feelings are probably mixed. They may be:

- embarrassed, perhaps with a twinge of sympathy;
- pleased that it is not them who is the butt of the derision; or
- excited by the bullying, but aware that it is sadistic and that they are weak not to intervene.

They can see that it is safer to be on the side of the bullies than on the side of the victim. The role they choose to adopt is pivotal in determining whether the taunts will die away or escalate.

> **Comment**: At this point, the students are much clearer about what is going on, and reframe the situation so that the onus for solving the problem is no longer on the victim of the bullying.

Step 7: revised solutions are made

The discussants agreed that most students on the bus did not like the name-calling, yet their shared passivity gave the impression that they all condoned it.

The class tried to work out some better solutions for Kristy, taking into account the various protagonists in the scenario and their roles. They came up with the following suggestions:

- When the bullying starts, it is important that the middle-seaters ask Kristy to sit with them.
- If anyone feels uncomfortable with the name-calling, they should either challenge it or talk about it with someone else on the bus.

- Middle-seaters should not support the behaviour by laughing.
- The middle-seaters should let Kristy know (off the bus) that what is being said about her is not true.
- They should take Kristy to see a teacher.

None of these suggestions requires the victim to take responsibility for the situation. Having realized what is happening, the peer group – the observers – decides to bring a halt to the bullying.

Comment: The class has now found a good way to stop the bullying. The solutions they have come up with are very important, but just as important is the process of deep learning they have gone through. What they have learnt can be applied to other bullying situations.

Step 8: an analysis and commentary are given

This final step is a summary and analysis of the whole experience. The students have gone through a process of reflective thinking and group problem-solving and, by doing so, clarified issues they had sensed but had not articulated. In providing a joint written analysis, they can integrate more fully what they have learnt.

They have learnt that the following dynamics make the bus an unsafe place.

- The name-callers, hearing the laughter, get confirmation that they are popular and funny and that everyone (except for Kristy) is enjoying themselves.
- The bystanders get the message that it is safer to laugh at Kristy than to be friends with her.
- Kristy gets a clear message that she is on her own.
- The driver hearing the name-calling dismisses it as 'a bit of harmless fun'.

If the bullying is not handled, things will only get worse. The back-seaters will continue their bullying and make increasingly outrageous comments as no one will oppose or stop them. The laughter will increase as the others desperately try to justify their inaction and cover up their discomfort. The bullying behaviour could escalate into attempts to humiliate Kristy physically or even sexually. Her feelings will not be considered and no one will empathize with her – they cannot afford to.

The driver will get fed up with the raucous behaviour and start shouting at everyone (indiscriminately) to keep quiet. She will tell the back-seaters to behave and that she has her eye on them. Kristy will become more withdrawn, isolated and fearful. Determined to maintain their power, the back-seaters will threaten her even more, safe in the knowledge that she will not tell. A culture of intolerance and lack of respect will have become embedded.

If the peer group is strong, however, and the middle-seaters tell the bullies to stop, then the bullying dynamic will be altered. The more the bystanders reject the bullying, the less danger there will be of confrontation and the greater likelihood there will be of the bullying coming to a halt.

How this exercise has been beneficial

The teacher and students have gone through an exercise to solve a bullying problem. The incident is imaginary but real enough for them all to relate to it. Carrying
out this exercise has produced the following useful results:

- It has helped students to clarify some of the issues and dynamics around bullying, which they can use in other situations.
- It has underlined the fact that the peer group has a choice either to support or to
  stop bullying.
- It has shown that the students (with facilitation from the teacher) can find their
  own solutions to bullying problems.

Practical outcomes of the scenario itself are that:

- Everyone is a winner if bullying stops. Kristy will no longer be bullied, she may
  make friends with those who support her and they will feel good about their
  prosocial behaviour. The back-seaters will channel their energy elsewhere and
  might develop more positive ways of relating.
- The driver will no longer need to keep one eye on the students and can concentrate on the road.

Social action drama

When we take part in or witness a piece of powerful drama, we come to understand the perspectives of the individual participants, what they are thinking, what
they are feeling and what personal power they possess (or do not possess). As char-
acters interact and events intersect, a sort of dance begins, and if we watch carefully
we can learn a lot. Using social action drama to create and deconstruct instances of
bullying is a very powerful way of getting inside 'the beast'.

Bullying is a dynamic event or series of events, and if it is likened to a play, then
there are usually three central roles:

1. the perpetrator(s);
2. the victim(s);
3. the bystanders, who can choose to:
   (a)   become actively involved in the bullying;
   (b)   encourage the bullying;
   (c)   watch;
   (d)   walk away;
   (e)   have an undefined role; or
   (f)   take the part of the victim(s) (see Salmivalli et al., 1998).

Although the main roles may appear to be those of bully and victim, the bystanders are crucial. If they as individuals and as a group assert themselves (which they often can just by force of numbers), they have the power to stop the bullying. The purpose of this intervention is to show how.

Twelve steps towards understanding

What follows is a description of a social action drama workshop that was designed to understand and find solutions to bullying at secondary school.

It is based on a successful workshop facilitated by Mark Cleary and me, with a group of 16- and 17-year-old final-year students in a multi-ethnic New Zealand secondary school. For the first half of the workshop, I was the only adult present. Mark was present in the afternoon. The workshop started at 10.00 a.m. and finished at 2.30 p.m. The process has also been worked on and improved using feedback from postgraduate education students in Ireland.

Step 1: preparing for the workshop

In preparing for the workshop, we needed to clarify aims and to arrange space, materials and provisions for the day.

The aims were to assist participants to:

- generate a consensual definition of bullying;
- identify common bullying scenarios based on their experiences and observations;
- write up and act out a selected drama;
- use the dramatic process to develop effective anti-bullying strategies.

The first consideration was to find a location. The school's audio-visual suite was ideal. It was a large, soundproof, windowless empty space away from the rest of the school, with wide carpeted steps, a stage area and a few pieces of school furniture stacked in a corner. We also had to gather together all the materials required to run the workshop effectively and to have food and drink available for the students.

Step 2: getting established

Once the group was gathered together, I explained the purpose of the workshop, introduced myself and asked the students to say who they were.

In this group, there were six girls and six boys. Two were exchange students, Paolo from Italy and Pieter from Germany. A boy and a girl (Maui, who wanted to be an actor, and Reihana, whose goal was to work in the airline industry) were indigenous Maori. The rest were New Zealand Europeans. Takis was a cellist, Mitch was a talented athlete and Mike intended studying politics at university. Katy, Lucy and Maria wanted to study art and graphic design, and Caroline tourism. Sharon wanted to become a teacher.

The students split up into four subgroups of three (of their own choosing). The subgroups were gender-specific comprising two of three girls and two of three boys. I gave them large sheets of paper and pens and asked them to discuss bullying for 10 minutes and to come up with a set of characteristics.

One of the girls' groups reported back first and articulately described three characteristics of bullying. I thanked them and asked for contributions from the other subgroups. Together they identified the following characteristics:

- acting superior;
- being insulting;
- unwanted physical contact;
- intimidation;
- emotional bullying;
- verbal abuse;
- mental abuse;
- pressuring people;
- sexual abuse, overtones or language;
- intentionally making someone feel bad/uncomfortable;
- lowering someone else's self-esteem;
- body language (for example, giving the finger);
- misuse of power;
- repetitive.

They summarized what had been discussed and written, and were later given a copy of the characteristics that they compiled.

This process took an hour, provided a foundation for the rest of the workshop, and established a sense of safety and rapport.

Step 3: identifying bullying scenarios

After a short break, students were requested to form into four mixed-gender subgroups of three people each. Each group was asked to discuss bullying and to describe a bullying scenario they were familiar with.

Step 4: writing a script

In this step, students choose one bullying scenario from the four to make a play about. These students selected what they called 'the sleazy scenario'. They were asked to number off as one or two (that is, there were six ones and six twos). All the ones gathered in the bottom right and the twos in the top left-hand corner of the room, so that they could work apart. Each group consisted of three boys and three girls. They were asked to develop their own scripts in two stages:

- to discuss the scenario and write down their thoughts;
- to write a short but realistic script based on their ideas.

In each group, a director naturally emerged.

Step 5: performing the drama

In step 5, the students perform the bullying dramas. (Only one performance is described here.)

The drama

Maui took on the role of director (and commentator). The first scene is set in the evening and features Adam phoning Heidi. Scene two takes place the following day at school and also includes Adam's and Heidi's respective friends, James and Michelle, and an unnamed female teacher. The group uses four plastic chairs as their props.

Scene 1: Sunday night. All is quiet when Heidi gets an unusual call. Take 1.

Adam:	Hello, is Heidi there, please?
Heidi:	Yes, this is Heidi speaking.
Adam:	Hey Heidi. This is Adam. How's it going? I've noticed you around school. I think you're cool. Do you wanna go out sometime?
Heidi:	Na.
Adam:	Why?
Heidi:	Cos I don't like you.
Adam:	Fuck you then, bitch. (He hangs up)

Scene 2: Monday morning. A very awkward situation in class. Take 1.

Heidi and her friend Michelle are sitting near the back of the class. Adam and James are sitting behind them throwing spitballs at Heidi's head and smirking and laughing. James is egging Adam on. The teacher is writing on the board with her back to the students, completely unaware.

Heidi:	(loses her temper and turns around and says to Adam) Stop it, wanker!
Adam:	(smirks and laughs)
Teacher:	(turns around, says to Adam) Stop that! (Says to Heidi) Don't use that language in my class!

The bell rings to signal the end of class. As they move out of the classroom, Adam shoves Heidi up against the wall. She bumps her shoulders and head. James and Michelle are close behind. Michelle shouts at Adam, 'Leave her alone!' There is a lot of jostling and Heidi runs off crying to the toilet.

The students had a quick 'dress rehearsal' and then performed it dramatically and fully.

Step 6: first impressions

Step 6 gives students the opportunity to discuss the drama immediately after it has been performed, in order to get a sense of its dynamics, to identify the nature of the bullying and to start thinking about strategies. Everyone agreed that the play was about sexual harassment but were confused about the rights and wrongs of what happened. They knew that it was nasty but didn't know how to change things. They decided on the following strategy:

> Strategy 1: Heidi needs to make Adam feel better.

Some students felt that Heidi had been mean to Adam when he rang her. One girl suggested she should have said that she did not want to go out with him now, but perhaps she would in the future. Most students felt uncomfortable with this strategy, however. More exploration was needed!

Step 7: coming to grips with the emotional content of the drama

Step 7 is intended to develop a deeper understanding of the nature and dynamics of the drama.

Everyone had either performed in or watched this drama and the group had come up with an initial but inadequate solution. I decided to approach things from a slightly different angle and said to Sharon (who had played Heidi): 'I am going to ask you what it felt like as Heidi when Adam phoned you.' The following dialogue developed:

> Sharon develops strategy 2: Informing Adam that Heidi does not want to go out with him because she already has a boyfriend.

Keith: Heidi, how did you feel when Adam asked you out?
Heidi: Well, I was surprised when he phoned me up out of the blue. He is in two of my classes but I don't really know him. It felt creepy.
Keith: How did you feel when he was abusive to you?
Heidi: I felt awful! Really awful! He swore at me!

This dialogue provided a new perspective and I decided to develop another angle and asked Sharon to speak as herself.

Keith: Sharon, did your experience as Heidi feel accurate? Would it have happened like that?
Sharon: Yes, it felt real. I know some people would have handled it like Heidi did but I would have done it differently.
Keith: What would you have done?
Heidi: I wouldn't have been so harsh. I would have let Adam down more gently.
Keith: What would you have said?
Sharon: Well, probably something like, 'Hi Adam. Thanks for calling. Look, I don't want to go out with you. I have a boyfriend already and everything is sweet.'
Keith: OK, let's do the first scene of the drama again and see how it feels.

Scenc 1: Sunday night. All is quiet when Heidi gets an unusual call. Take 2.

Adam:	Hello, is Heidi there, please?
Heidi:	Yes, this is Heidi speaking.
Adam:	Hey Heidi. This is Adam. How's it going? I've noticed you around school. I think you're cool. Do you wanna go out sometime?
Heidi:	Hi Adam. Thanks for calling. Look, I don't want to go out with you. I have a boyfriend already and everything is sweet. I have to go now. 'Bye.

The other main character in this scene is Adam. I decided to talk to Mike about playing Adam.

Keith:	Mike, how does that feel for you in your role as Adam? Is the new response from Heidi likely to change Adam's reaction?
Mike:	I'm not certain how Adam'd react. Heidi's new response is less of a put-down but as Adam, I'd still have been angry and probably still aggressive and abusive. Perhaps not as much though!
Keith:	Mike, I am going to interview you now as Adam, and I want you to answer my questions as you feel Adam would respond. Adam, can you tell me about your conversation with Heidi on Sunday night?
Adam:	Well, it was embarrassing. I telephoned her to ask if she wanted to go out with me. My mate James was there [new information] and she said she didn't want to go out with me and that she didn't even like me. Stupid cow!
Keith:	So how did that make you feel?
Adam:	Pretty crap! I don't wanna talk about it.
Keith:	When she turned you down, you swore at her. Was it OK to do that?
Adam:	She deserved it.
Keith:	(to Mike) Mike, do you want to change anything Adam's said?
Mike:	No, I'll leave it.

A dialogue for problem-solving

I suggested they try this new dialogue.

Scene 1: Sunday night. All is quiet when Heidi gets an unusual call. Take 3.

Adam:	Hello, is Heidi there, please?
Heidi:	Yes, this is Heidi speaking.
Adam:	Hey Heidi. This is Adam. How's it going? I've noticed you around school. I think you're cool. Do you wanna go out sometime?
Heidi:	Hi Adam. Thanks for calling. Look, I don't want to go out with you. I have a boyfriend already and everything is sweet. I have to go now. Bye.
Adam:	Fuck you then, bitch. (Hangs up)

Although Mike had chosen to use the same abusive sentence to finish the dialogue, he was not as convincing or as angry as in the original drama. He also looked slightly uncomfortable.

Checking things out with the characters

I then asked Heidi and Adam (in role) how this new dialogue felt.

Keith: Heidi, can you tell me how this dialogue felt compared to the first one?
Heidi: Well, Adam was still abusive to me so I didn't feel great, but I didn't bad mouth him so it's his problem if he reacts like that.
Keith: Adam, how was this second dialogue for you?
Adam: I felt angry and still swore at Heidi but I didn't feel as bad because she was nicer to me.

Step 8: developing alternate dialogues, finding solutions

The purpose of step 8 is to explore the dynamic of the roles and relationships in more depth in order to arrive at better solutions. I asked the audience for feedback in relation to the two variations of the drama they had watched and the two strategies for dealing with Scene 1 that had been suggested. This was intended to involve them further in the problem-solving/strategy development process.

I wrote Sharon's new dialogue on the board and got students to work in pairs (taking turns being Heidi and Adam) trying it out. The students were still ambivalent but now they knew why. They felt they needed to develop a third strategy.

> Strategy 3: Heidi needs to be assertive.

The group decided the best strategy was for Heidi to be assertive. She could tell Adam she did not want to go out with him in a neutral but firm voice. The students were sure that he would want to know why, be persistent and keep pushing for an answer. They agreed that Heidi did not have to give a reason. She could firmly repeat that she did not want to go out with him (the broken record technique). They stated that if Heidi lost her temper or became abusive to Adam, this would give him justification to be abusive back and an excuse to harbour long-term resentment.

It was underlined that Heidi was not responsible for creating this problem, but it was seen as important that she and other girls in this familiar situation be able to develop verbal self-defence strategies. The following mini-dialogue was created:

Adam: Why don't you want to go out with me?
Heidi: I don't want to go out with you.
Adam: But why don't you want to go out with me?
Heidi: I don't want to go out with you.
Adam: But why? Do I smell? Do you think I'm a jerk?
Heidi: I don't want to go out with you. I'm going now. Goodbye.

The group decided it was important to give a clear message, to be neither passive nor aggressive but to be neutral, polite and firm.

What also became apparent was that some of the boys were focused on the male point of view (and sympathized with and personalized the rejection), whereas the girls were more able to see both points of view. A way of extending the boys' restricted view was to have them go into the girls' roles, which they did. The group was no longer stuck and was able to move on and look at the rest of the drama.

The dramatic events

The group identified the drama as containing three distinct events. These were separated out and analysed:

Event 1: The telephone call. Adam was initially nice to Heidi because he wanted to go out with her. When she turned him down he immediately became angry and any pretence of being nice disappeared. He used obscene language and was verbally abusive.

Event 2: The classroom harassment. Adam with James's support harassed Heidi by throwing spitballs at her head. When the teacher became involved, her response to the boys was minimal, yet she chastised Heidi for using foul language. By making Heidi angry enough to retaliate, the boys doubly victimized her as they were able to lure the teacher into their web, as if pulling invisible strings.

Event 3: The assault as they leave the classroom. As the students were leaving class, Adam used the opportunity to push Heidi up against the wall, displaying his superior strength and hurting and jeering at her. Her friend Michelle tried to stop him while James gloated. Heidi, hurt and upset, ran to the toilets crying.

Analysing the three events

In relation to event 1, everyone agreed that there was little Heidi could do to make the interaction end pleasantly and that the final strategy of Heidi being assertive was appropriate. In relation to event 2, the students were clear that if Adam was asked nicely to stop throwing spitballs, he would have laughed and felt stronger. Building on the students' third strategy (Heidi being assertive with Adam when speaking on the telephone), I asked what would happen if Heidi stood up, turned around to Adam and James, and forcefully stated, 'Stop throwing spitballs at me!' The students thought this sounded like a good strategy and tried it out. They discussed how it felt. Those who played Heidi agreed it felt good. Those who acted in Adam's role thought Adam would be tempted to make a smart remark but in a classroom situation might refrain (although the spitball attack occurred 'under the teacher's nose').

The group was concerned about the teacher's lack of awareness and her inappropriate intervention. They felt that not only would it happen this way (with Heidi rather than the boys getting the blame), but that it also gave de facto approval to the escalation that followed. Adam was now free to turn from harassing Heidi with pieces of paper to physically hurting her.

Mark arrived during this discussion and decided to alter the dynamics by taking the part of the teacher. Mark and I created a revised scenario, with Mark playing the teacher and me taking up Heidi's role. The new drama went like this.

Changing the events

Scene 2: Monday morning. A very awkward situation in class. Take 2.

The students are in the classroom. Heidi and her friend Michelle are sitting near the back of the class. Adam and James are sitting behind them throwing spitballs at Heidi's head and smirking and laughing. James is egging Adam on. The teacher is writing on the board with her back to the students, completely unaware.

Heidi: (stands up, turns around and says firmly) Stop that!
The teacher: Heidi, please be quiet! Go and wait outside the room.
Heidi: But he was throwing spitballs at me!
The teacher: No, stop! Go and wait outside the room. I'll come and see you in a
              minute.

Discussion

The students were asked to comment on what they saw, but first they wanted to know how I had felt as Heidi. At first, I was incensed at how the teacher (Mark) had treated me, but I also realized the dynamics had changed. Rather than sitting passively while being showered with spitballs and feeling exposed and humiliated, I (as Heidi) felt angry (rather than humiliated), and my removal from the classroom had put me in a safer place. The teacher had asked me to '*please* be quiet', and told me she would come and see me 'in a minute'. Heidi was being treated in a more respectful way, despite the teacher's firmness.

Mark was asked why he had acted the way he did. He pointed out that the teacher needed first to be in control of the classroom and to defuse what could quickly have become an escalating confrontation. He explained that his intention was to split the students up and then, after a cooling down period, to talk to those involved and to set up a mediation process to find a fair solution.

The students came up with the following assessment:

- Heidi had moved from being a passive victim to being angry and active.
- Although the teacher appeared to be reprimanding Heidi for being disruptive, the intention was to take control and sort things out. The teacher was no longer part of the problem.
- Because of the teacher's actions, the school could now be seen as taking responsibility for solving a bullying problem.
- These changes would mean that the second part of this scene (the assault) should not occur because the momentum and potential escalation of the bullying had been halted.

The following ideas also emerged.

- If the problem had been handled at an earlier stage, the escalation would never have happened.
- Getting victims to react so they fall into a web of culpability is a common bullying tactic. So are lies told by the bully's supporters to place blame on the victim. This can be complex and difficult to deal with.
- Michelle was not a passive bystander, but alone she was relatively powerless.
- Positive interventions from teachers can help.
- Although it was laudable for Heidi to stand up for herself, others may not be able to. It is not the victim's responsibility to solve the problem.

Step 9: coming out of role and resolution

Social action drama is usually based on lived or observed experiences. In order to get into the roles, the emotions and feelings are often fully taken on. It is therefore essential for the facilitator to assist the actors to disengage properly from their roles. This can be done by using a short dramatic device, such as: 'Heidi, I want you to close your eyes. You will turn around twice to the right and then once to the left. When you open your eyes you will be Sharon again'. The facilitator then says, 'Welcome back Sharon'.

It is useful to ask each actor how they felt in their roles and what they learnt. It is also useful to return to the starting point of the drama and to see what characteristics of bullying are revealed by the scenario.

The group responded as follows.

- Adam was malicious towards Heidi (supported by James).
- It was repetitive (three incidents occurred).
- It was an abuse of power.
- It involved verbal abuse, harassment, intimidation, pressure and physical assault.

The students had managed to capture the feelings and nature of sexual bullying through their drama and to suggest useful strategies for dealing with it. The session was closed with comments from the facilitator to this effect.

Step 10: student evaluation

Evaluations provide useful feedback to a presenter and also help students process their learning. Below are the questions asked and a summary of some of the responses at this workshop.

1. **Did this exercise help you to understand more clearly what bullying is?**
   To varying degrees, everyone found the exercise useful.
2. **If so, what did you learn?**
   (a)   I learnt about how girls feel when guys harass them.
   (b)   Bullying if not solved can get worse.
   (c)   Bullying goes deeper than just name-calling and pushing and hitting.

(d)   Bullying is wrong and you should not be afraid to tell someone if you are being harassed sexually, physically or verbally.

(e)   Retaliation is not always a good idea.

3. **List three things you felt were good about this role-playing exercise.**

(a)   It gave me a girl's perspective so I won't bully girls now.

(b)   It showed me ways to avoid getting into a threatening situation.

(c)   It was very clear and thoroughly explained.

(d)   It involved everybody.

(e)   It showed how things can escalate.

(f)   It was better than just talking about bullying.

(g)   I got a good idea of how it felt to be bullied and be the bully.

(h)   I got to see what people's responses would be like.

(i)   I got to think more about how to handle bullying.

Step 11: facilitator reflection, self-evaluation and follow-up

The facilitator will find it useful to reflect on the day's events by:

1. noting what worked and what could be improved;
2. taking account of the student evaluations and issues that emerged.

In relation to point 1, I felt my delivery should be crisper, the experiencing of the drama and the discussions needed to be more equal; and having both a male and female facilitator is crucial.

In relation to point 2, I was concerned about the use of swearing but felt that if I took the moral high ground and set restrictive rules, the students would withdraw to some extent. What is more, there was a very strong reason for retaining the foul language, since it was instrumental to the bullying.

An analysis of the two uses of foul language is instructive.

- Adam used it as a weapon ('Fuck you then, bitch'). It needed to be there so we could learn how to deal with it.
- Heidi said 'Stop it, wanker!' to Adam in class. Adam provoked Heidi and she had an outburst. This caused the teacher to focus on Heidi's language rather than on what Adam and James were doing. This had the effect of putting Heidi 'in a bad light' with the teacher, and meant that if Heidi then complained about Adam's violent and threatening act, she would probably have been dismissed as 'part of the problem'.

I was also aware that one male student seemed to 'get a buzz' out of swearing publicly at school. When he was placed in Heidi's role, however, he said that he felt very uncomfortable and was surprised at how it made him feel. His initial provocativeness turned into empathy.

I decided I would not allow swearing in social action drama with younger classes or in assemblies; or if it would offend people for religious or other significant reasons.

Step 12: performance to other members of the school (optional)

Performing well-developed social theatre can:

* provide useful information about bullying and show that solutions can be found;
* act as a consolidation of understanding for those taking part;
* indicate that the school is concerned about bullying;
* have an impact on its target audience because of the immediacy of its language and culture.

While the performance context is very different from that of the workshop, the raw emotion of something meaningful may overcome this and engross even the most cynical members of the audience. The help of a talented drama teacher can also be invaluable.

References

Adair, V., Dixon, R.S., Moore, D.W. and Sutherland, C.M. (2000) '"Ask your mother not to make yummy sandwiches": bullying in New Zealand secondary schools', *New Zealand Journal of Educational Studies*, 35(2): 207–21.

Salmivalli, C., Kaukiainen, A. and Lagerspetz, K. (1998) 'Aggression in the social relations of school-aged girls and boys', in P. Slee and K. Rigby (eds), *Children's Peer Relations*. London: Routledge.

CHAPTER 13

HARNESSING THE POWER OF THE PEER GROUP

Introduction: bridging the two worlds

Within many schools (particularly at secondary schools), two worlds exist: that of the teaching staff and that of the pupils. These worlds come together in the classroom, where the teacher has the authority, owing to his or her position and role. But even here bullying can go on unchecked. Outside the classroom, much of what goes on is beyond the teacher's control.

In fact, most bullying is not reported to adults, partly because of fear of retaliation and a belief that nothing will be done, and partly because of peer group pressure. Whatever it is called – narking, grassing, ratting, snitching, splitting or telling tales – the unwritten rule is that children and young people should not tell on their peers. Loyalty is to the peer group, not to the adult world; to ask for interventions from that world is unacceptable. If students go against this code of conduct, they risk rejection not only by antisocial members of the peer group but also by the more prosocial members.

However, this power to include or not to include, to approve or not to approve, has just as much potential to be used positively as it does to be used negatively. If the culture in the school rejects bullying and encourages students to tell if they are bullied rather than to suffer in silence, then the greater good of a safe school will win out over fear of reprisals, rejection by the peer culture or tyranny.

Schools can advocate and create a safe culture through the encouragement of student leadership and the adoption of peer support strategies. Such strategies are among a school's best weapons for combating bullying. If students are fully involved in the solutions, then they have a very good chance of working. Leadership programmes and peer strategies can be supported from within the curriculum, or through initiatives embraced by a whole-school approach. In this chapter, I will discuss student leadership and a form of peer support – peer partnering – both of which are primarily preventative and/or ameliorative strategies based on a one-to-one relationship that reinforces the introduction or maintenance of a safe school policy. (Chapter 15 describes the interventionist peer strategies of peer mentoring and peer mediation.)

Student leadership

Leadership of any type exhibits the primary characteristics of power and status, and it is the use of this power and status that defines what kind of a leader someone is (see Figure 13.1). True leadership is less about top-down management than a relationship-based dynamic that is positive and extending. The literature on leadership in the business context, for instance, identifies it as coaching, enabling, encouraging, facilitating, inspiring, modelling, stewarding and visioning (see Parry, 2001).

Positive leaders use their power in positive ways. They benefit from what they do and also make a positive contribution to the society of which they are a part. Negative leaders misuse and abuse their power and status.

Those who bully are often negative leaders. They use their power and status in an antisocial fashion not only to subjugate their victims but also to create a web of manipulation and control within their immediate peer group. When this bullying dynamic is flexed, it spreads from the classroom and beyond into the school and wider community. Maines and Robinson's definition of bullying amplifies this point and helps explain how people use bullying to meet their needs: '[A bully is] a person behaving in a way which might meet needs for excitement, status, material gain or group process and does not recognise or meet the needs or rights of the other people/person who are harmed by the behaviour' (1992: 18).

The issues of actively participating in and leading group processes, securing material gain, and creating and participating in enjoyable and exciting events (particularly in adolescence) are driven by fundamental biological and social needs and are perfectly normal. It is the lack of recognition of others' rights or feelings and the resulting abusive and disrespectful treatment that makes the behaviour of bullies antisocial and negative.

Sociometry can be used to identify leaders (see Chapter 11), both those who are prosocial and those who are antisocial. For many students, their selection as leaders will come as no surprise. They will always have had their leadership acknowledged by adults and will be comfortable with their position in the peer group. They will have developed sound people skills, and will typically be assertive and empathic to their fellow students.

For others, this might be the first tangible recognition of their leadership potential. They will have been aware of their influence (as are their peers) but will not have been regarded positively by adult members of the school community. In particular, those leaders who are aggressive and self-centred and who lack empathy will

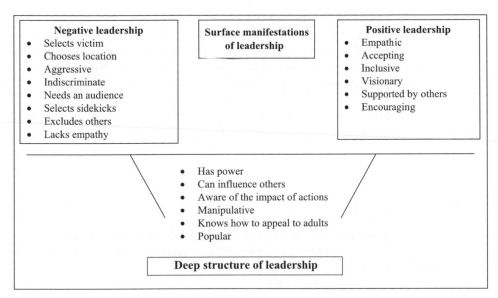

Figure 13.1   Deep structure and surface manifestations of negative and positive leadership

be more used to having their peer group power challenged by adults. They will have become skilled at being subversive and maintaining their position in spite of adult attempts to change their behaviour. Often these students will not have been successful either academically or in extracurricular activities and so will be even more determined to hold on to the status they have established over the years.

If a school recognizes the leadership qualities not only of its positive and obvious leaders but also of its negative and sometimes hidden leaders (as bullying is often hidden), and provides a platform for them to experience success, there are likely to be good outcomes for the individuals involved, their classmates and the school as a whole.

The main purpose of leadership training is to create a safe classroom and school environment. When students who bully are selected to take part in a leadership programme, they are immediately reframed in a positive light. Behaviour that has always got them into trouble, or about which they are secretive, suddenly ceases to be the focus of the school's response to them. Instead, they start to get positive feedback and to be noticed in a context of approval, and as they relinquish their hold on manipulation as a means of influence they are likely to become more attractive to their peers. As leaders they can have prosocial rather than antisocial influence, and their associates often move with them.

In addition to a general improvement in social climate and classroom safety that results from leadership programmes, trained leaders can take on other useful roles.

- They can be assigned specifically to help with conflict resolution, alongside their classmates.
- They can form the core of an anti-bullying team.

- They can aid and embody a process of team-based teaching, learning and classroom management that fully empowers the students. In this sort of setting a team approach can be more successfully introduced and sustained, encouraging constructive and cooperative learners within a resilient social environment.
- They can also become part of a peer support team.

The purpose of such a programme is to harness the abilities of both positive and negative leaders; to reframe the negative as active, energetic and powerful; and to encourage leadership potential through teaching new skills in a positive, experiential learning environment.

The leadership programme

Four of the most powerful students from each class, two who are regarded as prosocial and two who are regarded as antisocial, are selected by the teacher, using a combination of observation and sociometry.

The key objectives of the programme are:

- to give formal recognition to existing leadership and influence within the class group;
- to discuss what leadership is, how it works and what it can do;
- to help leaders identify their personal style of leadership;
- to allow leaders to reflect on whether this personal style is useful;
- to help leaders become aware of leadership behaviour and its influences, both positive and negative;
- to give students an opportunity to practise their leadership;
- to provide opportunities for them to develop understanding of the complex social dynamics that operate in groups of children/adolescents;
- to introduce the students to positive role models who are able to provide ongoing support;
- to empower leaders to act to help create a positive learning environment.

The process is as follows:

1. Leadership selection.
2. Initial training session.
3. Weekly meeting.
4. Follow-up training.

Leadership selection

The selection process begins near the end of the first term. The delay is deliberate as it gives students and classes a chance to become settled.

Teachers can use the tools of sociometry to develop an understanding of classroom dynamics and relationships, and can include students in making the selection, making sure that the aims and objectives of the programme are fully explained. In co-educational schools, the aim should be that two boys and two girls are chosen from each class, two of whom are prosocial and two of whom are antisocial. Negative behaviour can be recast as energetic or active to make the selection easier.

The following issues need to be considered:

- Who has the power and influence?
- Who are the recognized leaders?
- Who is the most popular and fun to be around?
- Who has the most friends?
- Who is the most feared?

Once selected, each student receives a letter of invitation to attend the training session. It helps if an off-site venue is used and senior school leaders are involved.

Initial training session

Here is a typical timetable for a leadership programme.

Time	The students	The facilitators
9.00–9.30	Ice breakers	Teachers, senior students
9.30–10.00	Explanation of the day's programme	Three teachers
10.00–11.00	Leadership styles activities	Teachers, senior students
11.00–12.00	Leadership and team-building exercises	Teachers, senior students
12.00–1.00	Lunch	Peer support students
1.00–2.15	Problem-solving	Two teachers
2.15–2.45	Putting it into action	Two teachers

Ice breakers

The students participate in a number of de-inhibiting activities (see Appendix 4).

Explanation of the day's programme

The details of the day's activities are then presented to the participants by the teacher responsible for the programme or the school's principal. This will include a short overview of what leadership is all about and why the school is undertaking the programme.

Leadership styles activities

The following leadership styles are described and explained by the teachers:

- authoritarian;
- laissez-faire/permissive;
- authoritative.

Ahead of time the senior students have prepared a series of short role plays to illustrate these styles. A scenario is presented.

> Rewi, a year 12 student, is walking down a corridor one day and notices that a year 9 girl is being jostled against a wall and that her lunch money is being taken from her.

The same event is played out by the seniors three times, each showing a different leadership style.

- In the first (authoritarian), Rewi rushes over, yells at the offender to stop immediately, threatens to report the incident to the principal, grabs the offender's hand and wrests the money out of it.
- In the second (laissez-faire/permissive), Rewi looks away, then comes back slowly, says, 'I guess you guys can handle this', and wanders off. He winks at the offender – he's friends with her older brother.
- In the third (authoritative), Rewi asks if the girl is OK, requests that the offender returns the money to her and apologizes, says, 'It's not cool to take people's money', and states that he will let the year 9 dean know about the incident, making it clear that he means it.

The students then break into groups to discuss what they saw. They take turns trying out similar roles, to see how each style feels. At the end of the session the teachers lead a discussion of the advantages and disadvantages of each style, and focus on authoritative styles, with their characteristics of clarity, encouragement, fairness and restoration.

Leadership and team-building exercises

To provide practical opportunities for students to experience leadership and team-building, the students are put into groups of four to six. These groups are each given the same task – to build the tallest tower using paper straws, for example.

The teachers and senior students observe and let the students carry out this activity on their own as much as possible, but help if asked. The students have to work out how to build the tower, the best way of going about it, how to include each other and how to intervene if it starts to go wrong.

Afterwards, they talk about their processes, who did what, whether they succeeded, what would have worked better, and if they managed to work well together and why.

Lunch

The lunch break can be used as a positive learning time by inviting local community and business leaders to share lunch with the students. The form teachers are responsible for organizing the guests, and each of the trainees and senior students is given a task to help make the lunch a success.

Problem-solving

After lunch the students work in different small groups of four to six and are given a number of problem-solving activities to undertake.

The first is an obstacle course. An imaginary river is drawn with chalk, and the students are given certain equipment to cross it. Each group might be given three tyres and three planks (that do not span the river), and they are told that they cannot touch the floor (the river bottom) on their way across. They have to work out together how to do it.

Once they have completed this task, they can be encouraged to discuss their solutions and strategies and to talk about what worked and what did not.

Next they are given problems for which they need to find strategies and solutions.

'We have a problem'

1. Your friends ask you to skip school for the afternoon.
2. You know who is stealing money from the teacher's desk.
3. You are invited to a friend's house at lunchtime and told that there will be drugs and alcohol available.
4. You know that someone in your class is always being left out and is very unhappy.
5. A friend confides that she is being abused by her stepfather.

Each group addresses a different problem and they then try to work out the best way to handle it as a group. After the activities, they are given the opportunity to talk about their discussion, whether they felt they came to a good decision and whether they had their say. In a very controlled manner, each member is given the opportunity to give their view on whether anyone dominated the group during the problem-solving exercises, and how. The students are asked what worked well and what did not. They are then asked to relate their experience to the earlier leadership styles exercise. The aim is for the students to identify the various forms of leadership and how different styles can be used in different situations.

They can ask the following questions.

- What did we do?
- How did we do it?
- What did we learn?
- How can we apply this to our daily lives?

The students usually arrive at the following conclusions.

- They realize they can talk about issues with their peers and usually find solutions.
- They realize they are not alone.
- They learn that if something dangerous, harmful, unfair or wrong is occurring, it is good to act responsibly.
- They realize they can refer problems to adults and that they do not have to handle things by themselves.
- They learn that there are always solutions.
- They learn that leadership is not about being a hero or being in charge. It is about helping to change the social dynamic.

Putting it into action

The teacher with responsibility for the programme explains how leaders can lead by example and role-modelling. When someone is being bullied, if they intervene, the bullying is likely to stop. If they have bullied others in the past and now stop behaving as a bully, the bystanders will notice and shift in relation to the victim as well.

The teacher can also explain how the leaders can take on particular jobs such as being in anti-bullying and anti-harassment teams. These teams are points of contact for other students and are not elite exclusive groups. They help maintain safe classrooms and give an anti-bullying message.

The teacher can explain how these leaders need to try to include others in their prosocial activities so that social responsibility becomes the norm throughout the school. The problem-solving and team nature of the position is emphasized, as well as the fact that the leadership programme is one of the school's strategies to maintain health.

Each class group of four is told that they will help their own class develop a charter. Their form teacher will help them do this, and they will have to overcome obstacles such as negative attitudes and sabotage when they undertake this task.

Weekly meeting

Typically, students are very positive at the end of the first training session. It is essential that there is immediate and high-quality follow-up to ensure that the momentum is not lost. The next session needs to involve the development of the class charter and the encouragement of a team-building approach, as well as feedback to the whole class about the programme and its aims.

At this stage the teacher should establish a regular meeting time for the leaders. The first few meetings should involve planning and debriefing over the class charter, while later other issues that arise can be discussed. These could include helping new class members settle in, addressing specific cases of bad behaviour or disruption to the learning environment, and the development of cooperative and group-learning strategies.

Follow-up training

The teacher in charge of the programme needs to organize at least two full training sessions at which the students are given more information about leadership and how to handle difficult problems and situations. One session can be devoted to explaining and practising the Support Group Method for bullying (Maines and Robinson, 2010 and see Chapter 16). Another can deal with harassment.

It is essential that these follow-up sessions give the students opportunities to ask questions and to raise issues of concern.

Conclusion

While many schools do run leadership programmes, they are often targeted at prosocial students and occur in a student's final two years at school. I am suggesting that leadership programmes have better results and are more useful if they include antisocial students and are run at various levels throughout the school, including in the first two years of primary and secondary schooling.

Student leadership is a crucial tool that is useful within classrooms, the whole school and the wider community. There are innumerable websites available describing both the theory and the practicalities of student leadership schemes. These outline ideas, training programmes, success stories and strategies that work.

For example, the New South Wales Public Schools website (schools.nsw.edu.au) outlines some of the advantages of promoting student leadership in schools:

Effective student leadership practices provide opportunities for students to:

- feel in control of their learning. This means significant input to rules and procedures, establishing learning goals and tasks, deciding how to work.
- feel competent. This means investigating and responding to issues of survival and quality of life, and solving real problems.
- feel connected with others. This means cooperative and collaborative learning, peer support, community linkages, mutual respect.

Peer partnering

Peer partnering formalizes friendship and assigns a more senior student to the role of befriender for a particular student who is at risk or has been identified as needing support. It can be used either structurally, such as when a new cohort of students arrives at a school, or there are significant ethnic groups within the school population; or specifically and individually, such as when a particular child is showing signs of low self-esteem, isolation or being bullied. This approach, which is suitable for use in all schools, is relatively undemanding yet effective, and aims to provide helpful and friendly support, to encourage confidence and to widen the befriended student's group of friends. Like student leadership programmes, it is an attempt to encourage and sustain prosocial behaviour throughout the school.

There are many ways in which peer partnering can be used, for example:

> Various buddy systems operate at Paparoa Street School. These range from pairing of senior school children/classes with junior school children/classes on a daily basis, to individual buddying within a class. We value the positive social relationships which develop throughout the school as a result of buddying. (Paparoa Street School, Christchurch, Information Booklet, 2009, see www.paparoastreet.school.nz)

In many high schools, an annual unhealthy and symbolic ritual of verbal and physical abuse and humiliation is visited on each new intake of students. This process quickly reveals who is resilient and who is a potential long-term victim. To stop this unhealthy process, some schools partner these newly arrived students with final-year students. Their job is to welcome, befriend and support them in their transition. In the process, they learn the school's processes, the written and unwritten rules, and how to keep themselves safe. This also signals that the school will not tolerate bullying or other forms of victimization.

In recent years, peer partnering has been used structurally in the UK with refugee children who have experienced traumatic life events, are lonely and perhaps do not have the support of their families. For example:

> An effective 'buddying' system offers support for pupils joining the school. The care of new pupils from minority backgrounds is very good. Wherever possible, a 'buddy' with the same home language is found to provide help and support … This very good provision demonstrates the school's commitment to the welfare of the pupils in its charge. (Blue Bell Hill Primary and Nursery School, Nottingham, 2004, see www.nottingham-schools.co.uk/eduweb/…/ABS%20Ofsted.doc)

Senior peer partners are chosen because of personal characteristics and their willingness to help. To learn the skills required, they need to be trained in both the procedures and qualities required by the school partnering plan. They must be helped to acquire a high level of tolerance and understanding so they can appreciate, rather than feel uncomfortable about, individuality and non-conformity. They need to be taught the difference between supporting and befriending, on the one hand, and being patronizing and 'rescuing', on the other. They also need to commit themselves to meeting regularly with each other (and the adult supervisors who are involved) so they can debrief, get feedback and so increase their effectiveness.

Once partners are chosen and trained, they need to be paired up with the student they will befriend. The supervisor can be present at the first meeting with specific or individual peer partners to help them set up a contract that specifies how they will work together and for how long. If a structural buddying system is created for a new group of incoming students, they can be talked to together and paired up with their partners at the same meeting.

Peer partnering is a preventative approach designed to stop a problem such as bullying from starting or growing. It is a temporary arrangement (usually for a term or a year). (See Demetriades, 1996 and 2003, on peer partnership in action.)

References

Demetriades, A. (1996) 'Children of the storm: peer partnership in action', in H. Cowie and P. Sharp (eds), *Peer Counselling in Schools: A Time to Listen*. London: David Fulton.

Demetriades, A. (2003) *Building Self-esteem First: A Practical Solution*. London: School of Emotional Literacy Publishing.

Maines, B. and Robinson, G. (1992) *Michael's Story: The No Blame Approach*. London: Sage – Lucky Duck Books.

Parry, K. (ed.) (2001) *Leadership in the Antipodes: Findings, Implications and a Leader Profile*. Wellington: Institute of Policy Studies.

CHAPTER 14

THE SCHOOL ENVIRONMENT

Introduction: making safe spaces

Although there must be a strong emphasis on strategies when examining anti-bullying procedures, it is also important to consider the physical environment of the school. This chapter suggests ways of preventing bullying in the school and playground by being innovative and inclusive, and by making the children the proud custodians of their school environment.

In class, children are in a small, defined group with established peer relationships and a teacher in charge. There is also usually a formal learning task in hand, with specific processes and goals. Because the classroom is a closed unit within a structured time frame, it is generally a safe environment. But bullying can occur in the classroom if the teacher is not vigilant: the research of Adair et al. (2000: 211) indicates that bullying often goes on very close to the teacher and that bullying can and does occur anywhere.

When children are out in the corridors and playground of the school, the structures and rules are less defined and the chance of being at risk is greater. From a finite set of relationships, the children move into a mass where different rules apply, where the social groupings are fluid and ever changing, and where there is little supervision.

And it is during this significant time that bullying occurs most often: in the playground, and elsewhere in the school between classes (see Chapter 2, 'Where does bullying take place?'). Smith and Shu (2000), for example, found that in British secondary schools most bullying takes place in the school yard.

Dealing with these areas is a management issue that requires creativity and vision.

An examination of violence-prone locations in American schools (Astor et al., 2001) came up with two concepts that are useful in analysing the socially and organizationally complex context of the physical environment of the school:

1. undefined public spaces (locations that are dangerous or violence prone because no one takes responsibility for monitoring and/or maintaining them);
2. territoriality (by which crime and violence can be reduced if people are appointed to safeguard spaces so that they become owned by the school).

Undefined public spaces tend to be unowned by school community members (students and staff) and are therefore more susceptible to violence and other antisocial behaviour. They include bathrooms, locker rooms, cafeterias, corridors and hallways, service areas, playgrounds, and routes to and from school. Although members of the school community are aware of the violence-proneness of these areas, neither students nor teachers think it their personal or professional responsibility to monitor them. A solution is that, from a territorial perspective, students and teachers (for school spaces), and the community (for travelling to and from school), should reclaim these spaces (see also Astor et al., 1999).

One way of tackling bullying in the school environment, therefore, is by extending control over areas where bullying is likely to occur and reclaiming unowned parts of the school. Control over the school environment can be both psychological, that is, children are taught to monitor their own behaviour and that of others, and physical, that is, teachers, and possibly parents and students, may be asked to patrol areas of the school outside class hours.

A second way to combat bullying is through the creation of a stimulating and enjoyable school environment. This involves the design and application of architecture, gardening and landscaping, and the use of the imagination, ingenuity and resources of the school community.

Extending control and reclaiming the school

In less controlled situations children can be bullied opportunistically. This can occur on a large playing field or in an enclosed space. For example, a group of girls find themselves near a girl alone in the playground. They think she is 'a bit of a loser' and notice that she is wearing a new jersey. They run past her, yelling abuse, and one of them grabs her sleeve and keeps hold of it until it rips. They call out, 'Sorry about the lovely jersey', and run off laughing. A group of older boys comes upon a single smaller boy in the toilets. No one else is there so they decide to have 'a bit of fun' by teasing him, and they start to push him around and force him to give them all his money.

The open spaces of the playground, and the corridors, toilets and other public areas of the school, are also perfect environments for more systematic forms of victimization. In the playground, relative anonymity and the general hurly-burly of play provide covers for this sort of bullying. In the unlikely event that it will be noticed by staff, it can readily be passed off as 'fun'. Bullying sometimes occurs as an out-of-class pastime when a group of bullies plan to 'get' their victim, and stalk him or her down. Such children often live in fear of going to the canteen, having to go to the toilet and walking down corridors. They are almost always alone, and they are targeted by bullies.

Extending control over these areas is the first step in discouraging and finally combating bullying. If a school adopts a whole-school approach, then one of its aims will be to encourage children to respect others, and to report bullying, both experienced and witnessed. In addition, it is important that bullying danger spots are identified to make proper patrolling of the school more efficient and to help create a safe school environment. In a safe school all areas are 'owned' by the members of the school, both staff and students.

An appreciation of the rights of others

In the playground, if there is a large group of children and only one or two teachers, all the teachers can manage is damage control. The law of the jungle prevails, and the stronger children dominate. In an unsafe playground, a number of trends occur:

* Boys' exuberant games tend to take up a large area and expand as they need to, dominating everything else. Girls, although half of a co-educational school's population, can be pushed into a small corner of the available space.
* In single-sex schools, this type of disparity occurs between the dominant, physical children and the passive, quieter children.
* Children who are isolated from their peer group, and special needs and ethnic-minority children, are vulnerable to bullying either from peers or groups of older children.
* Children who have been marked out to be victimized can be separated from the group and bullied in an unpatrolled area.
* The creating and breaking of rules that is part of children's growth and learning can be subverted into destructive behaviour that focuses on victimization.

Because this is a potentially anarchic environment, it is crucial that the school develops a clear set of rules about what is and is not acceptable. Concerns about bullying and not considering others should be part of a wider aim of making the playground safe. It is imperative that these rules stress the need to respect the rights of others. If these rules are grounded in a whole-school approach to bullying, then they are more likely to have some effect.

If the school has a play area with equipment, it is easy to encourage children to develop their own rules for the use of this area, in junior as well as secondary schools. These playground rules, for example, were developed by students and staff at Monta Loma Elementary School, Mountain View, California, in 2009.

Rules for using the playground

Play structure:
* No tag or chasing on or around the play structure equipment.
* No jumping from play structure platforms.

Slides:
* All slides should be 'feet first'. Students may not walk/climb up slides.
* One student at a time.

Monkey bars:
* One student at a time going one direction.
* Students are not to sit on top of the monkey bars.

Blacktop:
* Soccer/kick balls should be used in the basketball/field areas of the playground.
* Stay clear of organized games.

Field:
* Students may be on the infield of the ballpark if they are participating in an organized game. Games of tag are allowed in the grass area only.
* Students may not go into the bleacher or backstop areas of the ballfield.
* Students play touch football on the grass area of the ballpark. If the play in this game becomes too rough, we will discontinue.
* Students are only allowed in the Monta Loma Park if they are supervised.

Equipment:
* Any equipment checked out from the classroom or equipment area is to be returned to its storage location by the student who checked it out.
* All equipment is to be used in a safe and cooperative manner. Unsafe or disruptive use will result in loss of privileges in using equipment or participating in organized play situation.

Such approaches that attempt to provide ground rules about considerate behaviour and attitudes are in harmony with a whole-school policy that will also stress the importance of students letting staff know if they experience or see unfairness, rule-breaking or bullying.

Identifying the danger spots

Within any school there are danger spots – areas where bullying is more likely to occur. These may be places where people rarely congregate (a passageway or corridor), that are isolated (the periphery of a large playing field), or that are enclosed and not patrolled (certain toilets or the cafeteria).

Carrying out a survey of danger spots with students will give an accurate sense of where bullying occurs most frequently. This will also involve students in an anti-bullying measure, and may be a first step in signalling to bullying students that the school will no longer tolerate bullying, and will handle it rapidly and thoroughly if it occurs.

A survey can be successfully carried out by providing students with a photo-copied map of the school and asking them to mark on it where bullying occurs (a) very often, (b) quite often or (c) sometimes. By putting these responses together, an overall picture of a school's bullying danger spots can be drawn. Included in this survey should be questions about going to and from school (either on foot or by school bus or public transport).

The students can be shown the results of the survey and asked how to deal with these problem areas. Students may suggest that they patrol the danger spots, or that teachers or parents do. They may suggest altering them physically so that they lose some of their peripheral or enclosed nature. But, most important of all, if students start to think of the danger spots differently, they will begin to care about what occurs in them. If this process is repeated throughout the school, the danger spots may cease to be perilous places.

Patrolling the playground

Boulton (1994a, 1994b) argues that putting more people on duty and thereby increasing the policing is not enough. It will not stop children excluding each other, bring an end to vicious remarks, halt obscene gestures or stamp out physical bully-ing. It may deter some instances of intimidation and victimization, and increase the amount of reporting, but it will not make children feel more empathic or socially responsible.

Better and increased patrolling is, however, an immediate and practical response to out-of-class bullying, especially when the danger spots have been identified. A teacher recently told me that areas of his school were habitually not patrolled because teachers felt unsafe there. It became apparent that this was because they patrolled alone. The solution was that, rather than giving up this space to a gang of intimidating students, two teachers should patrol together.

In Chapter 13, I discuss harnessing student leadership. One of the tasks allocated to class leaders could be to help maintain order in the playground. Allied to this approach is the use of student monitors. In a school that encourages peer strategies for dealing with bullying, the appointment of monitors from the group of trained peer support students to act as playground monitors should work well. Alternatively, students who have shown an interest in the danger spot survey or who are directly involved in an anti-bullying initiative may make successful monitors. There are reports that when students manage their own playgrounds, or are at least involved in their monitoring and patrol, the incidence of bullying drops dramatically (Campbell, 2006, about the Zoneparc project in Great Britain and the Netherlands).

There are also ways to involve the community in playground monitoring. In some schools it is appropriate to ask for parent help at lunchtime. This can be done with minimal training and, in a school that is operating an anti-bullying initiative, can be part of the plan for a whole-school approach.

Community initiatives can also be adapted to the local needs of schools. For example, in New Zealand, the Tu Tangata (standing tall) programme (see Puketapu, 1988) has been developed by the Maori community but is not directed only at Maori students. It brings the community into the classroom through placing adults alongside students, and these same adults could also help patrol playgrounds as part of their contribution of time and commitment to the school. Adaptation of the programme should be relatively straightforward and could be suggested at preliminary meetings about setting up an anti-bullying initiative.

Creating a stimulating and enjoyable environment

There are a number of ways in which a school can be made a better environment for children, by thinking out the use of space and by introducing playground activities. This can involve specific professionals and tradespeople such as architects, builders and landscape gardeners, but it can also rely on the ingenuity and resources of the school population. It involves a change not only of the physical, but also of the psychic and temporal, environments.

Time management

School playgrounds vary enormously. Some are very small and overcrowded, some are massive and barren. There are practical ways of managing the use of space and providing the best conditions within the limitations of the school. For example, if the playground area is small, or there is a problem with overbearing and raucous play, lunch hours can be staggered so that there are fewer children in the playground at any one time.

Alternatively, classes can be rostered to use the playground at different times. This will relieve overcrowding and give the children a sense that it is a privilege to be allowed time out of class. For example, in a school with five different grades, one grade could be allowed to use the playground one day a week at lunchtime, and during breaks the class whose teacher is on duty could be allowed to use specific play equipment or to play in a specific area. This may simply be an extension of the rule that allows only a certain number of children on play equipment at any one time.

Rethinking the structure and aesthetics of the playground

Children and their parents can be involved in re-visualizing and modifying the space. For example, Newton Central School in downtown Auckland has the following statement on its website (newton.school.nz):

> Newton Central School is … in the 'heart' of Central Auckland … nestled on the side of the North Western Motorway above Newton Gully. Entrance to the school is off the main arterial route – Great North Road – down streets of concrete grey industrial buildings.
>
> However, the grounds are like entering into a tropical paradise.
>
> The development, regeneration, sustainability and beautification of the school grounds is a commitment of the school and wider community. The development of our grounds is not just about aesthetics. It is based on a philosophy of responsibility to ensure we put in place measures, strategies and systems that assist us to ensure a safe environment for our children while also providing information, knowledge and experiences to assist them to develop an understanding of Maori and world visions about 'Kaitiakitanga' [guardianship] and sustainability of the earth for now and the future.
>
> To this end the entire school community has contributed time, energy and resources to assist with the implementation of our vision to provide a model environment with systems, processes and plans for a healthy future of the earth and therefore us and for generations to come.

The driving force behind environmental change can come from regional or national agencies with local and voluntary input. In the USA, for example, many schools have been upgraded by urban development initiatives and Federal Work Programs. Jordan High School in New York State was totally transformed through a Federal Work Program that beautified an ugly wasteland of the Old Erie Canal and created a baseball diamond, gardens and playing fields for the school. In Australia, the Keep Australia Beautiful Tidy Schools competition attracts many entries in several categories, and encourages children to take pride in their school environments and to find ways in which they can improve them. It is supported and funded by Comalco. Some of these initiatives are part of a green school movement that is placing the school environment in the wider context of recycling, sustainability and environmental awareness.

Environments can be changed architecturally and spatially with imagination, little cash and a lot of hard work. In the school population, there are often parents with architectural, building or landscape skills who may be persuaded to help with such a venture. Alternatively, it is a good idea to ask the children what they want in their ideal playground and then to get students from a local architecture, design or recreational studies tertiary course to take on the project as an assignment. In some cases this will lead to the creation of detailed plans that can then be implemented with community help, and sometimes to the building or partial building of the design at minimal cost through the use of grants or subsidies. People from a government-funded job scheme can also be invited to participate.

If a play area is worn out and ugly, students can be asked to suggest ways to make it pleasant and stimulating again. Gardening and painting involve only minimal cost (and local businesses may donate plants and paint). Students can be asked to decorate areas of barren asphalt with games, roads and world maps. When graffiti has appeared, it can be painted over but a designated 'graffiti wall' created. Rusty, broken equipment can be painted and repaired. If children do the work themselves, with help, then they are more likely to take pride in the area and look after it.

Sometimes space is at a premium. Even then, there are usually ways to increase and improve space. All it may require is imagination, ingenuity and lateral thinking. If only a limited area is available, for example, it may be possible to build a multi-level adventure playground, using parental support and minimal funds.

In designing how best to use the space, it is beneficial to survey what the children do or would like to do. It is important to create spaces, both inside and outside, for all weathers, so that all children are catered for, both those who love exuberant play and those who enjoy quieter activities.

Children may want to see what playgrounds in other schools and countries are like (they can register with http://www.kidlink.org/; or visit a site such as global-classroom.org/play.html).

In a whole-school environment, cooperation between parents, students, teachers and the community is crucial. Although it may require out-of-school time and energy, it builds strong foundations that should make a resilient school resistant to bullying. Many side benefits result from working together like this.

Beating boredom

Many children are bored in school playgrounds. Television can make children passive and unimaginative, and they sometimes lose the ability to play creatively. If a school becomes proactive in its management of recreational time, there may be a reduction in bullying simply because there are more interesting things to do. For example, teachers can introduce children to traditional games for outside play (see Dunn and Winter, 2000) and to board and other games for inside play. This has the very important added advantage of giving teachers and children another way of getting to know each other and building stronger connections in a less formal setting.

Children can contact other schools to share descriptions of popular playground games. For example, there is a website that describes various games and includes and invites contributions from schools around the world (http://www.whitehall.waltham.sch.uk/game.htm).

It is worth considering the creative involvement of parents in both the recreational and academic functions of the school. Although in some schools it is common for parents to help with reading and other classroom tasks, for some parents the school exists behind a kind of imaginary barricade. An Israeli project in which I was involved (Lichman and Sullivan, 1999) had the larger intention of building bridges between Jewish and Arab children, but was also designed to bring parents into the school by getting children to ask their parents and grandparents about games they played as children. The parents and grandparents then came to the school and showed the children how to play the games. This benefited everyone concerned, giving the children something to do in their lunch hours and breaks, giving parents (sometimes for the first time) access to the school, and endowing the children and teachers with often lost cultural knowledge.

Playground time, as Briggs (1994) argues, can be seen as an educational opportunity.

References

Adair, V., Dixon, R.S., Moore, D.W. and Sutherland, C.M. (2000) '"Ask your mother not to make yummy sandwiches": bullying in New Zealand secondary schools', *New Zealand Journal of Educational Studies*, 35(2): 207–21.

Astor, R.A., Meyer, H. and Behre, W.J. (1999) 'Unowned places and times: maps and interviews about violence in high school', *American Educational Research Journal*, 36: 3–42.

Astor, R.A., Meyer, H.A. and Pitner, R.O. (2001) 'Elementary and middle school students' perceptions of safety: an examination of violence-prone school sub-contexts', *The Elementary School Journal*, 101: 511–28.

Boulton, M.J. (1994a) 'How to prevent and respond to bullying behaviour in the junior/middle school playground', in S. Sharp and P.K. Smith (eds), *Tackling Bullying in Your School: A Practical Handbook for Teachers*. London and New York: Routledge.

Boulton, M.J. (1994b) 'Understanding and preventing bullying in the junior playground', in P.K. Smith and S. Sharp (eds), *School Bullying: Insights and Perspectives*. London and New York: Routledge.

Briggs, S. (1994) 'Making the most of your playground', in A. McLean (ed.), *Bullyproofing Our School: Promoting Positive Behaviour*. Glasgow: Strathclyde Regional Council.

Campbell, F. (2006) 'No more playtime bullying', Radio Netherlands Worldwide, 21 February.

Dunn, O. and Winter, S. (2000) *Acka Backa Boo! Playground Games from Around the World*. New York: Henry Holt.

Lichman, S. and Sullivan, K. (1999) 'Harnessing folklore and traditional creativity to promote better understanding between Jewish and Arab children in Israel', in M. Leicester, C. Modgil and S. Modgil (eds), *Values, Culture and Education – Volume Three: Political Education and Citizenship*. London and Washington, DC: Falmer Press.

Puketapu, K. (1988) *Tu Tangata: A Management Perspective*. Wellington: Royal Commission on Social Policy.

Smith, P.K. and Shu, S. (2000) 'What good schools can do about bullying: findings from a survey in English schools after a decade of research and action', *Childhood*, 7: 193–212.

PART 4

INTERVENTIONS

CHAPTER 15

PEER MENTORING AND PEER MEDIATION

Introduction: defusing conflict and restoring balance

The potential for using the peer group to solve bullying conflicts is enormous. Although teachers and parents may have the best intentions in the world, the power of the peer group, from an early age but especially from adolescence onwards, is very great. This power is often a cause of bullying, but it can also be used to find solutions.

Peer mentoring and peer mediation are action-based strategies designed specifically to address the damage bullying can do, to individuals and within peer and school cultures, and to solve conflicts. They can be called upon when conflict is observed or reported; or by those in dispute who can ask for help to deal with their conflict. The intention is to defuse a situation as quickly and thoroughly as possible, and to address the aftershocks of bullying.

Encouraging peer support strategies is like running an anti-virus programme through a computer: it makes the system healthier and disinfects the problem areas. It also enhances relationships within the school, which are, after all, the foundation of its success as a social as well as educative institution.

Peer mentoring

Peer mentoring is a practical and effective anti-bullying strategy. It involves slightly older, more experienced students using their skills and energy to help stop bullying by giving support to younger peers (Cowie and Sharp, 1996). It can be utilized to deal with issues of bullying for middle and secondary school pupils, and specifically to:

- assist victims to recover from and avoid bullying;
- help perpetrators of bullying to find more useful ways of acting;
- support bystanders to develop the skills and confidence to resist and oppose bullying.

Peer mentoring and recovering from bullying

When someone has been in an accident and their body has been injured, we accept that time is required for a full recovery, for bones and bruises to heal. When someone has been bullied, they may be physically hurt but will also have emotional and psychological damage (which may be hidden and hard to detect). In Chapter 3, I discuss the trauma that results from bullying and how this can send the victim into a downward spiral. Those who have been traumatized by bullying need to be assisted through a recovery period to return to a normal non-traumatized state. When a person is being bullied, the first step is to halt it. The next is to assess the damage and create an action plan. These are the jobs of the school counsellor, anti-bullying team or psychologist. Depending on the duration and severity of the bullying and the personality of the victim, the effects will vary.

After an initial diagnosis and counselling (and the application of an anti-bullying strategy), the counsellor may suggest that a mentoring relationship be arranged to provide support and develop strategies to assist the recovery/change process. A similar process can be set up for those who bully or who are bystanders.

Peer mentoring normally includes the following four components.

1. **Befriending**. Being a friend, providing companionship, sharing ideas and activities, perhaps meeting outside of school.
2. **Coaching**. Sometimes those who have been bullied benefit from coaching about how school and student cultures work. This can be done by discussion, focusing on issues such as acceptance, expectations, fairness, friendships and rules (both written and unwritten).
3. **Problem-solving**. Whereas it is not the responsibility of the person being bullied to stop the bullying, it is important for them to learn how to avoid unsafe places and situations, and who they can go to if bullying recurs.
4. **Providing ongoing support**. The mentor provides a safe point of contact and a sense of constancy and reliability. The mentor can give practical help with organizational needs and academic problems.

A peer mentoring case study

This case study is based on setting up a peer mentoring scheme at a Canadian high school, and describes the preliminary processes, the training workshop, and the running and maintenance of the programme.

Stage 1: initial preparations

Step 1: creating a programme

In order for the programme to be accepted and supported, all staff at the school were given information about it and the opportunity to be involved in its inception and running. The school psychologist was in charge, and teachers with skills and enthusiasm were recruited. Through discussion, a time line and a specific structure and processes were developed.

Step 2: making students and staff aware

The peer mentoring programme was put forward at the beginning of the year and explained to students at school assembly; teachers were also asked to discuss it in class. The scheme was described as a strategy developed to provide assistance to victims, bullies and bystanders and to help tackle the universal problem of bullying in schools. Information about the extent of bullying was disseminated and organizers said they were looking for potential peer mentors in the senior school.

Step 3: Choosing the peer mentors

Suitable students were nominated, volunteered or shoulder-tapped. They were carefully screened and a shortlist was created. Generally, the shortlisted students:

- had a high degree of empathy, warmth and an interest in others;
- were not judgemental and were good role models;
- had a stable personality and lifestyle;
- had problem-solving skills.

In addition, suitable students who had been bullied and were now doing well were included. Those finally chosen had previously completed a leadership course and were judged good potential peer mentors. In this case, nine grade 12 (year 13) students were selected.

Stage 2: training the mentors

Step 1: the training workshop

The purpose of the workshop is to explain what peer mentoring is and to teach the skills required. The workshop is intended to be interactive so as:

1. to enthuse the students about peer mentoring;
2. to encourage 'ownership' of the peer mentoring programme;
3. to draw upon their knowledge about, and experience of, school culture as the basis for an effective programme.

During the training workshop, most activities are carried out in groups so that group processing can provide the foundation for ongoing and mutual support between participants as the peer mentoring programme takes shape.

Schools do not generally have the luxury of abundant free time. Therefore, while it would be preferable to run several consecutive training sessions, the reality is that most schools will have to find ways to present maximum information with optimum effect in minimum time. In this case, the training workshop was carried out in three consecutive sessions (with a snack and a lunch break between sessions 2 and 3) during one day.

Margaret, the school's psychologist, and Philippe, the head of discipline, ran the workshop. The principal (André) participated in the afternoon session. What follows is a description of the day.

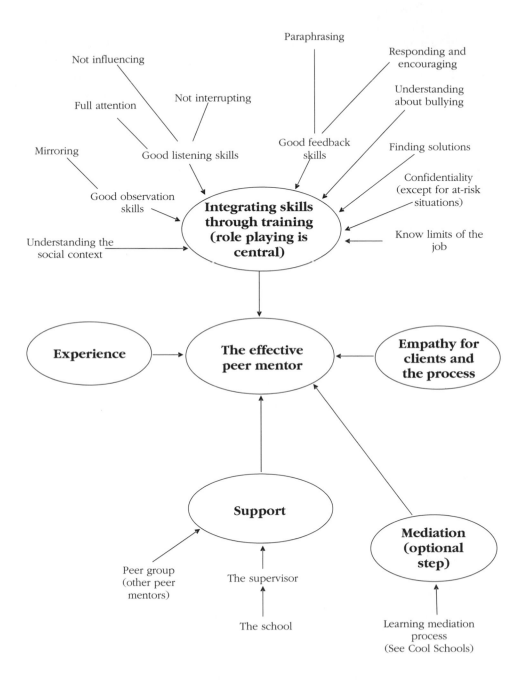

Figure 15.1 Requirements for an effective peer mentor

Session 1. 10.30–11.00 – Breaking the ice

> When starting off a workshop, it is important to create a pleasant, cooperative atmosphere and to establish a sense of trust.

First, Margaret and Philippe introduced themselves to the students and used an overhead transparency to explain what they would be covering. They then ran two ice-breaker activities (see Appendix 4 for examples).

Session 2. 11.00–12.00 Identifying the major issues

> The purpose of this session is to discuss bullying and come to an agreement about what it is, to talk about peer mentoring and to brainstorm how participants think they could be most helpful as peer mentors.

The process was designed to provide information and 'fill in the gaps'. It was also intended to draw upon the knowledge and experience of the participants as members of the student culture in order to create a programme that would enable meaningful connections and lead to good practice.

Four questions were posed. Brainstorming threesomes were formed and large sheets of paper provided for recording the findings from discussions. For each question, everyone changed groups. After each discussion, groups reported back. The results of the sessions were compiled, typed up and returned to the students before the end of the workshop. The four questions asked were as follows:

1. What is bullying?
2. What are the effects of bullying?
3. What is peer mentoring?
4. What should peer mentors do? What can we best offer as a peer mentor?

By the end of this session, the students had a clear understanding of bullying and its effects. They also knew that being a peer mentor meant committing about 15 minutes a week to a particular student for a specified length of time, as well as time to meet with their coordinator. They understood that they would be trained to provide support, to keep confidentiality, and to identify issues and incidents beyond their capability and responsibility, such as physical and/or sexual abuse, and suicidal feelings. They learnt that in such cases they should pass the students in question on to the coordinator for following up (see Appendix 3).

This session worked well. It was fast moving and the students changed groups readily and enjoyed themselves. It was also empowering because the peer mentor trainees were able to access and deepen their knowledge of the school culture and their place in it.

(Continued)

(Continued)

Session 3. 12.30–2.30 Teaching micro-counselling skills

The purpose of this session is to teach basic micro-counselling skills to the students. This was done by first providing an illustration of how not to mentor and secondly by showing how to do it correctly. After having seen good and poor mentoring in practice, students were given more information about what they should aim to achieve.

To mentor or not to mentor – how to do it badly, how to do it well
Philippe took on the role of the mentored student and André the mentor. First, they demonstrated how not to do it, and then how to do it well.

Take 1: how to mentor badly. Philippe and André came into the room allocated for their meeting. André did not tell Philippe where to sit and did not welcome him. He then got Philippe to talk but played with his trouser cuff, picked things off the carpet, looked around and kept glancing at his watch. When Philippe started to explain how he felt, André interrupted with interjections that stopped Philippe from expressing himself and focused on things that were only slightly relevant to his concern. When Philippe talked about having trouble with a teacher, André asked who it was and started to deride the teacher. He then stopped Philippe and said time was up, he had to go. Philippe was clearly frustrated and let down.

The students commented on the scenario, noting positive and negative aspects as follows:

Positive
- The mentored student was prepared to talk.
- The mentor shared some of his experiences.
- The carpet got cleaned [humorous comment!].
- The mentor was dressed well [humorous comment!].

Negative
- The mentor fidgeted.
- The mentor did not pay attention.
- The mentor criticized a teacher.
- The mentor side-tracked.
- The mentor made irrelevant conversation.
- A mixed message was given: I want to be here/I do not want to be here.
- The mentor could not read between the lines.
- The mentor kept looking at his watch.

Take 2: how to mentor well. When Philippe came into the room, André greeted him, made him feel at ease, showed him where to sit and explained pleasantly that there was a time limit. He asked Philippe how he had felt about being bullied. Philippe responded in general terms and, without being pushy,

André asked for further details. He listened to what Philippe had to say and paraphrased it, repeating it back to him. André said things like, 'That sounds hard to handle', 'I'd feel pretty bad about being treated like that', 'How do you feel?', 'Do you feel angry?', 'What would you like to do about it?' and 'Would you like me to speak to my supervisor?' He also said that Philippe could come back to talk again. When they finished, there was a sense that a relationship had been established.

The students commented on the scenario, noting positive and negative aspects as follows:

Positive
- The mentor offered a seat.
- The mentor warned about the time limit.
- The mentor opened up conversation.
- The mentor engaged in conversation and made eye contact.
- The mentor reviewed/gave feedback/paraphrased.
- The mentored student was allowed to talk.
- The mentored student was listened to.
- The mentor made himself available – he invited the mentored student to come back.
- The mentor offered to talk to his supervisor to ask for help.
- The mentor asked how the mentored student wanted to do things.

Negative
There were no negative comments.

After the scenarios had been played through and discussions taken place, André explained to the students that although he and Philippe were fairly familiar with counselling and mentoring strategies, they still had to figure things out and practise what to do in order to deal effectively with difficult situations and the unexpected. They said that this type of reflective thinking is important no matter how old or experienced you are. In order to become effective as peer mentors, it is not only OK but also important to think about what could go wrong and to develop role plays to find a variety of solutions.

The group discussed the following micro-counselling skills that they had just witnessed:

- active listening;
- providing useful feedback through paraphrasing;
- using 'I' statements, focusing on feelings and avoiding blaming;
- supporting people in making their own decisions.

Margaret, André and Philippe then led a wider discussion about the skills required for successful mentoring and how they could structure a typical

(Continued)

(Continued)

session. The germs of the discussion were summarized on two prominently displayed whiteboards as follows.

Fundamental mentoring skills (what you do)

Listening. Active listening means that you are involved, not just sitting back and nodding (but you also do not take over).

Paraphrasing. Summarizing. Repeat back what you have heard, and ask if you've got it right.

Clarifying. Ask questions to help yourself and the mentored person clarify the issue.

Naming feelings. For example, 'You seem to feel angry because the teacher didn't give you a chance to explain. Is this right?'

The four-step process

Engaging. Make sure that the mentored student feels comfortable.

Opening up. Ask questions, use paraphrasing, clarifying, mirroring.

Focusing. If there is a particular issue to resolve, focus on what the next step might be to resolve the issue. This may involve more dialogue or finding ways to arrive at solutions.

Moving on. Finish with an agreement about anything you have resolved to do, and when you will meet again.

Role play to practise peer mentoring

It was now time to introduce the students to role play in order to transfer theory into practice and to help them learn experientially. In three groups and with input from the adults present, they developed three scenarios on which to focus (see Appendix 2 for some useful bullying scenarios). They were then given the following structure within which to work:

> **Instructions**: In the role plays, you will be working in groups of three. One student will be the person being mentored. The second will be the mentor. The third student will be the observer/commentator. You need to experience all three roles.

The way it works is as follows:

1. The student being mentored states what his or her concern is.
2. The mentor responds.
3. This interaction is ongoing until the issues raised are satisfactorily dealt with.
4. The observer/commentator provides feedback to both participants about the scenario enacted.

Each group develops a role play for the first mentoring session for the protagonists in each of these scenarios. Time should be allowed for each of the students to take on each of the three roles: the mentor, the mentored student and the commentator/observer. This is an extremely valuable learning experience.

In a supportive environment, the students can learn:

1. how to listen (and how not to listen);
2. how to structure the session (the four steps);
3. the sorts of interactions and dialogues that may emerge;
4. what works and what does not.

Evaluation and acknowledgement

In order to get feedback, students were asked to fill out an evaluation sheet. They were asked the following questions.

1. List three things that you liked about today's training programme.
2. List three things that you think would help to improve the training programme.
3. Any other comments?

Step 2: follow-up

After the workshop, the programme organizers made sure the mentors received ongoing support. What they learned through listening, role play and discussion was tested when they put their training into practice. The mentors met regularly with a supervisor for debriefing and with other mentors in order to hone their skills.

Stage 3: running the programme

Step 1: carrying out the mentoring

The mentors were now ready to begin. Once they were paired up with the students they would mentor, they worked hard to establish trust and gather information. They then identified the main issues and began to put solutions and strategies into place. The sessions were well structured with clear beginnings and endings, and an emphasis on empowerment rather than the creation of over-reliance.

Step 2: mentoring support

The mentors were supported by having regular 'information and maintenance' meetings with the programme coordinators and through a mentors' support meeting.

They also met with their supervisors at least once a week to discuss how things were going and to receive support and feedback.

Stage 4: maintaining the programme

All schools are governed by regular cycles. Every year as one cohort of students in the upper school departs, a new group at the lower end arrives. Within the rest of the school, there will be comings and goings as families move in and out of the district. Similarly, there are movements within a school's staff.

It is always important therefore that someone is in charge of maintaining the peer mentoring programme and of overseeing the dynamics and its yearly cycle. If the job is passed on, then this should include full training in the running of the programme as part of the change-over process. In order for the programme to work, to develop its own ecology and safe regeneration, the school administration and teachers need to be informed about and involved to some extent in its process, running and success. That is why this school spent time at the beginning of the year familiarizing staff and students with the processes and aims of peer mentoring.

Peer mediation

Peer mediation is an action-based strategy designed specifically to solve conflicts. It can be called upon when conflict is observed or reported, or by those in dispute who can ask for help to deal with their conflict. The intention is to defuse a situation as quickly and thoroughly as possible. Whereas peer partnering and peer mentoring are based on one-to-one relationships that model acceptance, tolerance and prosocial behaviour, peer mediation is action based and involves the main protagonists in a dispute or antisocial conflict coming face to face with each other in the presence of a neutral peer. It is important therefore that mediators have specific skills that build on those required by peer mentors.

The process of peer mediation is as follows:

1. The disputants meet with the peer mediator and a set of ground rules is agreed upon. Both sides agree not to interrupt or be abusive in any way, to be honest and open, and to try to find a solution.
2. Each side in the dispute tells their story without interruption. The peer mediator listens carefully.
3. He or she paraphrases what has been said and repeats it to the disputants to allow any elaborations and corrections to be made. Both disputants are allowed to speak at this point and to seek clarification. This can go back and forth a few times and interruptions should not occur.

4. The disputants are each asked what outcome they hope for, and how they would like the matter resolved. This is discussed until an agreement is reached.

If at any point the disputants break the rules they have agreed upon, the peer mediator will need to point this out. If this continues, then the meeting should be stopped. The peer mediator can then decide whether it is best to bring in an adult or to have a 24-hour cooling-off period.

An example of peer mediation: the Cool Schools programme

The Cool Schools Peer Mediation Programme (usually referred to as Cool Schools) was developed in Auckland by Yvonne Duncan, Marion Hancock and Alyn Ware of the Foundation for Peace Studies Aotearoa/New Zealand. Cool Schools was designed initially for primary (including intermediate) schools (5- to 12-year-olds) to teach both classroom and playground mediation to students. Owing to its success, it has been expanded to include a separate programme for secondary schools and for parents; and it has also been taken up in Australia and Fiji, with plans for its introduction into Hong Kong.

The Cool Schools website (www.peace.net.nz) makes the following statement:

> The Cool Schools Peer Mediation Programme is a whole schools program that was developed in 1991. It aims to train students in the skills of mediation and conflict resolution, whereby children learn to mediate conflict amongst their peers. It is now in over half of the schools throughout Aotearoa/New Zealand.

Cool Schools addresses bullying both by providing processes for dealing with it, and by creating an atmosphere in which a mobilized and empowered group of students finds bullying unacceptable. As Yvonne Duncan explains, central to the Cool Schools approach is 'the belief that if you raise children's awareness and understanding of what conflict is about and teach them skills they can implement themselves, it is the most effective way of changing behaviour' (Duncan, personal communication, 5 December 1996).

Cool Schools has been very successful, for several reasons:

- It is very accessible, easy for teachers, pupils and parents to understand and use, and is practical and down to earth.
- Separate programmes have been developed for the primary and secondary sectors and for parents. This recognizes that the dynamics, needs and stages of development are different for the two sectors and for parents.
- Cool Schools is overseen by adults but relies on the participation and enthusiasm of students. In other words, it aims to alter the system of the school.
- Children often feel more comfortable talking to people their own age than to adults. The deputy principal of a New Zealand primary school ran a survey to determine the effectiveness of peer mediators' abilities to resolve conflict in the playground in his school. Over 80 per cent of the children surveyed felt they could approach a peer mediator and preferred doing this to discussing problems with the teacher on duty.

The Cool Schools website lists the benefits of the Cool Schools Primary and Secondary Programmes. Combined, these benefits include:

- Lifelong conflict management skills are learnt and practised by everyone in the school community.
- Students are empowered to help other students.
- It is a proactive programme to prevent conflict and becomes part of the school culture.
- An opportunity is provided for students to take on leadership roles that allow them to offer an important service as 'peace-keepers' in the school.
- Teachers can teach mediation skills and processes as part of their health curriculum.

Schools report the following benefits:

- Students develop an appreciation of conflict as something that can be handled positively and learnt from.
- Disputes between students are generally permanently settled in 80–85 per cent of cases.
- Students become equipped with valuable skills for handling conflicts both within and outside the school.
- A much improved and more cooperative school atmosphere develops.
- There are fewer incidents of troublesome behaviour beyond the school gates and a general increase in students' self-esteem.
- Teachers are more able to leave students to find suitable solutions to their problems, thus freeing teachers from a good deal of time-consuming dispute settlement and disciplinary action.

Philosophically, Cool Schools is based on a belief that mediation is preferable to discipline. Discipline involves a person in authority either dishing out a punishment or deciding on a solution, whereas, in mediation, the disputants themselves try to find a facilitated solution within a non-threatening structure. Because the disputants are in charge of their actions rather than being forced to act by an authority figure, they are empowered. It is also argued that, with an effective mediation system, the need for discipline is reduced.

Cool Schools intends to complement the aims of a whole-school approach. Its proponents argue that it works best within an environment and school philosophy that endeavours to handle conflicts constructively; works hard to enhance self-esteem; promotes cooperation and communication skills; acknowledges the diverse cultural, social and psychological backgrounds of pupils; involves pupils, where possible, in decision-making; supports teachers and pupils under stress; encourages the expression of feelings; and negotiates its way through problems rather than imposing a decision from the top down (Duncan and Stanners, 1999: 11).

Cool Schools is part of the resource and training material offered by the Peace

Foundation. It is also a model for the introduction of any similar mediation programme into any kind of school, anywhere in the world. It specifies the importance
of support and understanding within the whole school community, the selection and
training of student mediators, the publicizing and implementation of the scheme,
and its ongoing evaluation and improvement (Duncan and Stanners, 1999).

References

Cowie, H. and Sharp, S. (eds) (1996) *Peer Counselling in Schools: A Time to Listen.* London:
    David Fulton.
Duncan, Y. and Stanners, M. (1999) *Cool Schools Peer Mediation Programme: Training
    Manual.* 3rd edn. Auckland: Foundation for Peace Studies Aotearoa/New Zealand.

CHAPTER 16

THE SUPPORT GROUP METHOD

Introduction: from blame to empathy

George Robinson and Barbara Maines developed the Support Group Method (SGM), formerly called the No Blame Approach, as a creative reponse to a difficult bullying case they had been asked to solve. For many years, they had worked, both in individual and group settings, with children and young people who were struggling with academic and social problems and disabilities (George as principal of a school for 'behaviour-disordered' youth and Barbara as a practitioner psychologist). In the process, they had learned much about individual behaviour and social interaction and had come to the following conclusions:

- that despite the myth that says 'you have to stand up to bullies', most people do not and cannot (particularly if they have been targeted because the perpetrators know they can get away with it);
- that, with a few exceptions, those who bully are misdirected rather than pathological;
- that if the latent power of the wider peer group is harnessed, the bullying can be stopped; and
- that if students who expect to be punished and are intransigent are offered a genuine way out, in most cases they will cooperate and the bullying will cease.

In the programme that Barbara and George developed, the 'way out' was to shift the focus from punishing the bullies to helping members of the peer group (including the bullies) to empathize with the targeted and isolated student in question, and to support the group in finding ways of re-integrating the target (a less stigmatizing descriptor) into a now safer peer group (see Maines and Robinson, 2009; Robinson and Maines, 2008). In short, the Support Group Method is a prosocial response to bullying that aims to change the group dynamic so that the physical and mental health of the targeted student is supported and safeguarded, and the larger peer group and those responsible for the bullying are able to shift from being part of the problem to becoming part of the solution.

Some people are critical of the SGM because they regard its methods as a naive and irresponsible way of dealing with the serious and damaging problem of bullying. These people prefer for bullies to be punished and suspect that when the SGM is used, those responsible for the bullying will appear to go along with it while cynically laughing up their collective sleeve. However, the reality is that bullying among children and young people can be like Herbert's (1965) sandworm that weaves its way under the sand and only occasionally rears its head into the world of adults. If bullying is handled in a punitive way – when it becomes visible – licence may be given for revenge to take place once 'the worm' dives out of sight again and the bullying in fact escalates. In contrast, when the wider peer group is empowered to act responsibly, the social dynamic changes and a safer environment is created. In making this argument, I do not intend to belittle the concern and anger some people feel when severe bullying takes place and when more extreme sanctions must be adopted. Such cases are, however, relatively rare. I would argue that if good can be found in powerful bullies and their more humane side can be engaged, it can be beneficial to all, particularly when such aggressors are often long-standing victims themselves.

When it is clear that bullying is occurring, a teacher could round up the likely suspects and question them individually. Using basic detective work, the inconsistencies in their stories could be identified, and logical flaws, contradictions and lies uncovered as the guilty parties dig themselves deeper into an unsuccessful attempt at deception. The basis for punishment is established and those responsible can be given whichever punishment seems to match the severity of the incident. Rather than taking responsibility for the bullying, however, the guilty parties will consider themselves caught out and 'wronged', and will probably hold the targeted student responsible for their punishment and humiliation (even if the bullying came to light through another avenue). The aggressors will also actively seek the support or complicity of the wider peer group, and chances are that the bullying will continue but go underground. From the school's point of view, the problem will probably be considered to have been successfully dealt with since it will disappear from sight. Instead, however, matters will most likely have become considerably worse.

The SGM provides a pragmatic alternative to the above scenario and a solution that is straightforward and easy to use. When it is applied, it becomes clear who is responsible for the bullying and also that it is unacceptable. Not only does the facilitator ask for the group's help in solving the problem, but all of the participants are also given a chance to think about what is really happening as a result of the bullying. The process carefully avoids blaming or shaming the bullying perpetrator and his or her supporters, and instead gives everyone the opportunity to respond to the hurt the bullying behaviour is causing. The intention is that the perpetrator, still driven by the desire to be a dominant member of the group, will decide to find other, more prosocial ways of exhibiting leadership abilities or retaining status, and at the very least, that he or she will stop victimizing the targeted student.

The outcome is usually that, through having derived a better understanding of its effects, the peer group will neither condone nor tolerate bullying. The aggressors' hold is broken, not only over the bullied person but also over those who feel under threat and powerless to stop the bullying. The SGM provides a solution whereby bystanders and classmates can help make things better and also behave in new ways. With a focus on the targeted student's feelings and on finding a shared solution among members of the larger peer group, there is no justification or reason for those responsible to continue the bullying. They are not faced with blame, shame or the problem of ratting that would arguably justify a continuation of the victimization. The SGM is punishment-free and it is an appropriate method to use whenever there is a bullying problem in a school.

Furthermore, the SGM is educative in that it provides students with a model for developing solutions for a problem that many children, young people and adults would otherwise have great difficulty in dealing with.

How the Support Group Method works

The Support Group Method has a number of steps.

Step 1: talk with and listen to the targeted student

The targeted student's plight comes to the attention of a member of the school's anti-bullying team (through self-reporting, or being reported by another student, a teacher or a parent). A facilitator (usually a teacher, a counsellor or a school psychologist) is chosen to deal with the case and a meeting is arranged with the targeted student. The student's parents and teacher are informed that the SGM process will be initiated and why. The aims of this meeting are as follows:

1. to understand the pain the target is experiencing;
2. to explain the method and seek agreement to proceed;
3. to discuss who will participate in the support group;
4. to agree with the target about what the group will be told.

1. To understand the pain the target is experiencing

When bullying has occurred, the first thing for the SGM facilitator to do is to talk to the target and to reassure her that they will try to sort the problem out together. Whether she has been referred to the facilitator or has reported the bullying herself, it is important that the facilitator states that coming into the open is a brave and commendable thing to do.

The target is asked to describe the bullying she is experiencing and how it makes her feel. The facilitator can talk about how it feels to be bullied, sharing the experience and common feelings of loneliness that come from being isolated, and assuring her that she is not alone and that bullying can happen to anyone. In response, the student may state, for instance, that she is always being ignored or rejected by her classmates, is not part of group activities in the classroom or the playground, and that she is friendless and is always by herself. She is also regularly humiliated by insults and nasty remarks about her clothes or her body odour, and is constantly being jeered at and called stupid by a group of three girls in her class. The facilitator may respond as follows: 'So you are feeling lonely, upset and left out.' The facilitator's aim is to support the student by accurately reflecting her feelings back to her, and to gather information so as to develop an accurate description of how she feels so he can tell the support group when he meets with them for the first time.

Comment: At this stage it is crucial not to try to get to the bottom of things. It is most important to affirm that it is the behaviour of the bullying students that is unacceptable, not the target's, that she has done no wrong and has the right to be left in peace.

2. To explain the method and seek agreement to proceed

The facilitator now explains how the SGM works. His next step will be to choose a group of students who will act as a support group for the target. While she will not take part in this meeting she will be represented there by the facilitator. He explains that in introducing and discussing the issue, he will not blame or punish those responsible for the bullying but will seek the group's help (including the aggressors') to find a solution.

The Support Group Method is presented as an effective way to deal with the bullying. It is very important that the victim understands fully the processes and intentions of the approach and consents to its use. One of the pivotal keys to its success is getting those who are responsible for the bullying and some others in the class or group to experience how their behaviour or lack of support is affecting the targeted student. The focus will be on how the target is feeling rather than seeking to blame or punish anyone. If the targeted student fully understands this, she is usually relieved.

Comment: At this point, the target of the bullying is encouraged but not pressured to take part in the SGM. The adult makes the case in a way that is supportive and encouraging but lets her make the final decision. It is also often the case that initially the target may not wish to take part in the process and may need time to think about it. If this is so and the bullying continues, she will probably get back to the facilitator within a short period of time. If this does not happen, it may be necessary to contact the target again. An important consideration here is that she will feel disempowered as a result of being bullied. Supporting her to make a decision to go ahead with the SGM is the start of the re-empowerment process.

3. To discuss who will participate in the support group

The facilitator then asks the target who she thinks should be in the support group. He explains that it usually comprises some of those who are most responsible for the bullying (often two to three students, one of whom is usually dominant), some of those who contributed to or supported it, and some of those who watched but did not get involved. It should also include someone the target likes or admires. In terms of the mix of the group, the purpose is to achieve a positive result. Although the facilitator plays a major role and will be the most powerful individual present, the intention is (quietly) to shift the power of the group away from those who have carried out the bullying to those who will provide solutions and change the direction of the group (which those who are responsible for the bullying may or may not choose to be part of).

Even if the facilitator knows the students well, it is important to get a second opinion about the composition of the group from an insightful colleague (a teacher, psychologist/guidance counsellor or deputy principal, for instance) before making a final decision. Having the right balance within the group is crucial. Knowing which students are potentially proactive and will voice their concerns and contribute positively to creating solutions is crucial. It is also important to anticipate the range of responses that is likely to emerge (positive and negative) so as to be prepared for them and to have ways to deal with them.

> **Comment**: A group of six to eight students is ideal for the support group. They should include the main perpetrator, one or two supporters of the perpetrator, one or two bystanders to the bullying (not supportive of the perpetrator), and dominant/assertive class members who may have chosen not to intervene but would do so in a safer context. The composition of the group is central to having a positive outcome. It needs to bring together some of the powerful members of the class, who would disapprove of bullying and would say so in this context. These individuals have the influence and the ability to shape the attitudes of the group and to change the dynamic. Involving the non-bullying popular leaders gives them the opportunity to grasp fully the nature of the bullying behaviour and its effect on the victim. Experience has shown that these influential students often do not associate with either the bullies or the victims. They may have chosen to ignore the bullying (if they have seen it), or not to challenge the bullies' behaviour. The supportive process of the SGM enables such students to make a positive connection with the victim, to feel sympathy and to recognize that as members of the same community they have a responsibility to act.

4. To agree with the target about what the group will be told

Before bringing the meeting to a close, the target is asked to draw a picture or write a poem or a piece of prose that describes how she is feeling about being bullied. The facilitator will have gathered background information and will have a sense of what he will say to the support group about the target's experiences and how she feels. He can use this information to set the tone of the meeting and illustrate it with reference to the poem, piece of writing or drawing the targeted student has provided. The target is asked what she feels comfortable to reveal and what she does not. She could say: 'I am happy for you to say how sad it makes me feel, that I cry before going to bed and am having trouble sleeping, but don't tell them that I throw up because I get so scared.'

The facilitator, aware of her vulnerability, will tell the targeted student that he is happy to meet with her at any time before the SGM meeting with the students and also afterwards. In other words, the facilitator will support the target, as required, throughout the process and beyond.

> Comment: People are sometimes unsure how the target will respond to making a piece of art about the bullying or writing about it. The response is almost always spontaneous and creative because the pent-up reactions of hurt, frustration and incomprehension are released, and the work that results is often excellent and easy to empathize with. The perpetrators may also feel intimidated and shamed by it.

Step 2: convene a meeting with the people involved

The chosen students are asked to meet with the facilitator. They are informed that they will need to be at a particular location at a specified time. Short notice is given and details are not provided at this point. Having some refreshments and snacks on hand can be helpful in welcoming the students and implicitly underlining that the intention of the meeting is positive.

> Comment: Initiating a constructive dynamic is crucial here. The purpose behind this meeting is to invite the support group to take responsibility for working with the facilitator to address the bullying.

Step 3: explain the problem

In this meeting everyone, including the facilitator, (the target is not included in steps 2–7) sits in a circle, an arrangement that creates a sense of equal power among the participants. The facilitator explains that the group has been called together to help solve a problem that has arisen. He then explains, using the information gathered, what he knows about the bullying, how the targeted pupil is feeling and also that it is not her fault she feels this way. He says that the purpose of this meeting is not to blame or punish anyone but rather to help the student to feel safer and happier by providing specific and constructive support to her. He reiterates that no one is being blamed and that he is looking for suggestions for improving the situation. It is essential that the focus is kept on what the individual students can contribute themselves rather than what the student herself or other people can do.

The facilitator talks about how the target is feeling, and her piece of writing is read or her drawing is shown (with commentary) as the basis for discussion. He describes the target's unhappiness, her sleeping difficulties and her dread of coming to school (or whatever has been agreed between the target and the facilitator). Surprisingly, students typically respond that they did not realize how awful the target felt.

It is possible that defensive comments will come from those responsible for the bullying ('She asked for it!', 'She said stupid things to us!', 'She started it!'). This is a challenge to the truth of what is being described, to the authority of the facilitator and to the process. The perpetrators may also be testing whether it is true that no one will be punished and be defending their dominant status and issuing a veiled threat towards the other students. These challenges can be aggressive and the facilitator needs to be prepared for such reactions and to be calm, neutral and constructive in response.

This can be the most difficult thing the facilitator has to handle. At this point, he can reiterate that no one is being blamed. He may also inform the group that it was a concerned adult (or a student or teacher) who reported the bullying – that it was not the target. He may mention that the targeted student agreed to this meeting only on the condition that nobody would be blamed or punished. This may come as a surprise to those responsible for the bullying and to the group as a whole; it is usually seen as a point in the student's favour. It is clear to everyone present who is responsible for the target's sadness, that this is an opportunity to deal constructively with the situation, and that (by implication) consequences and/or punishment could occur if it is not solved in a benign fashion.

Once this is clear, it allows uneasy observers to the bullying and those who could be intimidated by it to intervene and make positive suggestions for helping find a solution. It is important that such students are part of the process. While they may not challenge the dynamic verbally, with support they may be able to challenge it by their actions and their expressed sympathy for the target. The main perpetrator(s) may resist contributing in a substantial way (as this could be seen as losing face), but will usually agree (sometimes apparently grudgingly, and in so doing acting more positively but still saving face) at least to have no more contact with the target (in other words, to stop bullying her).

Comment: This is where the scheme comes into its own. If the students have no experience of the Support Group Method and they expect to be blamed, their body language and prepared stance will probably be defensive and passive-aggressive. They know they have been caught and think that the person questioning them will blame them and punish them for what they have done. Their one satisfaction may be that they can get back at their victim later. Once it is clear that they are not being blamed or punished, however, they cease to feel threatened. This allows them to respond objectively to the act of bullying and to be part of the solution. Often, those who are leaders in the act of bullying can use the skills that bring them to the fore to find and endorse a more prosocial way of behaving.

Step 4: share responsibility

Responsibility for the bullying is shared by the group. Although blame is not attributed and punishments are not meted out, the act of bullying has to be acknowledged (rather than glossed over) so that the group can move on to the next stage. In focusing on the emotional state of the target, they are able to face the effects of the bullying more readily, and to feel empahty. It is made clear that:

- the purpose of the support group is to help solve the problem;
- no one is in trouble or is going to be punished;
- while the facilitator has the responsibility for organizing and implementing the process, if it is to work it will be because of the efforts of the peer group.

> **Comment**: In taking responsibility for the act of bullying and feeling remorse rather than facing punishment, the perpetrators can acknowledge the effects of their behaviour. The observers and bystanders can see that in doing nothing to stop the bullying, they were implicitly condoning it. Together, they are confronted with the main point: 'What are you going to do to contribute to finding a solution?'

Step 5: ask the members of the group for their ideas

The group is asked what they think can be done about the situation. After brainstorming, they each suggest solutions, how they feel they can help and what they will do. These suggestions should be clear, positive and concrete. Robinson and Maines (2008) suggest acknowledging this support by the issuing of a certificate.

> Thank you to (student's name is inserted here) for joining this support group to help support a peer who is unhappy, and for making the following suggestion: (for example, I will ask her to sit with me at lunchtime).

> **Comment**: Each group member is encouraged to suggest ways they can provide support to the victim, saying what they will do ('I will …').

The process

Strategy

- It is useful to focus first on one of the more thoughtful, confident members of the group to lead the way.
- If a student cannot think of anything, they can be allowed to pass but with an understanding that the facilitator will come back to them a bit later in the discussion. This will give them time to think without the spotlight being on them. It invariably works.

- The perpetrators of bullying can be left to last in case they have a negative (and defensive) response. This may also encourage them to shift into a more positive position.
- The students do not have to promise to do what they suggest.

Solutions

Solutions students come up with are usually straightforward and logical, such as:

- 'He/she lives just down the road. I could walk to school with her.'
- 'I'll offer to sit with her in maths and help her with her work.'
- 'I'll ask if she want to come to the cinema with us [a small peer group of girls] on Friday night.'

The perpetrators can react in a variety of ways.

- They may not have regarded their behaviour as bullying and be shocked into stopping.
- They may not have realized the effects of their bullying and may decide to do something positive for the victim.
- Or, after becoming aware how the group is feeling, they may decide the bullying reduces their attractiveness and withdraw gradually from it.
- They may realize it is more important to be accepted by the group than to be admired or feared for negative behaviour.
- They may say, 'I'm not going to do anything' (this is a typical reaction that should be openly welcomed as a solution that would be most helpful!).
- In order to maintain a position of high status they may take on a leadership role and organize the support being developed for the victim.
- They may deny any responsibility and continue to bully, but in the face of the changed dynamic and loss of support they may forfeit their audience and have to stop.
- They may continue with the bullying and will need to be dealt with through consequences, suspension or the CPR approach. This is the least likely result of the SGM process.

> **Comment**: The processes of peer support and problem-solving are helpful and, when done in a concerted fashion, create a sense of the students working together positively. This is a practical problem-solving session. The solutions sought are intended to support the reintegration of the victim into the class, not to 'rescue' her – that is, they are assertive and empowering, not patronizing, solutions.

Step 6: leave it up to them

Responsibility for carrying out their suggestions is left up to the group. They go away feeling they will do something positive that is supported by the facilitator who has conducted the session and in conjunction with the efforts of their peers.

Comment: With the understanding that the facilitator will meet with them again individually in a week's time, the group members are free to carry out their solutions or suggestions. Step 6 is useful because it turns theory to practice, stops the bullying and gives a constructive focus for the group's energy. One of the important outcomes of this method is that, even if a perpetrator of bullying remains intransigent, he or she will probably have lost the support of the peer group, which means either that there is no audience to applaud and encourage and therefore no reward for doing the bullying, or that observers may now intervene and stop it because they realize how it feels to be bullied.

Step 7: meet members of the support group again

About a week later, the facilitator has a short meeting with all members of the support group as well as with the targeted student. The meetings are on a one-to-one basis and the students are asked how things are going. Did they manage to carry out the tasks that they had agreed to? How are they feeling? How is the target feeling? Have there been noticeable changes?

Comment: An individual meeting with each support group member allows them to discuss what they have done to provide relief for the target. It can both affirm the effort and provide a framework and timeline for students to carry out their chosen tasks, giving them a sense of success, both as individuals and within their peer group. They have created a safe place for the student who was a target and for themselves. This also provides reinforcement for the concept that it is better to be supportive and positive than to bully, and that students acting as a group have the power to stop the bullying. The most important outcomes are, first, that the bullying has stopped, and second, that the peer dynamic has shifted: these are of greater significance than the hope that all members will have carried out their intentions.

The ongoing step: meeting with the targeted student as required

Although the process is carried out on behalf of the targeted student, he or she is not involved with the group meeting processes. The facilitator will meet with the target when establishing the process and to check to see how things are before Step 7 takes place. If the bullying had been going on for some time, it is important to check several times to verify that the positive effects of the SGM are continuing. If they are not, other methods will need to be considered.

Effectiveness of the Support Group Method

The Support Group Method is popular because:

- it deals with potentially complex situations in a straightforward way;
- there is no need for extensive and difficult investigations;
- students see bullying addressed in a constructive, non-threatening manner;
- it brings about change quickly;
- it is easy to use;
- it works.

It works for several reasons.

- The first thing that the SGM does is to focus on how the victim is feeling. By focusing on feelings rather than on what happened or who did what, attention is drawn away from blame, cause and sequence and towards empathy, which is the most powerful catalyst for change in this dynamic.
- The SGM causes the bully and supporters to think about the impact of their behaviour.
- It draws the bystanders and non-involved students in to finding a solution to the problem. They are forced to be involved.
- The group members are asked for their help. The facilitator makes it clear that it is up to them – it is their process.
- It is a non-confrontational, prosocial approach.
- No one has to hide behind an untrue picture of what happened as no one is going to be blamed for anything that occurred.
- It powerfully reinforces the fact that bullying is a problem that is best solved by those who are enmeshed in the behaviour. While adults facilitate the method, they do so by seeking the help of the students and thus empowering them.
- Those who are responsible for the bullying are given a way to be part of the solution, to help to solve the problem by assisting the person being bullied or at the least to desist from bullying. Everyone knows, however, what their role has been and therefore what their personal responsibilities are. Although this process is constructive and positive, the implication is that if it does not work there are consequences or punitive-based approaches that can be used instead.

All the participants are given the opportunity to empathize with the victim, the bully perhaps for the first time. The bystanders are given an opening to voice what they may have been thinking but were lacking courage to express. This process subtly changes the power structure within the group. Its effectiveness lies somewhere between the encouragement of empathy and the fact that when people do something helpful they usually feel good about it.

Bullying relies on an audience and on support from the bystanders. The Support Group Method erodes the bully's power base, humanizes the target and causes the other students to lose interest in or support for the bullying. The intimidation stops.

The Support Group Method has been found to be particularly useful for the upper primary and the middle and lower secondary school sectors.

References

Herbert, F. (1965) *Dune*. Randor, PA: Chilton Books.

Maines, B. and Robinson, G. (2009) *The Support Group Method Training Pack: Effective Anti-Bullying Intervention*. London: Sage – Lucky Duck Books.

Robinson, G. and Maines, B. (2008) *Bullying: A Complete Guide to the Support Group Method*. London: Sage – Lucky Duck Books.

CHAPTER 17

A CIRCLE OF FRIENDS

Introduction: modifying behaviour and supporting change

Drawing in particular on the research of a colleague, Tina Axup, Barbara Maines and George Robinson created an excellent programme entitled 'A Circle of Friends'. The thinking behind the programme is that children with emotional and behavioural problems, who are often a focus for bullying as well as being bullies themselves, need teaching and support rather than punishment and isolation (which their behaviour often brings).

At the time, Maines was employed by Bristol City Council as a support teacher for young people with emotional and behavioural difficulties. Alex, an 11-year-old, class 6 boy, had been identified as having behavioural problems that seemed to be getting worse. Maines discovered that his mother had been diagnosed with a life-threatening illness and that he was worried and frightened. Maines felt that Circle of Friends could be used to support Alex through his mother's illness, and that it might also help to solve some of his emotional and behavioural problems. She and George decided to film the process in action, and were given permission by Alex, his classmates, their families and the teachers involved. The resulting video and accompanying booklet is called *All for Alex: A Circle of Friends*.

How Circle of Friends works

A Circle of Friends is conducted in three parts:

1. Part one: arranging the Circle of Friends
2. Part two: the meetings
3. Part three: follow-up and evaluation

Part one: arranging the Circle of Friends

The planning for Circle of Friends requires a number of steps:

Step 1: permission from the young person

In step 1, Maines discussed Circle of Friends with Alex and explained how it worked. She and Alex decided that she would talk to the class about how he was feeling, without him present. A group of volunteers would be asked for and chosen as his circle of friends. It was important to negotiate this with Alex so that it was clear he agreed and felt safe to go ahead.

> Comment: In this step Maines makes sure that Alex wants to take part, that he knows he has the power to say no and that he can negotiate the terms. He is also warmed up to the process.

Step 2: planning with staff

The next step was to speak with Alex's teacher and to get his agreement to create a circle of friends for Alex. An important and sensitive consideration was that, in providing the class with information, Alex's mother's illness would be discussed publicly.

> Comment: If a programme like Circle of Friends is to be successful, the teacher's role is central. He or she must understand both the intentions and processes of the initiative, provide advice and monitor it on a day-to day basis, and support the efforts of the circle. By implication, if the teacher supports the programme the circle can be widened to include the rest of the class as secondary participants.

Step 3: talking to the whole class about Alex

In step 3, Maines talked to the class, without Alex present, about his mother and about his distress. Maines's intentions were to reframe Alex's behaviour as sad and troubled rather than as difficult and naughty, and to encourage the group to feel empathy towards him. She asked the children to volunteer to be members of the Circle of Friends by writing their names on pieces of paper and placing them in the box provided.

> Comment: In this step, Maines presents not only the process but also lays the groundwork for a better and less punitive response to Alex and for his acceptance by the class. The aim is also to create a positive atmosphere and to encourage more prosocial behaviour from Alex.

Step 4: talking to the whole class about Circle of Friends

In step 4, Maines answered questions about the process from Alex's classmates. She closed by thanking the children for their time and attention.

> **Comment:** This is a useful exercise in clarification. The questions the pupils ask are: 'What does the Circle of Friends do?', 'Can I drop out?', 'How do you choose the Circle of Friends?', 'Will Alex get to know what the circle is doing?' In her answers, Maines is able both to provide specific details and to give a sense of the method's intentions and philosophy. Such explanations also allow children to feel closer to the aims of the programme because they understand it better, even if they do not volunteer or are not chosen as members of the circle.

Step 5: choosing the circle members

After meeting with the class, Maines went through the names of the volunteers with the teacher. They chose some children whom they knew to be reliable and also chose two students who were known to have conflicts with Alex.

Seventeen children volunteered and six were chosen. Wanting to encourage a sense of support in the class generally and to acknowledge those who put themselves forward but were not chosen, Maines wrote a note of thanks to each of them.

> **Comment:** The circle of friends is balanced by including both boys and girls (in co-educational settings), and supportive as well as challenging children. Two girls are chosen because they are close friends and in their friendship have excluded Alex (they have written on their piece of paper, 'Take both of us or neither'). It is particularly important to select people who are at odds with Alex because, if their attitudes towards him can be turned around, this will affect the way others treat him. The remaining children are known to be reliable and stable. Their presence gives a sense of legitimacy and acceptance to what the circle children do in their contacts with Alex.

Part two: the meetings

Maines had half a term (the remainder of the school year) to plan meetings and to implement the programme. She decided to arrange four meetings but to avoid the daily follow-up that some facilitators use. She decided that Alex would not be at the first three meetings but would be at the last.

During the period in which the circle was meeting, Maines arranged short visits with Alex so that she could be sure things were going well for him, and so that, if any problems arose, she could support him and incorporate these difficulties into the meetings.

The meetings were organized as follows:

- Meeting 1. Forming the group, planning the action.
- Meeting 2. Monitoring progress, giving praise and encouragement.
- Meeting 3. Reflecting on the work, planning the final meeting.
- Meeting 4. Talking with Alex, planning the celebration, closing the Circle of Friends.

Meeting 1: forming the group, planning the action

The purpose of this meeting was to welcome and thank those who had volunteered, to validate them for the special gesture they had made, to revisit the purpose of the group, to set ground rules in place and to help all members of the group come up with a positive intention towards Alex. Maines closed the session by thanking the participants again.

> **Comment**: In the video, Maines is able to elicit a positive commitment from each member of the circle of friends to do something constructive to acknowledge or help Alex. Any of the children are allowed to pass the first time around but the next time round they are asked for a contribution. Now that they have seen other people's suggestions, they have a sense of what is needed.

The process of helping the students decide what to do is interesting. Maines reflected their suggestions back to the children. This helped to clarify what they would do and also made it possible for them to each do something different but along similar lines. Here are two examples.

Dialogue number 1

Nicky (a girl): Well, you could give him special attention when he's in quite a good mood, and when he's sort of in a bad mood, you could just keep out

	of his way.
Maines:	That would be like focusing on the good things rather than paying attention to the bad. That's really good.

Dialogue number 2

Matthew:	I would tell him not to take any notice of people that crack jokes about him.
Maines:	Right. Can you explain that a bit to me, what happens when somebody cracks a joke?
Matthew:	Normally he just goes after them and starts pushing and punching.
Maines:	Right. He sometimes takes things that are not meant to be serious too seriously and too personally.
Matthew:	Yes.
Maines:	So how would you remind him or help him not worry about that too much?
Matthew:	Just to put it away and tell them to think about things that have happened to them in the past.

Matthew's last statement is slightly unclear, but it is supportive of Alex, and the intention is to try to find a solution rather than meeting him head on (which is probably what has happened in the past).

Meeting 2: monitoring progress, giving praise and encouragement

The purpose of this meeting was to carry out a maintenance check: to get feedback from circle members, to help them modify their plans if they did not seem to be working, or to give reassurance or encouragement. A major purpose in touching base was to keep the momentum going.

> **Comment**: Maintaining the programme, giving pats on the back and reassuring students that what they are doing is good even if they do not see the results immediately are all part of the hidden but essential work in setting up such a programme.

Meeting 3: reflecting on the work, planning the final meeting

The group had been working for three weeks at this point. Maines expressed amazement at the pupils' insights and their commitment towards Alex. Two themes emerged from the meeting:

- The group members stated they had a different view of Alex and they felt they now understood him better.
- They felt that he might be blaming himself for his mother's illness.

The meeting closed with a decision to invite Alex to the next and final meeting.

Comment: The group has obviously learnt through their experiences. As their efforts have met with a positive response from Alex, they have seen, first, that they have the power to change things and, second, that it is better not to have quick, angry responses to all situations but to learn to reserve judgement and give others a chance.

Meeting 4: talking with Alex, planning the celebration, closing the Circle of Friends

The last step acknowledged the circle's efforts and achievements. During this final meeting, Maines acted as facilitator and allowed the individuals from the circle to express what they had done to help or support Alex. They decided (at Maines's instigation) to celebrate their achievements by giving certificates to those who had participated and (at their own instigation) that these should be presented by Alex. The principal of the school was invited to say a few words and to call out the names of the children in the circle so that Alex could present their certificates.

They chose to have the celebration in the classroom to reinvolve the whole class who had been part of setting up the circle, and to include any who had felt left out. The occasion turned into a party, with drinks and biscuits. Maines felt that this had a very positive effect and that the whole class took ownership of the process.

I particularly liked the understated way, throughout this and other meetings, in which Maines was able to encourage change while allowing the participants to retain their personal power. Alex was never patronized or demeaned.

Comment: This last meeting is very important because it both values the children's contributions and reinforces the positive behaviour the circle has been exhibiting. (Remember that some of these children had been meeting Alex's aggression head on with their own.) It also gives Alex the opportunity to see that he has truly been supported, and it acknowledges that his peers think he is worth it. The facilitator must bring things to a close when the goals have been achieved, rather than letting the programme drift on and peter out.

Part three: follow-up and evaluation

The final meeting coincided with the breakup of this class before its move to secondary school. Consequently, no follow-up was done. Maines suggests that, if circumstances were different, if it were a younger class or had this happened at an earlier point in the year, then they might have continued for longer, changed some of the group members and followed up at a later date.

Maines's evaluation is a reflection of Alex's circumstances and the effect of the Circle of Friends method. She points out, first, that Alex was a pupil who had been referred because of difficult behaviour before his mother's health worries arose and, second, that his anxiety caused his behaviour to deteriorate and made it harder for him to be at school.

Maines observed that the Circle of Friends initiative brought about an improvement in Alex's behaviour for two reasons:

1. Alex was clearly and genuinely supported by his circle of friends.
2. The circle's expectations changed: they wished for, looked for and reinforced improvement as they felt a sense of ownership towards the Circle of Friends and all it entailed.

Like other strategies and interventions developed by Maines and Robinson, a Circle of Friends is straightforward, well considered and effective. I recommend this programme as a useful tool, particularly for children in the primary and intermediate sectors.

Reference

Maines, B. and Robinson, G. (1998) *All for Alex: A Circle of Friends*. Video and booklet. Bristol: Lucky Duck Publishing.

CHAPTER 18

THE PIKAS METHOD OF SHARED CONCERN

Introduction: tackling the hard with the soft

When I visited the Tayside Anti-Bullying Initiative late in 1995, I was impressed by the seriousness with which the anti-bullying team tackled the problem of bullying in local schools. In the UK during the early and mid-1990s, as well as a major commitment from the Scottish Council for Research in Education, various local authorities spent money developing resource kits to deal with bullying. Walsall, Islington, Strathclyde and Cardiff are notable for their efforts. None, however, had created a full-time team to combat bullying (comprising teachers, social workers and psychologists) as was the case with the Dundee-based Tayside initiative.

In setting up anti-bullying initiatives to meet the varying needs of schools in their catchment area, the team had examined a number of schemes and chose to use the Pikas Method of Shared Concern. As with the Support Group Method, this programme tries to find practical solutions to break dysfunctional patterns, and provides an opportunity for those committing antisocial acts to come up with prosocial alternatives. The most hard-nosed opponents of such feelings approaches think that it is important to make people see the error of their ways by giving programmes a consequences or punishment base; they believe that, particularly with tough cases, a 'touchy-feely' approach will not work. But members of the Tayside team whom I interviewed in December 1995, and Alison Duncan (1994) in her report of the use of the Pikas Method of Shared Concern in Dundee, argue that this method was very successful, even with very difficult cases. The method has also been used successfully by schools in Australia (Rigby, 1996) and in Scandinavia (Björkqvist and Osterman, 1999), among other places.

The foundations of the Method of Shared Concern

Anatol Pikas's Method of Shared Concern has been widely applauded as an effective way of dealing with bullying behaviour. Several anti-bullying scholars have written about it. Sharp and Smith (1994), Duncan (1994), Fuller and King (1995) and Rigby (1996) have provided useful information about the method and its applications, and this information is distilled here.

Professor Pikas, a psychologist formerly in the Education Department of Uppsala University, Sweden, devised this method to deal with the bullying of one or more children by a group of children (a type of bullying referred to in Scandinavia as mobbing). According to Pikas (1989: 93), the concept of the 'mob' is important in finding a solution, because the thoughts and feelings of the group are simpler than those of any of its individual members, and the members of a group strive towards what he calls a 'common psychological denominator', or a collective mind.

This means that the actions of the group are predictable so, when bullying is involved, it is possible to handle the situation and to find a solution.

Pikas has constantly refined his method (see Pikas, 2002); and in 2009 he drew attention to the way it can be used to prompt bullies to cooperate trustingly with the adult counsellor (whom Pikas calls a therapist), and to reveal clandestine bullying by the particular use of class discussions with teenagers (see his website, http://www.pikas.se/scm)

How it works

Step 1: the first meetings

The procedure

When a decision has been made to address bullying (either through self-reporting or referral), then it is important to initiate the procedure straight away. Pikas insists that his procedures be followed strictly because he has created a clearly mapped out series of interrelated steps that cause subtle changes, creating an emotional climate designed to produce results.

During the first step, the counsellor speaks with the ringleader and then with each of the other suspected mobbers (usually three to six) for 10 to 20 minutes each. These meetings should be held consecutively and all at the same time so that the individuals involved cannot converse with each other. It is important not to interview the victim(s) before all the bullies have been interviewed so they cannot assume that the victim has told tales.

The counsellor should be non-threatening and make it clear that there is no intention to attribute blame. He or she should stress that the victim is being made miserable by the bullying. Each of the bullies is asked how things could be made better for the victim. The counsellor sits opposite the child being interviewed so that their eyes are at the same level and they are communicating on equal terms, and always makes sure that eye contact is maintained.

The process

The counsellor doing the interviewing starts.

1. 'I would like to talk to you because I've heard you've been mean to Justin/Julia.'

This is an assertive statement of fact. It is not accusatory and is intended to get to the bottom of things. It is said with empathy and no anger.

2. 'What do you know about it?'

The second question is intended to get the bully to talk about the bullying. Most people will talk freely at this point. If, after several attempts to initiate a conversation there is no movement, then the counsellor should finish the session.

> **Comment**: This is the most important part of the proceedings. It aims to help the bully take responsibility without feeling shame or resentment towards the victim. Pikas says that it is vital at this point to reinforce the person's answers, and to ask further questions so that the process moves towards a predetermined goal of shared concern.

This sharing underlies the interaction: a problem of bullying has been identified and it should be solved together. The counsellor must proceed with an expectation that the two of them can construct a solution. In doing this, the counsellor models empathy and support but is not too friendly (or patronizing).

At this stage, barriers to success may appear that will need to be removed to hasten the process. Sharp and Smith (1994) suggest that the following may occur:

- The child has no idea of any solutions. If a child genuinely cannot come up with solutions, the adult can suggest some. It is important not to hurry the child.
- The child is uncooperative. It is best not to try to force a child, but to be silent and wait. If there is no response after a reasonable time, the counsellor could say, 'We don't seem to have anything to discuss today. You can go back to class.' This usually makes the child want to talk.
- An impractical or impossible solution is provided. If this happens, the counsellor should not respond negatively but ask, 'Do you think that would stop the bullying?' and then move towards other solutions.
- Involving others in the solution. If it is suggested that the solution lies with another person, for example, the ringleader, then it is important to emphasize that the person being interviewed must provide the solution. The counsellor could say, 'I was thinking more about something you could do.'

- There is a complaint about the provocative behaviour of the victim. Any discussion of the bullying at this stage is helpful so it is important to encourage talking and to listen patiently. Some of the information that emerges may aid the process of finding a solution for provocative and passive victims. It is then essential to return to the fact that the pupil being bullied is having a hard time and that this is the issue that must be resolved. The counsellor could say, 'Thank you for this extra information. Julia is feeling very sad and miserable because of being bullied. What can you do to change this?'

There is no need either to blame or to get the absolute truth: the focus is on solving the bullying problem.

3. 'All right, we've talked long enough. Let's move on.'

When the counsellor has enough information, it is important to move things along pleasantly and clearly. If the discussion has been difficult and there is no sense that any progress has been made, this can be a crucial point in the proceedings. This statement underlines the fact that the point of the intervention is to find a solution, not to blame or punish.

> **Comment**: By now, there is enough information about the bullying to focus on a solution. There is a sense of relief and a reduction of tension when it becomes clear that no hidden blame or punishment waits around the corner.

4. 'What can you do? What do you suggest?'

It is at this stage that the discussion culminates in the bullying child making a suggestion about how to proceed. This may take the form of a solution or a promise to stop bullying.

5. 'That's good. We'll meet again in a week, then you can tell me how you've been getting on.'

The final statement is meant to reinforce the relationship that has been established between the counsellor and the student, and the fact that they are working together to find a solution to the bullying. The counsellor says goodbye and the student returns to class. The counsellor then sees the other members of the bullying group one by one.

> **Comment**: The last stage of the first meeting emphasizes the gravity of the effects of the bullying on the victim, rather than focusing on blaming or punishing. The perpetrator(s) and supporter(s) of bullying are given the opportunity to act positively, to speak as individuals and to reclaim their personal power. In this way, the power of the 'mob' is broken and the 'common psychological denominator' of the group

is undermined. Although it has not been stated, the fact that the ringleader has been taken out of the class will have indicated that something is afoot. That person's return to class gives two messages: to their fellow mobbers, 'It's OK, I've had to deal with this and so will you', and to the victim of bullying, 'Maybe I'm going to be nicer to you'. The removal of punishment takes away the likelihood of retaliation, and tension and aggression are defused.

Step 2: meeting with the victim

Immediately after the first series of meetings, the person who has been bullied is interviewed and encouraged to talk about the bullying. Pikas states that, in his experience, victims are not afraid to speak. This meeting allows the counsellor to establish whether the person being victimized is a passive or a provocative victim, as solving the problem differs with the type of victim, as well as with each individual.

Comment: If someone provokes the bullying, this does not mean that the bullying is excusable, but it does mean that their behaviour is a contributory factor. This needs to be acknowledged assertively, and without the counsellor attributing blame or judgement. The provocative victim can make suggestions about how they can improve things. For a passive victim, the counsellor proceeds in a more fully supportive fashion.

Step 3: meeting with the individuals again

A series of further meetings is held to meet individually with students to see how things are going. Often, the student has not done exactly what was agreed to in the first meeting but he or she has usually left the victim alone. If this is not the case, then the counsellor will need to go through the procedure again in order to invoke a commitment from the student to do what was agreed. The counsellor and the student should decide to meet again to see what progress has been made. About a week later, the talks are repeated, either with the individuals involved in the bullying or with the group as a whole.

Comment: Because this method relies on follow-through, the school must be committed to dealing with bullying. The students can process what is happening, to think and to realign how they will act over a period of time. They are also given an opportunity to correct their behaviour without being punished.

Step 4: the group meeting

When it is clear that the bullying group have changed their behaviour, they must meet the counsellor and consolidate their changed behaviour. It is critical for them to discuss the person being bullied and to make positive comments about him or her. When it feels safe, the victim(s) should be invited to enter. The chairs should be in a circle and the victimized child must be able to come in and sit down without having to run the gauntlet (it is probably best that she sits next to the counsellor).

The group should be praised for having created a positive situation out of a negative one. If positive statements have been made about the victim, the students who made them should be asked to repeat them.

> **Comment**: Even if there has been a successful resolution, this meeting is necessary, for several reasons. It rounds things off and tries to reintegrate those who have been bullied safely into the group. It is also important to acknowledge that a bullying situation has been turned around. The counsellor can ask what can be done to make the new dynamic a long-term one, and enlist both ideas and commitment from the group, with the victim being equally involved in this venture.

Two case studies

The following two case studies of the Pikas Method of Shared Concern are taken from the experiences of two teachers from Tayside, Scotland, after they had been trained in the method by Professor Pikas (Duncan, 1994). These examples show how the method works in practice and indicate that it is effective when accompanied by the creative and practical problem-solving skills of experienced teachers and counsellors.

A primary school case study

A P4 pupil (7 to 8 years old) named Nicola was brought into the school by her mother one morning because of a series of bullying incidents to which she had been subjected. These included physical aggression and name-calling, both at school and outside by a group of similar-age children consisting of three boys and a girl (the ringleader). Nicola's mother thought her daughter was being victimized because she was different from the other children – she was well dressed, well cared for, and regularly went on outings and on holiday with her family. Nicola could be described as a passive victim.

Her teacher said that, as a result of hearing about the bullying, she followed the Shared Concern Approach by:

- talking individually with those doing the bullying;
- talking with Nicola, the victim of bullying;
- talking with those doing the bullying in a group;
- talking with those doing the bullying and the victim of the bullying together.

She was surprised how quickly the children's responses changed afterwards.

Although they were young and had difficulty saying why they had bullied, they established empathy with the victim very easily. Apparently, a reason for the bullying was their envy of Nicola's more stable home background.

At the meeting between the bullies and Nicola, she was understandably apprehensive, but those who had bullied put forward their suggestions for solving the problem and were very pleased to be part of the solution. The meeting finished amicably. The teacher thought their age made these children open to changing their ways; she felt older children might be more cynical. Of the method, the teacher says:

> Professor Pikas' Shared Concern Method has much to offer primary schools. The non-authoritarian, patient approach of the therapist pays dividends in offering bullies shared responsibility in resolving problems and my limited experience of this method to date has been positive and rewarding. (Duncan, 1994: 8)

A secondary school case study

Caroline went to the assistant head teacher (AHT) of her secondary school to complain about being bullied by a group of former friends (see Duncan, 1994). She related a recent scene in the canteen when she was kicked, punched and whispered about, and had a label placed on her back with an insulting name written on it, which she wore for a long time before realizing it was there. When Caroline was picked on, she received support from her friend Pauline.

Both girls then became the target of the bullies and were victimized: they were called names, cold-shouldered, ignored and in the public areas of the school – the corridors, the canteen, the playground – were jostled and pushed. Both girls were so distressed they told their parents what was happening.

Caroline's parents wanted the situation handled. She had been picked on at primary school and some of the same girls were teasing her again. Pauline's parents asked her older sister, a pupil at the school, to defend her, and they threatened to remove Pauline from the school if the bullying was not handled.

The AHT listened first to Caroline and then to Pauline and comforted them. She then called a meeting of all the girls to attempt a conciliation. Caroline's mother arrived uninvited as she did not want her daughter to be unsupported amid her tormentors. The result was an unproductive meeting that ended with bad feeling. Caroline's parents were angry with the school and wanted the bullies punished.

On the following Monday and between classes, Caroline was kicked and punched by a member of the bullying group. As a result, the AHT asked an outside counsellor who had been trained in the Pikas Method to try to sort things out.

The counsellor felt her first task was to get the girls' parents to agree to the use of the method. She explained to them that the purpose was to help the girls to work things out between themselves. The parents of the victims reluctantly gave their permission for the intervention to go ahead.

Step 1: the first meetings

The bullies and victims were interviewed separately. The final student to be interviewed was Jenny, who was identified as the primary bully. When she arrived in the counsellor's room, she appeared nervous, was uncommunicative and said that everything was OK. With the counsellor's gentle probing, she admitted that recently Caroline had been having a hard time and seemed upset. She avoided saying why. (The counsellor suggested to Jenny at this point that it might be because Caroline was being left out. In retrospect, the counsellor decided that she probably should have followed Pikas's script and not prompted Jenny.)

Jenny latched on to this suggestion and said that Caroline was feeling left out because she had recently moved to a different part of town and was being given much less freedom than her peers.

At this point, the counsellor decided to have a group meeting the following day rather than waiting a week, as is suggested by Pikas. She did this for two reasons: she was responding to the sense of urgency surrounding the case, and she came away sensing that Jenny would 'crow' to her friends about pulling the wool over the counsellor's eyes. (In retrospect, she realized that missing out this 'stand-down' period was a mistake.)

Step 2: the group meeting

As she anticipated that a lot of mediation would be required, the counsellor went straight to the group meeting rather than meeting the bullying group first. If she had met with the bullying group first, she could have reinforced and consolidated the positive sense of shared concern. Instead, it was immediately apparent that there was an oppositional feeling in the meeting, with a lot of giggling and sneering. (She later said this short-cut was another mistake.)

The bullying group, with Emma (rather than Jenny) as their articulate spokesperson, told of the group's keenness to move towards a solution. Caroline and Pauline, however, were distrustful and repeatedly referred to the hurt the bullies had caused them. In response, Emma defended the group and provided counter-arguments against the alliance of Caroline, Pauline and Pauline's older sister. As the arguing continued and it was clear that Pauline and Caroline were becoming angry, distressed and distrustful, it was decided to call a halt.

Trying to salvage the situation, the counsellor suggested that they would all meet again soon when they felt fresher and keener. She suggested optimistically that this meeting had not been a failure, but had given everyone the opportunity to say how they felt. She also told the group that they could meet as many times as required to come to a resolution.

When the bullying group departed, the counsellor spent an hour with Caroline and Pauline and told them that when they were feeling ready she would arrange another meeting with the bullying girls to try to find a solution. A major issue that emerged from the post-meeting discussion was the prominence in Caroline and Pauline's thinking of their parents' anger, which was acting as a barrier to progress.

An unusual thing then occurred. Led by Emma, those who had done the bullying asked for a meeting with the counsellor. She reassured them that her original intention of finding a resolution remained intact; it was not her intention to get revenge for Pauline and Caroline but to work out a way for them all at least to coexist.

The process was marred by messages from both Caroline and Pauline that their parents would not allow them to meet with the bullies again. After 10 days of gentle persuasion and a letter home to their parents, Caroline and Pauline agreed to attend a further meeting with the girls who had bullied them. (The counsellor noted that it was good to listen to parents' advice but it was Caroline and Pauline who had to live with those girls every day at school.)

This meeting was more productive and provided a resolution to the bullying problem. The mood was generally positive, although Pauline and Caroline were distrustful. The counsellor made it clear that they did not have to be friendly with their former tormentors, but merely had to agree to be tolerant and to develop a working relationship. Fine details were discussed, such as how to greet and reply to each other. The group agreed to meet a week later.

Step 3: the follow-up meeting

When the whole group met the following week, they all agreed that the bullying had stopped after the first meeting. Discussion was brief but positive, with progress reported by all. Another group meeting was arranged after the impending holidays. In the meantime, the counsellor met Pauline and Caroline three more times and both reported that everything was OK.

The counsellor stated that she knew this case would be hard and complex, that she had spent approximately five hours spread over several weeks on it and that six months after the intervention the girls were getting along fine.

A comment on this case study

We learn by our mistakes, and I applaud Alison Duncan's honest description of this case study. What Pikas says in his description of the Method of Shared Concern is that the person applying the method must be calm, clear and in charge. In this case, the sense of urgency meant that the procedures were changed. The counsellor did not, therefore, follow Pikas's procedure and allow her initial meeting with bullies and victims to take effect over the following week.

Although there were alterations to the prescribed formula and problems with the various stages, the counsellor persevered. Eventually, the bullying stopped and an unhealthy interaction pattern between this group of girls was halted.

Note:

Anatol Pikas stresses that he is available to provide free workshops about the Shared

Concern Method. For contact, write to anatol@pikas.se, and refer to his website (www.pikas/.se/Scm/).

References

Björkqvist, K. and Osterman, K. (1999) 'Finland', in P.K. Smith, Y. Morita, J. Junger-Tas, D. Olweus, R. Catalano and P. Slee (eds), *The Nature of School Bullying: A Cross-national Perspective*. London: Routledge.

Duncan, A. (1994) 'Resolving group bullying in schools. Anatol Pikas' Shared Concern Method in Tayside's experience 1993–94', unpublished paper, Tayside Regional Council, Dundee.

Fuller, A. and King, V. (1995) *Stop Bullying!* Melbourne: Mental Health Foundation of Victoria.

Pikas, A. (1989) 'The common concern method for the treatment of mobbing', in E. Munthe and E. Roland (eds), *Bullying: An International Perspective*. London: David Fulton.

Pikas, A. (2002) 'New developments of the Shared Concern Method', *School Psychology International*, 23(3): 307–26. (www.pikas.se/SCm/Anatol_SchPs_Inter2002.pdf).

Rigby, K. (1996) *Bullying in Schools and What To Do About It*. Melbourne: Australian Council for Educational Research.

Sharp, S. and Smith, P.K. (eds) (1994) *Tackling Bullying in Your Schools: A Practical Handbook for Teachers*. London and New York: Routledge.

CHAPTER 19

CPR: COLLABORATIVE PROBLEM-SOLVING AND RESOLUTION

Introduction: foundations of the CPR process

Collaborative problem-solving and resolution (CPR) is a student-centred dispute resolution process developed to address bullying problems and to create constructive, immediate and long-term solutions.

In its design and processes, CPR combines elements of collaborative law, counselling skills, restorative justice and critical professional practice, within a socio-ecological framework.

Collaborative law

Collaborative law is a non-adversarial approach to settling disputes, especially in family law. It was conceptualized by Minnesota lawyer Phil Webb in the 1990s and developed further by Pauline Tessler (Tessler, 2009). Collaborative law is client-centred and entails cooperation between both parties, full disclosure of facts and an intention to reach a settlement that is fair, transparent and acceptable to both parties. Besides having legal representation, each client has a coach to assist making the case, to support them through the stages of the process, to ensure all relevant information is brought to the table, and to make certain that both sides are treated respectfully and that the principles of natural justice are adhered to.

Success depends upon each side listening fully and taking in the other side's perspective, arguments and experience. If the process has been transparent and fair, the case has been explored fully and the parties involved are satisfied that the outcome is mutually beneficial, then the foundations for resolution are established.

Counselling skills

The CPR process uses adult mentors rather than coaches. Usually, they are psychologists or counsellors with the training, skills and experience to take on this role. Teachers who have excellent interpersonal skills can be trained as CPR mentors. Counselling skills are based upon having both a useful framework within which to work and the ability to respond creatively to confrontation and challenge.

Restorative justice

Criminal acts can be devastating and have far-reaching effects for victims, their families and their communities. Restorative justice is a process developed to address these effects; to assist perpetrators to take responsibility for their acts; and to restore balance in the lives of victims, families and communities. Restorative justice can also usefully be applied to bullying.

The restorative justice component of CPR seeks to create a resolution that constructively restores the balance that bullying purposely disrupts. In this process, the victim's voice needs to be heard clearly and the pain and short- and long-term effects of bullying made clear to the perpetrator. The bullying needs to be acknowledged, responsibility accepted and amends made. The intention is not to punish and humiliate but to teach about effects, feelings, consequences and responsibility.

Critical professional practice

When bullying occurs, it is important first to stop it but then to deal with the underlying issues and the needs of the participants, both victim and bully. There are many reasons why someone may bully, and the repercussions of bullying are far-reaching. This wider context needs to be considered or it will be only the symptoms – the fire currently alight, not the underground inferno that feeds it – that are addressed.

Using our experiences and critical skills to find fair and constructive solutions is central to the CPR process. As teachers, counsellors and psychologists, we bring a variety of personal skills and insights to cases we deal with. Being comfortable as a professional, gathering and sifting as much information as possible, suspending judgement and retaining our humanity are crucial to being an effective practitioner.

Working within a socio-ecological framework

The ripple effect, the downward spirals and the bullying triangle (see Chapter 3) are models that demonstrate the bullying dynamic and its deep and wide-ranging effects. The bullying dynamic does not occur in isolation. Collaborative problem-solving and resolution addresses this dynamic and is informed by the underlying issues and wide-ranging effects of bullying upon the social networks in and beyond the school.

Carrying out a CPR process has an immediate effect upon the bullying relationship in question. Although largely the domain of the students involved, this relationship also exists within the fabric of the school's culture. When it is dealt with constructively and ecologically, the social health and overall wellbeing of the school are enhanced.

Participants and their roles

The following personnel are involved in CPR:

- school principal;
- head of school discipline (HSD);
- CPR mentors;
- student participants.

In order for the process to work, it is crucial that those involved are clear about their roles and the structures and processes they will follow.

School principal

The principal is the overall head of the school and may be the first point of contact when a concerned parent, teacher or student reports bullying. Such reports are then referred to the head of school discipline (often a deputy principal).

Head of school discipline

The HSD deals with school bullying and is in charge of CPR processes.

> **Comment**: The role of the HSD is formal and symbolic, and represents 'the voice' of the school. In dealing with the students, the HSD is pleasant but authoritative. If agreements are broken, the case will be referred back to the HSD for enforcement; if the process does not work, the HSD will initiate the next stage of the school's anti-bullying policy.

CPR mentors

The CPR mentors administer and run the process. The bullied person and the perpetrator each have a mentor. The responsibilities of the mentors are as follows.

Administration

- Developing and running a student-centred process.
- Educating their assigned students about the process.
- Encouraging transparency and sharing of information and viewpoints.

- Being knowledgeable and clear about school rules and regulations and any relevant legal issues.
- Being the interface between the school and students in the process.
- Discouraging an adversarial and encouraging a collaborative approach.
- Setting agendas for meetings and explaining procedures.
- Developing a process for record-keeping.
- Preparing for and conducting constructive one-to-one meetings with their assigned students and preparing for and participating supportively in four-person meetings with the other student and mentor.
- Meeting prior to or after a four-person meeting with the other mentor in order to discuss an appropriate way forward, and being transparent with the student about the nature and content of these discussions.
- Cooperating with the co-mentor to facilitate a process that leads to a fair and mutually acceptable resolution.
- Overseeing that appropriate confidentiality is maintained.

Support, advice, trust

- Acting professionally and ethically in the best interests of the mentored student and of the other parties involved.
- Preparing their student-clients for each step.
- Advising and counselling the mentored student about different views and options that may arise.
- Working with the student to establish the facts of the case and to assist the student to state clearly their perspective and to fully understand that of the other side.
- Conducting a safe process.
- Suggesting possible and likely outcomes.
- Building a relationship of trust and rapport with the mentored student.

Comment: The mentors are central to the success of the CPR process as they take their assigned students through it. Building and maintaining trust with the students is crucial to the process.

Student participants

The student participants are:

- the bullied person;
- the perpetrator of the bullying; and, sometimes,
- the onlookers.

The CPR process is prepared and guided by the mentors but is designed to bring out the student participants' voices: it is student centred. Its first aim is to arrive at a clear understanding of the events and then of the effects of the bullying.

If the bully agrees to stop bullying, then the issue can be resolved there and then and an agreement signed to this effect. If the major contributors to the bullying do not show remorse or agree to cease bullying, then students identified as having taken part in the bullying or urging it along may also need to be interviewed by the mentors. When the major bullying energy is neutralized, the wider peer group dynamic is usually neutralized as well.

A case study using the seven steps of CPR: Belinda is bullying Alicia

Background information

This case study is based on real events that occurred in an American school. Its purpose is to show how the steps of the CPR process are organized and put into practice, with the aim of finding an agreed solution towards which the students are guided, first by the school head of discipline and primarily by their mentors.

Mount Joy School for the Arts is a small school (426 students) with both junior and high school sections. Teachers are aware that bullying has been a difficult and recurrent school problem and that it needs to be handled more effectively. The Support Group Method (see Chapter 16) was chosen to address bullying in the elementary and lower senior areas, but several cases of bullying have proven difficult to solve, especially those occurring in the middle and upper high school. The school decides to adopt the CPR process for such cases. The school's counselling team administers CPR and consists of half-time school psychologist Maria, and Cathy who is the school's guidance counsellor and drama teacher.

Step 1: establishing whether this case of bullying is suitable for a CPR process

Bullying is reported

Alicia's mother tells a former class-teacher that her daughter is very distressed and has recently been missing school because she feels intimidated and bullied by Belinda, a recent arrival.

An investigation is undertaken by the HSD

The case is referred to the principal, and to John, the HSD. He initiates an investigation by talking to Alicia's mother, Alicia's teacher and other staff at the school. He forms a picture of what may be happening.

Alicia is 13 and is in her first year of high school. She transferred to the school four years earlier, largely because she had been severely bullied at her previous school. Although that school had attempted to deal with the problem, Alicia's parents decided to remove her. Because she is artistically talented, she was accepted at Mount Joy. Since being there, Alice has made several friends and become best friends with Sara. Belinda arrived at the beginning of the current school year (three months ago) and immediately got into conflict with several girls in her class. This quickly escalated into an ongoing campaign of aggression focused on her classmate, Alicia. She has teased her cruelly and made particular fun of her early physical development; she has also gradually undermined Alicia's relationship with Sara, who has now become Belinda's best friend. Since Belinda's arrival, Alicia has gradually reverted from being happy and outgoing back to being sad and withdrawn as she was when she first arrived at the school. Some of the staff are concerned that Alicia's inability to stand up to Belinda is making her more and more vulnerable. They are worried about her mental health. They are concerned about Belinda as well, and her behavioural indications of disturbance and unhappiness. Although the evidence of wrongdoing is clear, the school considers it better to find a solution than to punish Belinda.

Belinda's parents argued strongly for her to come to Mount Joy. She is both very intelligent and extremely artistic, and they felt that attending this highly regarded school of the arts would be the best thing that could happen to their precocious daughter. Belinda had been excluded twice from previous elementary schools but, based on their past successes with talented but difficult children, the teachers felt that they would prove equal to any problems she brought with her.

A decision is made about CPR's suitability for the case under consideration

The HSD discusses the case with the guidance team and they feel very concerned for Alicia. They question whether, based on her history, the school made a good decision in admitting Belinda. On the other hand, they are aware that Belinda is intellectually gifted, artistically talented and is liked by her teachers. Their first priority is to stop the bullying and they feel that, if done effectively, a CPR process could find a constructive solution to the problem Belinda has created. The HSD informs both sets of parents of the school's decision to initiate a CPR process to deal with the bullying. He also explains what the process entails.

Step 2: initiating a CPR process

Appointing CPR mentors

In anticipation that CPR will be used, the HSD has asked Cathy and Maria if they will respectively be Alicia and Belinda's mentors. He shares his thinking with Cathy that as both a counsellor and drama teacher with a talent for drawing out shy students, she may be very helpful as Alicia's mentor. Maria has a reputation for being clear, fair and kind, and well able to handle difficult students. She is regarded as a good choice to mentor Belinda.

HSD and mentors meet with the victim of bullying

John, Cathy and Maria meet with Alicia. John explains to Alicia that he has heard she is being bullied and left out and that Belinda is making her life difficult. He states that he has decided to initiate a CPR process to try to solve the problem, that her participation in the process is crucial and that, if she agrees to take part, he will make certain she is safe and treated respectfully. He briefly discusses how CPR works and asks how she feels about participating. She is subdued but agrees to take part, signing a document that outlines the contract to participate fully in terms of the spirit and specifics of the process.

HSD and mentors meet with the perpetrator of the bullying

With the two mentors present, John then talks with Belinda. He states that since arriving at the school, she has been doing very well academically and seems to have a good future there. He then adds that he has investigated claims of bullying made against her and would like to hear her side. Although no names have been mentioned, she immediately refers to Alicia, saying she is pathetic and that she deserves what comes to her. John informs Belinda that he intends to initiate a CPR process and is about to tell her about it when she angrily bursts out that she has not done anything wrong and should not have to go through any process. She walks out and slams the door. John then telephones Belinda's mother to explain what has happened.

Later that day, Belinda's father arrives at the HSD's office with a red-eyed daughter. He says he has talked with her and that she agrees to take part in the CPR process. Belinda snaps back that she will not. John explains that the process is intended to find a constructive solution that works for both Belinda and Alicia. Furthermore, it only works when both parties are committed to finding a solution. He explains that if the CPR process is either not undertaken or breaks down, the next step in the school's bullying policy is to consider excluding Belinda. He suggests Belinda has a cooling-off period for two days to decide what she wants to do. During this time, she is to have no contact with Alicia.

Belinda comes back the next day, apologizes for her behaviour and says that she wishes to participate in the CPR process. Like Alicia, she signs a contract of cooperation.

> **Comment**: Step 2 is designed to introduce students to CPR and to get their agreement to participate in and sign up to it. They are introduced to their mentors, and the distinction is made between the HSD's role in supporting the school's authority and the application of its anti-bullying policy, and the mentors' role in supporting the students and taking them through the CPR process.

Step 3: one-to-one meetings

Mentors speak together before meeting their assigned students (1 hour)

> **Purpose**: Preparation for meeting individual students for the first time.

The mentors are responsible for jointly conducting the process, for keeping a record of what happens and for setting agendas for each of the meetings. This initial meeting focuses on sharing the information they have to date and deciding who will do what organizationally. Cathy and Maria decide to share the agenda-setting and to each keep notes of all meetings.

Agenda for first student and mentor meeting

1. Introductions (mentor and student introduce themselves)
2. How the CPR process works (mentor)
3. The role of the mentor (mentor provides the details and student reflects it back)
4. The nature and extent of the bullying (student provides this information and mentor reflects it back)
5. The agenda for the next meeting (student and mentor)

Cathy and Maria agree to follow normal procedure for their first one-to-one meeting: introducing themselves, providing information about how the process works and what their roles are, and gathering information from the girls about their interpretation of the bullying to date. They will also ask their respective students to write one or two pages about the purpose of CPR, how it works and their perspective of the bullying situation. This will constitute the minutes of the meeting, which the students will present verbally and in writing to their mentors at the second one-to-one meetings.

First one-to-one meeting between mentors and their assigned students (1 hour)

Purpose: Generating information, introducing students gently to the process and establishing trust.

Alicia and Cathy

Although initially cautious, Alicia had become enthusiastic about CPR. When she meets Cathy, however, she seems 'down'. She says that, if left alone, things will probably work themselves out in time. Cathy is puzzled by this, but rather than commenting she changes the subject and talks about the upcoming play she is directing. She suggests there are one or two roles Alicia might be interested in trying out for. She gains Alicia's attention, and then says she does not understand Alicia's first response and asks what has been happening. Alicia hesitates then blurts out that it is just not fair, since the girls in her class heard the school was going to deal with the bullying, they have been treating her as if she has ratted! She thinks Belinda is stirring things up. She feels this is a no-win situation, which makes her want to go and hide.

Cathy agrees this is unfair and says it is probably all the more reason why the case should be handled. She then explains how the process works and underlines that it is non-confrontational and constructive, assuring Alicia she will be safe at all times during the process. She explains CPR as follows: 'I am going to ask you to tell me about the bullying and I will take notes. When you have finished, I will tell you, in my own words, what I think you said and you can then tell me if I got it right. When we've finished I'll tell you what my job as your mentor entails and you will similarly reflect back what I told you. Do you have any questions? OK, let's begin. Tell me about the bullying.'

Alicia's answers are reflected back to her, either verbatim or through paraphrasing.

Cathy asks Alicia to write an overview of CPR; the role that Cathy, as mentor, will play; and a description of the bullying that has occurred.

Belinda and Maria

Maria is aware that Belinda may be defensive and that, although she has agreed to take part, she may resist the process and try to manipulate the others involved and attempt to undermine it. Belinda arrives very troubled and conflicted. Maria explains how the process works and lets Belinda talk. She describes how both her parents have high-profile jobs and have never had time for her; she says that girls like Alicia have it easy – she is pretty, well liked and has found it easy to make friends. She claims she is entitled to take Sara away from Alicia because she is more intelligent and interesting than Alicia and is a far better best friend for Sara.

Maria prompts Belinda to describe what has been happening between her and Alicia, and how she has been treating her. Maria then reflects back to Belinda what she has said and explains her role as mentor.

Maria asks Belinda to create a set of notes to present to her providing an overview of the purpose of CPR; the role that Maria, as mentor, will play; and a description of the bullying that has occurred.

> **Comment**: The first meetings between mentors and students facilitate a full explanation of the purposes of CPR, the role of the mentor, the gathering of in-depth information about the bullying and the start of establishing trust. The mentors' purpose is to gather information accurately and to listen carefully. Both students have strong feelings about what has happened that need to be expressed and explored: the perspectives of each will be different and some probing may be required to establish the truth. It is important to look for the truth about the feelings involved as much as the actual events. What either participant says may lead to other questions, such as: 'How did the bullying start?', 'Once it started, what happened then?', 'Who else was involved?', 'How were they involved?', 'When did it happen?', 'How often?', 'What was the nature of the bullying?', 'Is there anything else you would like to tell me?', 'How did it feel?'
>
> The first one-way meetings are crucial in paving the way for four-way meetings and the continuation of the process.

Follow-up meeting between the mentors (½ to 1 hour)

Purpose: Reflection on first one-to-one meetings with students.

The mentors brief each other on the state of mind of Alicia and Belinda, the details of the bullying and the potential outflow of its effects into the wider social context of the school.

Second one-to-one meetings between mentors and their assigned students (1 to 1½ hours)

Alicia and Cathy

At the second meeting, the bullying is discussed in greater depth. Alicia describes how she has not only lost her best friend but has also been humiliated in front of the whole class. She tells of multiple instances of being made fun of, called names, ridiculed and sidelined.

She says that their teacher, Michael, does not understand girls and has been no help at all. She feels completely unprotected and unsafe in his classroom. Alicia and Cathy talk about how to present their case at the first group meeting.

Maria and Belinda

Belinda says that she has been having trouble since she was little. She is overweight and ugly, unlike Alicia, who she says is gorgeous. She says how she has been able to create a place for herself in the class by making sure the other students ostracize Alicia. She finds it easy to be cruel to Alicia – it makes her feel better, more powerful, more at the centre of things. She also feels sick, angry and anxious if she thinks about what she has been doing.

She mentions that Michael does not understand girls and lets everything get out of hand. She finds him patronizing and stupid, and gets a buzz out of behaving badly in his class.

Comment: The first one-to-one meeting is designed to establish trust, openness and some of the facts; and the second to address all relevant procedures and issues prior to going into the four-way meeting. It is important that mentor and student discuss the bullying and its context in earnest so that, as much as possible, concern and/or difficult issues emerge here rather than unexpectedly in the four-way meeting.

Meeting between mentors before first four-way meeting (½ hour)

Purpose: The major purpose of this meeting is to clarify how the mentors feel they are progressing towards guiding the two students to a resolution, and to prepare for the first four-way meeting.

Cathy and Maria meet and discuss what they have understood to be the root causes and complexion of the bullying. They feel things are going well and that they are prepared for the four-way meeting. They summarize what they know and how each of the students is feeling and behaving. They then set the agenda for the coming meeting.

Agenda for the first four-way meeting

1. Discussion of the rules of engagement: no bad language, no putting down, respect for each other.
2. Discussion of the bullying: starting with the victimized person and followed by the aggressor, each student will describe what happened and will be listened to without interruption. They will reflect back what they hear.
3. The mentors will comment on what has been said, taking into account the information provided: all four participants will discuss the situation.
4. Review of a range of solutions.
5. Discussion of contingency plans: use of time out, termination of the process if disruption is extreme or opting out is chosen by either student.

Comment: It is crucial to the process that all four-way meetings are fully prepared for. Agendas are created and rules and expectations established. The fact-finding and careful listening that have already occurred should reduce the possibility of unexpected issues and outbursts, which will contribute towards the sense of the security for both students. This in turn will create an environment where constructive solutions can be found.

Step 4: the first four-way meeting is held

Students and mentors meet together to discuss the bullying (1 hour)

The air is tense. Before the mentors can open the discussion, Belinda blurts out that their teacher is a man and does not understand what is going on. Alicia angrily mutters, 'Don't blame the teacher'. Belinda shouts back, 'What would you know, you fucking moron'. Alicia cries and so does Belinda.

The two mentors have to improvise in response to the outbursts. They begin to outline the agenda and the rules of engagement. They talk about the process so far and some of what they have learned. Somehow they need to bring the openness of the discussions they have had in the one-to-one meetings into this four-way forum.

Alicia is asked to put her case, encouraged by Cathy. She tentatively turns to Belinda. 'You came here to this school – my home away from home – and you wrecked it for me. It was great before you came. Not only did you make fun of me. You called me a slut and criticized me for being more physically developed than you. I can't help it. I don't flaunt it. It's just what was given to me, and I'm not as clever or creative as you. We all have our talents and the other stuff we can work on, but that's life! The awful thing that I thought I would never recover from was how you tore me down and ripped me apart in front of everyone. I would never have done that to you or anybody else. It was horrible. Why did you do it? It was so cruel.' Through all this, tears are rolling down her cheeks.

Belinda responds. 'So what, you're pathetic. Your parents are so middle class. You have everything you could fucking well want. Life is hard for me. What are you going on about! You got what you deserved! I have nothing. I am nothing – a piece of shit!' And she crumbles and starts to sob.

Cathy and Maria are aware that things are getting out of control but are stopped in midstream. Alicia goes over and touches Belinda's face. Both girls are crying. The mentors quietly watch to see what will happen. In this calmer atmosphere, each is asked to speak again and then to present the perspective of the other. The mentors facilitate a discussion about solutions and ways forward.

> **Comment**: The first four-person meeting is expected to establish boundaries and procedures in which the waters are tested and the discussions and negotiations are begun. It is also meant to establish that this is a fair process whereby all participants will benefit. Crucial to an effective meeting is effective preparation. From the point of view of the victim of bullying, when encountering the perpetrator there may be a build-up of fear and anger. The mentor of this student needs to have prepared the student both emotionally and in terms of the specifics of the case. It is important that steps are taken to ensure that the victim is not re-traumatized in the presence of the bully. The perpetrator of the bullying needs also to have described what has happened and to have become aware of the emotional and social effects as a way of working towards taking responsibility.

Step 5: follow-up to the four-way meeting

One-to-one meetings between mentors and their assigned students (1 hour)

Alicia and Cathy

Alicia says the process is awful. Some progress has been made but she feels frightened and upset. Cathy tells her that she has done very well: Belinda has come some way towards taking responsibility and has had to confront what she has done. They discuss the outcome and what will help heal the deep divisions that have occurred. Alicia says she does not want anything from Belinda – she just wants to get on with her life.

Maria and Belinda

Belinda says she is sorry for repeatedly losing her temper and agrees she was mean to Alicia. She still says Alicia has it easy. Maria points out that Alicia is unhappy and that Belinda has taken away her only friend. They discuss what Belinda should do. She suggests she will say sorry and 'will give Sara back'.

Follow-up meeting between the mentors (½ to 1 hour)

The two mentors agree that they had to improvise more than is desirable in the volatility of the first four-way meeting, but feel that their discussions together as well as their personal skills and the inherent honesty of the two girls have enabled them to establish enough equilibrium for open disclosure and active listening to have occurred. They agree that they will call for time-out if Belinda becomes abusive towards Alicia again.

Step 6: the second four-way meeting is held

The four meet to decide what needs to be done (1 hour)

The agenda is about what options there are for bringing things to a conclusion. Restorative justice is applied.

- Belinda is asked to accept responsibility for the bullying and to think about what she could do to compensate for the pain she has caused Alicia.
- Alicia is asked what she would like to say.

At this second four-way meeting, Alicia is more confident, having challenged Belinda and been coached by Cathy. She says she wants Belinda to make a full apology for having made her life miserable and to promise that she will not bully her again.

Belinda says it will be completely embarrassing and humiliating to apologize but knows that she must. She states that she knows she was wrong to steal Sara away from Alicia and that she can tell Sara to become friends again with Alicia.

Alicia responds that it is not Belinda's job to tell Sara what she should do and that Sara has shown herself to be a poor friend in deserting her anyway; although she will not bear a grudge, she does not want Sara back.

Alicia says again that she wants an apology for the hurt and humiliation she has been subjected to in the face of the whole class. Belinda looks shame-faced and nods her head.

The two students are asked to mirror back each other's perspective on what has happened and the outcomes and options now available. Alicia is forgiving and Belinda is surprised. With their mentors facilitating, they discuss responsibility, consequences and punishment.

Belinda reflects back what she has done, how it has affected Alicia, and how thoughtless and cruel it was. The mentors write up an agreement that Belinda will not bully Alicia again and that Alicia will report it to John if she does so. Both girls sign the agreement.

Mentors stay on to plan for step 7 (1/2 hour)

The mentors discuss what has occurred and are satisfied with the outcome.

Step 7: final meetings are held – closure and issues for follow-up

Closure of the CPR process (third and final four-way meeting) (½ hour)

This has been a difficult case to handle, but important changes have occurred. Each girl is given a certificate of achievement and copies of what they agreed at the last four-way meeting.

Belinda thanks them all for sorting things out. She seems quiet and withdrawn. Alicia appears also to be shy, but when she gathers up her courage she is very articulate and says how much she appreciates the work of Maria, and Cathy in particular. She says that when the process started she hated Belinda all the time: when she saw her she felt physically sick. She does not think they will ever be friends but she does not hate her anymore.

Following Alicia's lead, the girls shake hands and nod to each other. The mentors close the proceedings

Following-up (final one-to-one meetings to discuss any issues needing to be followed up) (½ to 1 hour)

In this case, the follow-up proves to be important for both girls.

Alicia Meets with Cathy

Cathy says that she has two suggestions to make. First, she would like Alicia to audition for one of the major roles in the upcoming play she will be directing. Second, the school has a peer mentoring programme and Cathy knows that Emily, a final-year student who experienced similar bullying to Alicia three years ago, would be willing to become her peer mentor for a term. Alicia agrees to both suggestions.

Belinda Meets with Maria

Maria discovers that Belinda has been cutting herself and knows that, far from being brash and confident as she pretends to be, she is very vulnerable. Maria is very concerned about her and meets with her parents. She then makes a psychiatric referral to a colleague who is well regarded for her excellent work with disturbed teenage girls. Maria also suggests that she will also support Belinda at school by meeting with her once a week.

Final meeting between mentors (up to 1 hour)

The mentors decide that the case raises two issues that the school needs to consider:

1. Although it was generous of the school to allow Belinda to enrol, nothing had been done to prepare for her arrival. Clearly, her expulsion from two primary schools indicated a major problem. As a consequence of her admission, a pupil who was vulnerable because of previous bullying was exposed to particularly damaging bullying in an unsafe environment.

2. In addition, both girls commented that their male class teacher responded well to the boys in his class but did not know how to deal with teenage girls: as a result, the dynamics of bullying among girls in the class were neither contained nor addressed by him.

No answers to these issues were immediately available, but the school had been given an opportunity to develop a process of self-examination and follow-up.

> **Comment**: The CPR process is designed, first, to deal with bullying, but second it enables other issues to be addressed that may affect the entire school community and culture.

Reference

Tessler, Pauline (2009) *Collaborative Law, Second Edition: Achieving Effective Resolution without Litigation.* Chicago, IL: American Bar Association.

PART 5

FOLLOW-UP AND CONCLUSION

CHAPTER 20

FOLLOW-UP AND CONCLUSION

For a person who has been bullied, perhaps quite seriously, there are no miracle cures. But it is clear that anything that can be done to increase personal confidence in an environment of social health will help begin a process of healing and growth. As an adjunct to anti-bullying programmes, schools can promote strategies that will enhance social health – strategies such as assertiveness training, anger management, and self-defence and martial arts.

Assertiveness training

Assertiveness training is based on an assumption that the dynamics in relationships can be changed by developing strategies that will empower the protagonists. Passive or aggressive individuals can learn how to be assertive, and those who like to rescue others can learn to be supportive, which allows the relationships to remain equal.

Bullying is a dynamic rather than a static process. Rather than there being bullies, victims and bystanders trapped in their roles, an event occurs in which the roles are assumed and are fluid. Assertiveness training, because it focuses on behaviour rather than entrenched roles, can successfully be used to change the dynamics of bullying.

Changing the dynamic: bullying, rescuing and support

When bullying occurs, someone is victimized by a person who is more powerful than they are. The event is usually watched by others. There are at least three types of interaction that can occur: bullying that goes unchecked, bullying that is challenged and halted by an onlooker who rescues the victim, and bullying that is challenged by an onlooker who supports the victim who is then able to stand up to the bully.

The point of assertiveness training is to teach students how to be assertive for themselves and how to be supportive of others. It promotes confidence and an ability to know what is and is not acceptable. It focuses on enhancing personal power and knowing the difference between aggression and assertiveness, and rescuing and being supportive.

> **The scenario: Jasmine, Andrea and Melanie**. It is a rainy lunchtime. The pupils have been let into their class after eating. The teacher is marking assignments at the front of the classroom. At the back of the class, Jasmine is looking through the new illustrated storybook the teacher has put on display. Andrea leaves her group of friends, comes up quietly behind Jasmine and snatches the book away. 'Give that to me', says Andrea. 'Let someone with a brain have a look.' She walks away and adds as she does, 'My God, your shoes are ugly. They are so uncool.' The teacher does not seem to notice.

This is a typical bullying event. The protagonists are Andrea (the bully), Jasmine (the victim), Melanie (the principal onlooker), the class (the inactive onlookers) and the teacher (who in this setting is also an onlooker). If the event occurs as described with no intervention and the life of the classroom goes on, then a bullying dynamic will be allowed to flourish and to become even more deeply entrenched than it is already. Each such event hardens the roles and reinforces the imbalance of power. But if Melanie were to step forward, things could change.

Sometimes when an onlooker becomes active, they in effect rescue the victim. What happens in this dynamic is that the power balance still lacks equilibrium, because it is now the rescuer who has power over the victim. If Melanie were to tell Andrea sternly to give the book back to Jasmine, and then to put her arm around Jasmine and whisper that she'll look after her, then Melanie has placed herself between Andrea and Jasmine and is now in the superior position. Jasmine is still subordinate and powerless.

On the other hand, if Melanie were to stand closer to Jasmine and to say, 'Hey, don't do that', and Jasmine were then to demand the book back in a clear and firm voice, the dynamic will inevitably change as the power imbalance has been righted. The other children are more likely to react with disapproval of Andrea, and the teacher may also begin to take charge. The bullying dynamic is likely to flare and die out in such an assertive environment.

Assertiveness training programmes and safe environments

Assertiveness training that goes hand in hand with attempts to change a school from an unsafe to a safe place will usually focus on:

- teaching victims of bullying to be assertive;
- establishing an assertive culture in the school for everyone.

Any course should run once a week for about an hour (or less for young children) over a six- to eight-week period.

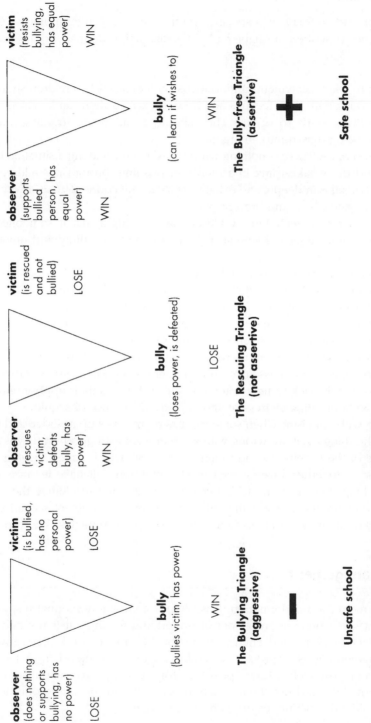

observer
(does nothing or supports bullying, has no power)

LOSE

victim
(is bullied, has no personal power)

LOSE

bully
(bullies victim, has power)

WIN

The Bullying Triangle (aggressive)

Unsafe school

---

observer
(rescues victim, defeats bully, has power)

WIN

victim
(is rescued and not bullied)

LOSE

bully
(loses power, is defeated)

LOSE

The Rescuing Triangle (not assertive)

---

observer
(supports bullied person, has equal power)

WIN

victim
(resists bullying, has equal power)

WIN

bully
(can learn if wishes to)

WIN

The Bully-free Triangle (assertive)

Safe school

Figure 20.1 An assertive approach to bullying – the three bullying triangles

The skills taught

Each session should focus on a specific skill the students can then practise (see also the techniques described in Chapter 12, on social action drama; and in Chapters 13 and 15).

- Learning to use 'I' statements and to focus on feelings. The children should learn to be in touch with their feelings and how to express them under stress (such as when bullying starts to occur). They should avoid being insulting, attributing blame or being drawn into an argument.
- Learning to relax. There is nothing wrong with calmly leaving a situation or learning to find the weakest link in a mob and pushing through it. Children can be taught to breathe in deeply and exhale slowly to the count of 10 as a way to keep their pulse rate down and prevent panic.
- The broken record technique. Children can be taught that if someone ignores their reasonable request, they can repeat this request, calmly and quietly, until they get a response.
- Masking out the noise. When children bully, they often use a lot of insults and name-calling to make the victim feel bad or to provoke an attack. Children can be taught to block out insults and not to react to them.
- Focusing on body language. Body language is a good indicator of a person's strength, weakness or resilience. If children are trained to stand and look assertive, this will help them to avoid difficult situations. It is useful to show the body language of an unassertive and an aggressive person. An assertive person stands with their back straight without being stiff, looks their opposite number in the eye without being aggressive and is pleasant but not obsequious.
- Agreeing with criticism. When someone sets themselves up as judge and jury and lists all the things that are wrong with another person, a good strategy is to agree with one of the statements and to ignore the rest. This is called fogging.
- Putting it all together. Over several weeks, children will have learnt a series of skills to help them respond to bullying assertively and to change the nature of difficult encounters. Towards the end of the course, a series of scenarios can be provided to allow the students to try out the learned strategies (see Appendix 2).

Anger management

Anger is a natural human emotion. It is often a completely rational response to a situation; at other times it erupts out of underlying feelings. It is not bad in itself and is in fact essential and energy-giving, but it can be used in negative ways. Anger management is a process whereby anger is accepted as a feeling but managed constructively. It is possible for teachers to learn some anger management skills and use them, when appropriate, in the classroom; or schools can hire a skilled practitioner from an outside agency.

If an angry child is told to stop being angry, the anger is likely to go underground or to erupt. Children need to be taught acceptable ways of expressing their feelings. A strong feeling like anger cannot be ignored; it should be recognized and met. But if it is destructive it must be controlled and redirected.

Children who are habitually angry often lack basic skills. They do not know how to get along with other people, they retaliate rather than compromise, they see only their own point of view, they blame others when things go wrong and they frequently misinterpret what others say to them. Often, such children grow up with little sense of self-worth and feel that the world is an unjust and unsafe place. For them, vulnerability, sadness and despair are the horrors that loom in the darkness. In order to keep these at bay, they hit out and mask their true feelings. In their cases, anger management awareness in the classroom and the school will help, but outside intervention from therapists or anger management professionals may be essential.

Anger management in the classroom

Teachers have developed various strategies for dealing with anger. Many use a 'cool-down area' where children can go when they feel stressed and on the verge of losing their tempers. Some teachers institute signals for children to use when they are upset, or they have objects like stress balls that children can use when they need to. Others teach special social skills programmes or hire outside experts to teach them. These can cover such areas as anger management, empathy training and impulse control.

For younger children, anger management strategies involve the recognition of anger followed by relaxation techniques, such as deep breathing and counting, and the use of self-statements such as 'calm down'. At the intermediate and secondary school levels, they comprise the recognition of anger cues and triggers, the use of positive self-statements and relaxation techniques, and reflection on the anger-provoking incident. While younger children may require adult assistance in using these techniques, older children can use the techniques by themselves once they are trained, and this knowledge will be invaluable to them throughout their lives.

Teachers can use role play to show ways of dealing with anger. In these role plays, children can identify the best ways for dealing with their own and others' anger. They can learn such things as:

- recognizing triggers and deciding to signal that a trigger has been tripped;
- expressing the anger with calm words, not fists;
- stopping to think before acting;
- owning their feelings and not blaming someone else for how they feel;
- thinking how the other person might feel;
- separating big issues from small issues, and talking out the big issues and letting the small ones go.

In a classroom where everyone is working together to deal with anger, there is a chance that healthy support and change will develop.

Self-defence and martial arts training

Much of the focus of contemporary anti-bullying programmes is on finding non-confrontational, non-violent solutions to physical bullying, rather than advocating the more old-fashioned approach of standing up to the bully. It is a myth that, if bullies are confronted or spoken to sharply, they will run away. This may be a little like the commonly held belief that if you tap a shark on the nose, it will swim away. Confrontation with a violent bully is more likely to end in an escalation of violence.

I have a black belt in karate, and when I lived in New Zealand I taught Kyokushin karate, which includes a self-defence component, for over 10 years. Since I took up karate, I have had to defend myself only once. I was attacked in the street by an angry and deluded man who was a similar height to me but weighed less. He grabbed me around the neck and tried to strangle me. I quickly removed his hands and could very easily have knocked him to the ground. Instead, I chose to move away from the situation. Knowing that I could call on karate techniques allowed me to act rationally, to be calm and to cause the least amount of damage. Having managed to avoid conflict, I felt that my martial arts training had served me well.

For children who have been the victims of bullying, a course in self-defence techniques or taking up a martial art may be helpful. But this is because the knowledge gained will give confidence, not because it will encourage them to try to inflict damage on anyone who attacks them.

Self-defence

Self-defence may be taught within any martial art, or separately as a specific programme. Self-defence programmes usually teach techniques that people can use to get out of dangerous situations. Good self-defence courses develop people's natural skills and confidence so that, if threatened, they can react spontaneously and assertively.

Self-defence skills are usually based on the use of excellent natural weapons such as elbows, hands, knees, the forehead, the side of the head and feet, with fast escape as the ultimate defence. Basic martial arts techniques, such as some easy-to-use kicks and punches, are also taught.

But 95 per cent of self-defence is more about attitude than fighting ability, so that although specific techniques may not be remembered after the course, the person is able to stand more confidently and know that there is a way out. Self-defence also arms each person with the ability to identify potentially dangerous situations. For instance, if a girl on the way to school sees a group of girls ahead who have been tormenting her, then it will be sensible for her to stay close to nearby children or adults, remain far behind her potential tormentors or take another route to school (as long as this does not put her in more danger).

Children who are victimized often lack the self-assertiveness or anticipatory skills to assess potential danger. A good self-defence course can start to reverse years of poor avoidance techniques.

Recently, there has been a lot of emphasis on teaching women self-defence, and a number of excellent courses specifically for girls and women have been devised.

Martial arts

Aikido, judo, karate, kick boxing, kung fu and tae kwon do are all forms of martial arts. Martial arts teach sets of techniques for self-defence and attack that are learned individually, practised thoroughly and put together as combinations. They are also grounded in well-established philosophies, and learning a martial art also means becoming familiar with this philosophy and becoming a member of a large extended family.

Taking up a martial art requires much more commitment than doing a self-defence course. When people watch martial arts films, they see very dexterous opponents executing a series of difficult and impressive techniques. These are the outward manifestations of a process of physical and psychological growth and development. People with some degree of accomplishment in martial arts tend to be calm and confident, which are good body language signals to give to potential bullies.

It is true that some people who study martial arts lack self-discipline and want to use their skills to show off. Such attitudes are, however, antithetical to the discipline of all martial arts, and such people have neither the staying power to train to a good standard nor the personal qualities to allow them to grow within the art. Bullies are not tolerated in martial arts.

If it is taught well, a martial arts training does several things.

- It teaches a series of skills, such as hand locks, kicking, punching, rolling, throwing and various disabling techniques that can be used either in competitive tournaments or in defence.
- Through repetition of basic techniques it teaches the ability to respond without thinking in a challenging situation.
- It develops physical stamina through hard training.
- It builds both physical skills and a sense of self-esteem and confidence.
- Martial arts teachers discourage people who show off or bully as a result of learning martial skills.

Conclusion

Although bullying is a difficult problem, we increasingly understand how it works and have developed a range of excellent strategies for stopping it. A strong and resourceful global anti-bullying movement has emerged, with three complementary perspectives that are personified in the researchers, the programme developers and the practitioners. There are crossovers between these perspectives, but most of us gravitate towards one of them.

- Researchers have gathered information about the complexion, extent and nature of bullying. They have monitored the understanding and experience of those involved and evaluated various approaches and programmes for their effectiveness.
- Programme developers have responded to bullying, sometimes using the information provided by researchers, sometimes instinctively, and have produced programmes to deal with bullying, and to improve the safety of individual students and schools.
- Practitioners include teachers, deputy principals and guidance counsellors/psychologists. They take note of research and deal with the problem of school bullying on a day-to-day basis, selecting particular programmes they think will work.

The informal partnership that has developed between these three groups has nurtured the development and improvement of our understanding and ways of dealing with bullying. A concerted effort supported by modern technology has ensured that the excellent anti-bullying resource base now available is inexpensive and readily accessible by telephone, fax, email or the Internet.

This book has provided an overview of what I think is the best that is available and has made suggestions for developing workable anti-bullying processes and programmes. As such, the book also paints a picture of a healthy and safe school environment that will, inevitably, help create and sustain more healthy and safe societies for us all.

APPENDICES

A SCHOOL ANTI-BULLYING POLICY

Our policy

This school believes that, in order for students to learn to the best of their ability, this school must be a safe and friendly environment. We therefore declare the school to be a no-bullying zone.

We have discussed matters thoroughly with the school's community – students, teachers, parents, trustees and the wider community – and, in order to make the sort of school we all want, we have created an anti-bullying policy. In this policy, we define bullying and outline what people should do when they experience it, see it happening or hear about it.

A definition of bullying

Bullying is a conscious and wilful repetitive act of aggression and/or manipulation and/or exclusion by one or more people against another person or people. It is also an abuse of power by those carrying out the bullying, which is designed to cause hurt. Bullying contains the following elements:

- harm is intended;
- there is an imbalance of power;
- bullying is often organized and systematic;
- bullying is repetitive, occurring over a period of time; or it is a random but serial activity carried out by someone who is feared for this behaviour;
- hurt experienced by a victim of bullying can be external (physical) or internal (psychological).

Bullying can be either physical or non-physical.

- Physical bullying can include biting, hair-pulling, hitting, kicking, locking in a room, pinching, punching, pushing, scratching, spitting or any other form of physical attack. It also includes damaging a person's property.

* Non-physical bullying can be verbal, which includes abusive telephone calls, text messages or messages sent by computer; sending (often anonymous) poisonous notes; extorting money or material possessions; intimidation or threats of violence; name-calling, racist remarks or teasing; sexually suggestive or abusive language; spiteful teasing or making cruel remarks; and spreading false and malicious rumours.
* Non-physical bullying can also be non-verbal, which includes making rude gestures and mean faces; manipulating relationships and ruining friendships; and purposely and often systematically ignoring, excluding and isolating someone.

Bullying can be any one of the above or a combination of them. It includes racist bullying, sexual bullying, bullying of special needs children and the bullying of children with a different sexual orientation.

Dealing with bullying: what you need to know and do

What students need to know

Students have the right not to be bullied. Bullying is harmful to everyone, in both the short and long term. No one has the right to bully anyone else. All cases of bullying brought to the school's attention will be taken very seriously and all necessary steps to stop it will be taken.

In order to stop bullying occurring, students need to tell us when it happens. The unwritten rule of the code of silence for many students is 'Don't tell adults about things that are occurring in your group', 'Don't rat on your mates'. The best weapon bullying pupils have is their misuse and abuse of this code of silence. No one has the right to be protected by their peers when they physically or psychologically abuse others.

If students are being bullied or know of instances of bullying, it is important to tell somebody. Bullying only gets worse if it is not stopped, so it is important to do this right away. You can do this by speaking to a teacher, by taking a friend in trouble to a teacher, by going to the deputy principal or another staff member, or by asking your parents or another adult to help you follow things up. All incidents of bullying brought to the school's attention will be investigated and taken seriously. In dealing with such matters, confidentiality for those concerned will be safeguarded.

A strong anti-bullying stance by students contributes in a major way to making the school a safe place. Another major weapon of those who bully is that they may seem 'tougher' than their peers, and individual bullies often have a small group who encourage their bullying behaviour. If most students decide that bullying is not acceptable and support each other in letting adults know or in intervening assertively and showing their disapproval, much of the bullying will stop.

What parents need to know

If you know or suspect that your child is being bullied, contact the school immediately. You can contact any staff member. We all take bullying very seriously. All matters will be thoroughly followed up and appropriate action taken. We will also assure confidentiality in our contact with you. When the school knows or suspects that a child is being bullied, we will contact the parent(s) of all children involved, seek their advice and support, and keep them informed of progress with the handling of the bullying.

What teachers need to know

Bullying can grow to become very serious or it can be nipped in the bud. If teachers know of bullying or suspect that it is occurring, they should report this first to the deputy principal. After discussion, it may be decided the teacher can handle the bullying satisfactorily. A brief report is important so that the matter is on record: if another incident flares up later it can be seen as part of a pattern, not an isolated occurrence. This is not intended to label people as victims or bullies, but it is important to track bullying behaviour.

Because teachers cannot be everywhere at once and because bullying is often a clandestine activity, it is important for teachers to encourage students to tell about bullying.

The process

The process for dealing with cases of bullying is as follows.

1. The bullying must first be reported to the deputy principal, either directly or via other staff.
2. A brief report will be made detailing the nature of the bullying, who was involved and what happened. This should go on file.
3. It is important to inform parents (of victims and bullies) that bullying has occurred and that it is being dealt with.
4. The teachers of those involved and the deputy principal and school psychologist will discuss how best to find a solution to the bullying. Together they will devise a strategy that may call on a programme that the school has adopted.
5. If, after adopting a course of action, the bullying has been resolved, a report should be written and put on file.
6. If the bullying is not resolved, those trying to find a solution will need to meet again to decide what should be done. An account of this meeting should also be put on file.
7. When a solution is found, it should be decided if back-up strategies are needed (for example, referrals, peer support, other interventions).

APPENDIX 2

USING BULLYING SCENARIOS

Bullying scenarios can be used in classroom and other school-based activities to explore how bullying works.

- The use of scenarios helps students enter into *all* the dynamics of bullying.
- The immediacy of the scenarios may encourage empathy and understanding, and lead to a cessation of bullying.
- A major vulnerability in the bullying dynamic is the fact that one bully has inordinate power over a large group, which could in fact intervene and bring a stop to the bullying. When students work together to solve a problem, they not only think about what is happening and come up with answers, but also realize that together they can be strong and combat bullying. The potential power of a group of students acting against bullying cannot be overestimated.

The scenarios presented here can be used by teachers in classroom work on bullying and in preparation for the adoption of and training for preventative and interventionary programmes. The scenarios of the physical beating up of a boy in the school grounds (scenario 1), and the harassment of a gay/effeminate boy (scenario 2), are intended for use in secondary schools; the scenarios of the racist bullying of a Punjabi boy (scenario 3), and the isolation of a young girl (scenario 4), can be used in primary/intermediate settings. These scenarios can be adapted and changed in discussion, and others generated using the format provided here.

Scenario 1: physical bullying – the beating up of Ben by Shane and his friends

In the playing fields of a large secondary school, far from the main teaching blocks, Ben, aged 14, marches towards a prearranged spot looking very determined. When he gets there he is surprised to find a crowd of about a hundred teenagers restlessly milling around. It seems as if everyone has heard about what is going to happen and has come to watch. Soon, a self-assured and slightly older and bigger boy called Shane arrives with a group of his friends who are sniggering among themselves.

When the fighting starts the crowd becomes noisy and there is a sense of excitement in the air. Some of the boys yell out to encourage Shane ('Come on, Shane. Give him what he deserves') or to discourage Ben ('Go home, loser!'). The verbal support fans Shane's aggression, and almost immediately it is apparent that he will win. He is obviously a much better fighter and has many other advantages – more weight, more confidence and the support of friends. Ben is knocked to the ground and Shane's friends start to kick him. He tries to protect himself by contracting into a foetal position and covering his head with his arms. Shane and his friends then walk off with a sense of camaraderie, of a job well done. As they leave, they make taunting and threatening remarks to Ben. The crowd disperses and leaves Ben lying on the ground, alone, humiliated and hurt.

Ben knows better than to go to the school authorities, first because, despite the savageness of his beating, he would be transgressing the ultimate taboo of 'ratting on his peer group' but, perhaps more important, because even if the school supported him over this incident, he knows Shane and his friends will get back at him and that in the long term his prospects will be very poor.

There are several useful pieces of background information that are relevant to this incident.

- Ben has been bullied by one boy in particular, Shane, who has been supported by a group of boys.
- The bullying of Ben started off in a low-key way, with one of Shane's group accidentally-on-purpose tripping Ben as he passed him in class and making low-grade insulting remarks, such as 'Who cuts your hair, your mummy?' Things have gradually got worse.
- With some encouragement from his father that he should stand up for himself, Ben decided enough was enough. He responded to Shane's challenge to fight him.
- Unlike so many Hollywood movies when the good guy wins and the bully, who is always a coward, either runs away or loses the fight, Ben does not have the skills or support to do anything but lose and lose badly.
- The school's principal will defensively state that bullying does not occur in this school. He will agree that there is some rough play: 'All right, there may be odd incidents, but boys will be boys! You have to learn how to stand up for yourself – it's good preparation for life.'
- A huge amount of research indicates that there are innumerable myths about physical bullying, including how to stand up to it and how to 'beat it'. (See also Chapter 2, and bullyonline.org.)

What observations and inferences can be made about this incident?

- This school is not a safe place for Ben or, by implication, for other pupils.
- Many people were watching the fight. They vastly outnumbered the bullies, yet nobody intervened or provided any vocal or physical support for Ben.
- Those involved in the bullying treated Ben as a 'non-person' and did not seem aware or to care that Ben could suffer serious, long-term, physical and psychological harm. They lacked a sense of empathy towards him.
- The principal may have acted defensively in response to the suggestion that there is a bullying problem at the school. He may also truly believe that bullying does no harm but is character-forming. In either case, he lacks adequate strategies for dealing effectively with bullying, as does his school.

Scenario 2: Jamie is bullied because he is gay

Jamie is average in many ways: average height, average weight, average academically. One attribute which has set him apart from his male peers ever since he started school is that he is effeminate, and many people think that he is gay.

Jamie has been teased from an early age and is frequently beaten up. He seems to be without any aggressive tendencies and does not have any real friends. Some of the teachers are ambivalent about him and treat him as if he brings his victimization on himself.

Jamie tries to avoid other children at lunchtime by going to the library. There is a teacher on duty and a few children are scattered through the room working. While he is sitting and making notes in an alcove by himself, two boys come in to look for him. They signal to some other boys down the corridor, then go past the duty teacher and make their way to the alcove where Jamie is sitting. They sit down on either side of him. The door to the library opens and closes again, and they know their friends have arrived. These boys sit down in the next alcove.

The first boy grabs Jamie by the knee and pinches hard. Jamie pulls away and looks as if he may cry. The boy then pats him on the head and says, 'There, there, cry baby. Isn't mummy here to blow your poofter nose?' The other boy giggles. The second boy pulls the book away from him. 'What ya reading, freak? Trying to find out how to bugger boys?' He pushes Jamie hard so that he falls against the other boy.

The boys in the next alcove are watching and listening. They start to mutter, 'Faggot, faggot', and to make sarcastic comments. They laugh. The first boy pushes Jamie back so hard that his head slams into the wall behind him. 'Poofter, poofter, his brain'll be mashed', he jeers. 'If he's got one', says the other boy. They grab the pages on which Jamie has been writing, scribble over them and screw them up.

The duty teacher calls out, 'What's all that noise? No noise in the library or you'll be thrown out.' 'Yes, sir, no sir', chorus the boys. They giggle again. The two on either side of Jamie hiss, 'Teach you a lesson, homo freak. Just go die somewhere', and one punches him hard in the stomach. The others file past and stare at him with disdain. A couple make obscene gestures.

Jamie stays still and silent until they have gone, gasps for breath, and then tries to wipe his face, straighten out his clothes and his pages, and get ready for the afternoon.

There are several useful pieces of background information that are relevant to this incident.

- Jamie feels very confused about his sexuality, especially in light of the disgust with which he is treated. He lives with his mother who is a solo parent. She loves him and supports him, but is low in self-esteem herself and does not have many resources for helping Jamie to survive in the world. He never sees his estranged father who detests the idea of having 'a poofter' for a son.
- Children of gay or lesbian sexual orientation are likely to be bullied. The Mental Health America website (nmha.org) reported in 2009 that, 'While trying to deal with all the challenges of being a teenager, gay/lesbian/bisexual/transgender … teens additionally have to deal with harassment, threats, and violence directed at them on a daily basis. They hear anti-gay slurs such as 'homo', 'faggot' and 'sissy' about 26 times a day or once every 14 minutes. Even more troubling, a study found that thirty-one percent of gay youth had been threatened or injured at school in the last year alone!' (See also Chapter 4.)

What observations and inferences can be made about this incident?

- In this school and community, there is clearly a sense of homophobia.
- The pupils treat Jamie with scorn and hatred. This is not stopped by the school.
- By doing nothing, the adults directly and indirectly condone the bullying.
- This school is a very unsafe place.

Scenario 3: racist bullying – Nilish replies to harassment and racist teasing with violence

Nilish is working by himself in the classroom. The door opens. 'What are you doing, paki boy?' taunts David. 'Did ya fall in the shit, black boy?' He struts closer. 'Are you reading something? I didn't know you could read.' 'Hey, nigger', the other boys say as they start to filter in and see Nilish on his own.

Instead of ignoring these taunts and provocations (as he has done four or five times over the last month), Nilish loses his temper. He turns on David. The two boys fight and Nilish is clearly a better fighter and is winning. David's friend Acbeh steps in, grabs Nilish around the neck and pulls him away from David, throwing him on the ground. He helps David up. The duty teacher arrives, and David and Nilish are taken to the deputy principal's office. David is crying and says he was just having fun and that Nilish went 'psycho' and really hurt him. When questioned, Nilish is surly and insolent and is suspended from school for a week for fighting and being rude to the deputy principal. David's friends back him up, saying Nilish went 'psycho' for no apparent reason. David is given a warning about fighting but is largely seen as the innocent party.

Nilish is identified by those in authority as the aggressor. He is not listened to. Instead, the boy with more credibility in the school is believed.

There are several useful pieces of background information that are relevant to this incident:

- Nilish is one of only a few Punjabi children in this Somerset school.
- Nilish is seen as having a bad attitude. He is regarded as violent, with a tendency towards bullying.
- Nilish has shown he is tough and can stand up for himself.
- The school sees him as causing the situation.
- The school authorities believe racism does not exist in their school.
- Research all over the world points to the high degree of racism and intolerance in society and also in schools. A BBC news story on 23 April 2009 reported that nearly half of 802 British teachers surveyed said that racist bullying occurred in the schools in which they worked. (See also Chapter 4.)

What observations and inferences can be made about this incident?

- Although there is a strong element of racism in this scenario, the school authorities believe the aggressors and discipline the victim.
- These boys will probably not bother Nilish again.
- Nilish, however, will probably harbour a grudge against the boys, will be angry at the racism and will turn against the school because of its inability to address the problem justly.
- It may set him on a path to antisocial acts based on a sense of grievance and injustice towards society at large.
- The other boys will turn their attention to somebody else they can victimize more easily.
- The other boys may grow to think racism is acceptable.

Scenario 4: psychological bullying – Rachel's exclusion by Charlotte and her peer group

Rachel is 9. She is playing in the school yard by herself. Four girls from her class, led by Charlotte, come up to her. 'You can't play here. This is our area', says Charlotte. They push Rachel aside, purposely ignoring her as they do so, and start to chalk in hopscotch squares. She does not resist, even though she is taller than they are.

'Can I play?' she asks.

'No, you dress funny and you're too dumb and ugly to play with us', replies Charlotte in a sweet voice that contradicts her words. It seems to be a bit of a joke, as if perhaps she does not mean it, and even Rachel laughs. Charlotte flashes her winning smile at her friends as she says this. They all giggle at her comments.

'You can come over to Anna's house after school, though. We're going to watch a DVD', Charlotte says condescendingly, giving a knowing look towards the circle of admirers. Rachel's instincts tell her things are not as they seem but she really wants to go to Anna's house; she wants to be accepted.

Rachel walks to Anna's house by herself after school and knocks on the door. No one answers the door. She knocks several more times. She sees the curtain move and hears the quiet giggling of several girls on the other side of the door. Her heart sinks. After a few more quiet knocks and no response, Rachel gives up and walks home despondently. Later that evening, Rachel answers the telephone. 'Hello, this is Rachel', she says. Someone laughs at the other end of the line, says, 'Weirdo freak', and then hangs up.

There are several useful pieces of background information that are relevant to this incident.

- The school in this scenario is in an affluent neighbourhood. It is academically very successful and much value is placed on material possessions.
- Charlotte's father is a successful lawyer who is well known in the school community.
- Charlotte is an attractive child, does well at school and is highly thought of. She is her teacher's favourite pupil. She is widely recognized for her leadership skills, and is seen as having all of the hallmarks required for success at school and in the world at large.
- Rachel is unusual in her dress and thinking. Although she is creative, interesting and intelligent, she is also introverted, quiet and whimsical, and sometimes appears to be sullen. She is not popular with the teachers. She is an average achiever and her teacher feels ambivalent about her. She either does not notice or is willing to overlook teasing or exclusion of Rachel by Charlotte and her friends, not only in the playground but also in the class. (See also Chapter 10.)
- Becky, one of the girls who is part of Charlotte's circle of friends, once invited Rachel to play but told her not to tell Charlotte or the other girls. Becky was invited to Rachel's house several times but she never came.
- Events like this happen to Rachel almost daily. It has become routine and nobody seems to notice.
- Rachel suffers from a common form of bullying that occurs especially among girls. This is generally referred to as relationship bullying. (See also Chapter 2.)

What observations and inferences can be made about this incident?

- The crowd of girls around Charlotte has no empathy for Rachel, nor do they feel in any way responsible for what is clearly an act of bullying.
- This sentiment is echoed by the teachers. They do not consider the purposeful exclusion of Rachel by her peer group to be bullying, they do not take it seri-

ously and they see it largely as Rachel's problem.

- Although not subjected to physical abuse, Rachel is still the victim of bullying. It is manipulative and cruel, and could have as detrimental an effect on Rachel as physical bullying has on Ben.
- This school is not a safe place for Rachel.

APPENDIX 3

ETHICS AND CONFIDENTIALITY

The important issues of ethics and confidentiality are applicable to all bullying inter-ventions, and particularly to peer support programmes. All matters discussed in a bullying or peer support session are confidential to that session, and none of the matters that arise there should be the subject of idle discussion or gossip with staff, students or anyone else.

Much anti-bullying work is collaborative and therefore relies upon discussion and conferring, and much of this can be done without using names. Staff directly involved will know the students being discussed anyway, so confidentiality is more a matter of discretion, respect and keeping information within anti-bullying groups.

In cases of peer support, students giving support need to state at the beginning of a relationship that confidentiality will normally and routinely be kept, but they also need to specify that they have to be able to discuss problems and/or progress with their own supervisor. In addition, most peer support programmes rely on sup-port groups of peers who meet regularly to talk about their work, any difficulties they are having and how to improve their effectiveness. Such discussions can usu-ally refer to issues rather than specific and identifiable students, and any matters discussed in the peer support group are confidential to the group and should not be discussed outside it.

However, there are exceptions to the rule of confidentiality in the case of both anti-bullying groups and peer strategies and interventions. When a person being supported says something that suggests she is at risk, for instance, 'I feel so bad today that I want to end it', what does the teacher or counsellor do? In such cases, it is important that other professionals are involved. For the peer supporter, it is even more imperative to seek help, which will inevitably involve breaking confidential-ity. These students are neither trained professionals nor adults. In all cases where there is talk of self-harm, the threat of harm from someone else or disclosure of sex-ual abuse, then the supervisor must be informed. The bottom line is that all students are the legal responsibility of the school when they are at school, and this includes both students needing support and students offering support. This is a health and safety issue as well as a legal requirement.

APPENDIX 4

ICE BREAKERS

Ice breakers are useful methods that can be used to 'break the ice' and establish ease and rapport when working in groups. They can be selected to match the ages of the students present. Three are suggested here.

The throwing and naming game

A soft ball or toy is thrown around the group. The teacher starts off by saying their name and the name of the student they are throwing it to (for example, 'Anil to Clare'). That student then throws it to someone else ('Clare to Raman'), and so on. The use of names is important: those present get to know each other, and humour and fun enter the activity.

Balloon game

All participants are given a balloon and a small piece of paper. Sitting in a circle, they are asked to write something interesting about themselves, to roll the paper up, insert it into the balloon, blow it up and tie its end. The balloons are then thrown into the circle and each student grabs one. Taking turns, they burst their balloons, extract the paper and read it to the group. They then have to guess who this is about. This works well to 'break the ice'.

Dyads

The students are asked to pair off with someone they do not know well. They tell each other about themselves and then introduce their partner to the rest of the group. This helps create a sense of mutual interest and trust.

INDEX